*The* COACHMEN *of* NINETEENTH-CENTURY PARIS

The
COACHMEN
of
NINETEENTH-CENTURY
PARIS

*Service Workers and Class Consciousness*

NICHOLAS PAPAYANIS

LOUISIANA STATE UNIVERSITY PRESS
*Baton Rouge and London*

Designer: *Glynnis Phoebe*
Typeface: *Bembo*
Typesetter: *G&S Typesetters, Inc.*
Printer and binder: *Thomson-Shore, Inc.*

Library of Congress Cataloging-in-Publication Data
Papayanis, Nicholas.
    The coachmen of nineteenth-century Paris: service workers and
class consciousness / Nicholas Papayanis.
        p.      cm.
    Includes bibliographical references (p.) and index.
    ISBN 0-8071-1814-1
    1. Coaching—France—Paris—History—19th century.   2. Coach
drivers—France—Paris—History—19th century.   3. Class
consciousness—France—Paris—History—19th century.   I. Title.
HE5749.F8P36   1993
388.3'24'0944361—dc20                                                    93-834
                                                                          CIP

Some information on the Compagnie Générale des Voitures à Paris in this study
appeared in the *Journal of Transport History* (March, 1987). Parts of Chapter 3 and
Chapter 6 appeared in a different form in the *Journal of Contemporary History*, XX
(1985) and in *Le Mouvement Social* (July–September, 1985), respectively.

*To Marilyn*

# CONTENTS

# ILLUSTRATIONS

# Tables

# PREFACE

A major investigation of male service workers in the nineteenth century, this book fills a significant gap in the literature dealing both with Paris and with its working class, for it seeks to account for the class attitudes of a portion of the Paris working population hitherto neglected in labor and social history. Questions concerning class consciousness and collective action have traditionally been tested against the history of such groups as artisans, factory workers, and miners. This study brings the male service worker center stage. Moreover, despite the plethora of publications on the urban history of Paris in the nineteenth century, not many deal with transportation in the French capital during the era of the horse-drawn carriage.

To explore the position of the Paris coachmen in the nineteenth century from multiple interlocking perspectives, I have organized this book to deal with the important factors that shaped the work, the lives, and the ideas of these men. The first two chapters describe their work environment. As will become clear, company and government rules and the size of the individual firms influenced not only the way coachmen went through each day but also their ability to become entrepreneurs. The structure of the cab industry and the many rules governing it were the setting within which general attitudes were forged, class loyalties and unions developed, and strikes took place. Chapters 3 and 4 present a statistical profile of coachmen and explore their social and family status. Chapters 5 and 6 examine the formation of class consciousness. Chapter 5 focuses on the formation of coachmen's unions and the introduction of coachmen's newspapers, with special attention to the discourse emerging from these two sources and the shift from a corporate to a revolutionary ideology among Parisian coachmen. In Chapter 6 this shift is dramatized by the great coachmen's strikes during the Paris expositions of 1878 and 1889. These two chapters also discuss the role of economic crisis and revolutionary syndicalism in the formation of class consciousness.

The last chapter, Chapter 7, deals with the most fundamental technological innovation in the cab trade, the coming of the motorcar, and illustrates that coachmen accepted this technological transformation without protest. Although in theory the introduction of the motor cab might have had a devastating effect on the occupation of coachmen, in fact the motorized vehicle accomplished for coachmen all that the horse-drawn cab had and in the process made the workday easier and more efficient (provided, of course, the cabbie could master the necessary skills). This outcome is consistent with the view taken here that issues of social improvement, integration into the life of Paris, control, the structure of the industry, wages, and the nature of the workday were the primary concerns of coachmen. This study includes information from all the decades of the nineteenth century, but its focus is on the midcentury and thereafter, since it is from that time on that more than merely anecdotal material on coachmen is especially abundant.

The French word for coachman, *cocher,* denotes any person who conducts a horse-drawn vehicle, be it cab, omnibus, tram, or private conveyance for an individual employer. The coachmen who are the subject of this book are only those in the cab industry. I eliminated private servants because my focus here is on public transportation. I found it necessary to distinguish between the mass transportation system of nineteenth-century Paris (omnibuses and trams) and the cab industry, because after 1855 they comprised two distinct spheres of the public transportation system. The coachmen of the cab industry and those of the omnibus and tram systems were, for all the similarity of their skills, two distinct segments of the Parisian work force.

At first glance the English word *cabman* might seem a more accurate and appropriate designation for these drivers of carriages. The French word for cabman, however, is *cocher de fiacre,* denoting the conductor of only one of the two major kinds of nineteenth-century Parisian cabs. Parisians and the cab conductors themselves usually refered to a cab conductor by the all-embracing word *cocher.* Throughout this book, therefore, unless otherwise noted, the word *cocher,* or *coachman* (or an English equivalent such as *cabbie*), refers to a cab conductor of a horse-drawn carriage.

While it would be impossible to mention all of the many people who took an interest in this project, I would like to record my deep gratitude to a few individuals on both sides of the Atlantic whose assistance has been especially important. My work on Paris coachmen grew out of several conversations with Michelle Perrot; I am grateful for her continued interest in this enterprise. Madeleine Rebérioux welcomed me as a member of her seminar in the University of Paris and let me present some of my early research to her students. Alain Cottereau, Alain Faure, and Andrew Lincoln, three of the most pleasant colleagues imaginable, freely shared with me their extensive knowledge of Parisian history sources. Debra Perry kindly let me see her notes on the Bixio family. For advice and information on crime statistics and coachmen, I thank Barrie M. Ratcliffe and Scott Haine. During one summer in Paris, I also enjoyed my many conversations about this project with Lenard Berlanstein. Michelle Bonnard, a librarian at the Bibliothèque Nationale, provided me with assistance above and beyond what was required; she also became a dear friend. As always, Patrick Fridenson helped make my stay in Paris a warm and pleasant experience.

I owe a very special acknowledgment to Roger Médori, president and director of the Compagnie Générale de Voitures de Paris. Monsieur Médori, deeply interested in the history of his firm, granted me (a complete stranger at the time of our first meeting) total and unrestricted access to his company's rich collection of materials dealing with the nineteenth century. His welcome could not have been more hospitable, and I shall always be grateful to him for his generosity. Nor could I have completed my research of the CGV's extensive files without the many favors extended to me by Marc Levaire, formally of that company.

I would also like to acknowledge Brooklyn College of the City

University of New York, from which I have received support. Following my sabbatical year in Paris, the school's administration provided me with aid for several semesters, which I put to good use in transcribing a considerable amount of statistical data. For assistance in this task I wish to single out Ping F. Louie. For providing me with student programmers who could process my data from the CGV archives and with other technical services, I thank three members of the computer and information science department of Brooklyn College: Michael Barnett, Yedidyah Langsam, and Aaron Tenebaum. My friend and colleague in my own department, Philip Dawson, an accomplished programmer as well as historian, also wrote a program for my needs in respect to this data. Wang Chi Wong, faculty liaison officer with the Academic Computing Center of Brooklyn College, has provided me with more services than I could possibly account for in this space. The research for this study was supported (in part) by a grant from the City University of New York PSC-CUNY Research Award Program. John Merriman, Philip Nord, Donald Reid, and two readers for the Louisiana State University Press read all or parts of this manuscript; I have borrowed freely from their many valuable suggestions.

L. E. Phillabaum, director, Catherine Landry, managing editor, Julie Schorfheide, production editor, and the staff of the Louisiana State University Press made the experience of seeing this work published enjoyable. To Margaret Fisher Dalrymple, editor-in-chief of the Louisiana State University Press, I owe a special acknowledgment for her interest in, and support for, this project. I would also like to thank my copy editor, Christine Cowan, for her advice.

I have benefited from my wife Marilyn's careful reading of this study. More important, she has been my best friend and companion, a deep source of love and support; the dedication is an inadequate expression of my feelings.

# Abbreviations

ACGV — Archives de la Compagnie Générale des Voitures à Paris

AN — Archives Nationales, Paris

AP — Archives de Paris

APP — Archives de la Préfecture de Police, Paris

BHVP — Bibliothèque Historique de la Ville de Paris

BN — Bibliothèque Nationale, Paris

BNSR — Bibliothèque Nationale, Service des Recueils

CGO — Compagnie Générale des Omnibus

CGV — Compagnie Générale des Voitures à Paris

CGVPP — Compagnie Générale des Voitures de Place de Paris

CIV — Compagnie Imperiale des Voitures à Paris

EGC — Enterprise Générale des Citadins

FNMT — Fédération Nationale des Moyens de Transport

*The* COACHMEN *of* NINETEENTH-CENTURY PARIS

# INTRODUCTION

On May 1, 1878, the president of the Third Republic of France, Marshal Patrice de MacMahon, rode an open coach from his residence to the Trocadéro, where he was officially to open the Universal Exposition in Paris. He was greeted by the minister of commerce and agriculture on a specially built platform overlooking the exposition grounds. From there he and his official cortege proceeded by foot to the Champs de Mars, the main grounds of the exposition. Saluted by military bands, the sound of cannon fire, and eighty thousand troops, MacMahon and the officials in his party filed between a double row of soldiers, traversed the gardens of the Champs de Mars, and entered the Palais de l'Industrie, where he was welcomed by France's leading political and intellectual leaders, among them members of the Conseil d'État, magistrates, ministers, members of the Senate, and academicians. Following a strict protocol, he next toured the buildings of the foreign nations at the exhibit.

France was well on the road to recovery after the Franco-Prussian war of 1870 and had prepared this festive exhibition as a symbol of its revival. The exposition was by all accounts a great success, as local chroniclers noted: "During the evening all Paris celebrated. The very animated appearance created during the daytime by houses covered with tricolored flags gave way to a fairy-like decor of illuminations at night."[1] The architectural centerpiece was the huge, semicircular Palais de Trocadéro built on Chaillot Hill. Before the exposition was over, sixteen million people from France and abroad would have come to Paris to visit the Trocadéro Palace and the sights on the Champs de Mars.

On August 5, 1878, with the glamorous activities of a world exposition in full swing, almost half the Paris coachmen went out on strike.[2] Their action resulted in considerable confusion on the streets, especially near railway stations, as visitors to the exposition, many with luggage and families in tow, had to compete with each other for the remaining cabs or had somehow to make their way to omnibuses.

Two unrelated decisions, one by public authorities and the other by the CGV, the largest Paris cab company, were immediately responsible for the strike. First, the prefecture of police issued an ordinance on July 16, to take effect on August 5, requiring each cab to display a sign indicating whether it was free or taken. Second, effective on the opening day of the exposition, the CGV raised the daily target fare for cabs (that is, the amount it expected each cabbie to turn over to the company) to an exceptionally high level. These two policies would effectively prevent the coachmen from making more money during the especially busy time of the exposition. The first made illegally pocketing a fare more difficult, because the police would be watching coaches carefully for unrecorded rides; the second made it impossible for coachmen to profit from the increased receipts the tourists generated. There was an additional grievance. Since the start of the exposition, the coachmen had complained to the public authorities and the populace at large that the CGV mistreated its horses. Thus, on August 5, the day the new police regulation regarding coach signs was to take effect, the coachmen of the CGV struck, claiming they could no longer stand by while the company overworked its coachmen and its horses.

There were about twelve thousand public cabs in Paris at that time, and the strike affected almost half of them. Just when France

1. Jean-Jacques Bloch and Marianne Delort, *Quand Paris allait à l'Expo'* (Paris, 1980), 61–62.
2. See Chap. 6.

wished to present its best face to the world, Paris coachmen began a twelve-day action that dislocated traffic in the capital, seriously inconveniencing Frenchmen and foreigners alike. Conservative newspapers and the CGV's management questioned the patriotism of the coachmen. Even the liberal press wondered whether the strike would harm the exposition. The authorities need not have worried; the CGV successfully broke the strike. Visitors to Paris continued to enjoy the exposition, and talk of ill treatment of cabbies and horses faded away. The coachmen, however, did not forget. They had struck during the Paris expositions of 1855 and 1867 and would strike again during the expositions of 1889 and 1900. They walked out during every Paris exposition in the nineteenth century (though they never attained their main objectives).[3]

Here were two events, one staged by the successful and confident elites of the state, attracting millions of French and international tourists to Paris, the other planned by workers to disrupt the official festivities in order to press their claims. Among other abuses, the cab companies expected the cabbies to work single shifts of fourteen to seventeen hours for the comparatively low wage of four to five francs per day. These two events also illustrate two kinds of attractions offered by Paris. The city and its monuments had always drawn tourists, and it was especially attractive during the expositions of the nineteenth century. The capital was also a magnet for men with minimal skills seeking relief from rural unemployment or looking for seasonal labor as coachmen. Thus, the Paris of lights, fireworks, and festivities for the well-to-do and the Paris of low-paying jobs for native Parisian and migrant laborers came face to face.

These two elements indicate the major concerns of this study, which recreates the world of the Paris coachmen within the context of the urban history of Paris during the nineteenth century.[4] It also

3. This was first pointed out by Michelle Perrot, *Les Ouvriers en grève, France, 1871–1890* (Paris, 1974), I, 333.

4. For studies on domestic workers, see Theresa M. McBride, *The Domestic Revolution: The Modernization of Household Service in England and France, 1820–1920* (New York, 1976), and Pierre Guiral and Guy Thuillier, *La Vie quotidienne des domestiques en France au XIXe siècle* (Paris, 1978). An important recent work on cafe workers is Henry-Melchior De Langle, *Le Petit Monde des cafés et débits parisiens au XIXe siècle: L'Évolution de la sociabilité citadine* (Paris, 1990). Lenard R. Berlanstein's *The*

discusses the economic and structural history of the cab trade, the mass transportation system of Paris, the Paris expositions of 1878 and 1889, the Imperial Cab Company (later the CGV), founded in 1855 by Napoleon III and, finally, the impact of the automobile on Parisian transportation.

Coachmen were a central presence in Paris. They constituted a work force ranging from about five thousand in 1860 to about fifteen thousand in 1911, scattered throughout the city. Such a ubiquitous group must always attract attention, and opinions about coachmen varied from the extremes of pity, sympathy, and affection to those of fear and hostility. At the positive end of this range, in a short story about a coachman, Alexandre Dumas stated that he preferred conversing with a coachman to a boring play or show. One he met quite by chance, Cantillon, became his favorite because the man was quite well read and had a literary bent. Victor Hugo invited a coachman, Charles More, to dinner when the latter, recognizing the great poet, refused to accept his fare. More happily accepted the dinner invitation: he wished to show Hugo some of his own poetry.[5]

---

Working People of Paris, 1871–1914 (Baltimore, 1984) demonstrates that Paris was increasingly becoming a service-oriented city as manufacturing tended to locate outside the capital in the last part of the nineteenth century; Berlanstein's work is important for the portrait it provides of the different kinds of workers in Paris within the context of structural changes at this time. For a sampling of a few important works on the history of Paris, see Norma Evenson, Paris: A Century of Change, 1878–1978 (New Haven, 1979); Jeanne Gaillard, Paris, la ville, 1852–1870 (Paris, 1977); Pierre Lavedan, Histoire de l'urbanisme à Paris (Paris, 1975); David H. Pinkney, Napoleon III and the Rebuilding of Paris (Princeton, 1958); Anthony Sutcliffe, The Autumn of Central Paris: The Defeat of Town Planning, 1850–1970 (Montreal, 1971). For transportation, see Conservatoire National des Arts et Métiers, Centre de documentation d'histoire des techniques, Analyse historique de l'évolution des transports en commun dans la région parisienne de 1855 à 1939 (Paris, 1977); Christian Gérondeau, Les Transports urbains (2nd ed.; Paris, 1977); Philippe Laneyrie, Le Taxi dans la ville: L'Ervers du mythe (Paris, 1979); Joseph Jones, The Politics of Transport in Twentieth-Century France (Montreal, 1984); John P. McKay, Tramways and Trolleys: The Rise of Urban Mass Transport in Europe (Princeton, 1976); Pierre Merlin, Les Transports parisiens: Études de géographie économique et sociale (Paris, 1967). One contemporary book that deals with transportation in the era of horse-drawn cabs is Bernard Causse, Les Fiacres de Paris aux XVIIe et XVIIIe siècles (Paris, 1972).

5. Alexandre Dumas, "Le Cocher de cabriolet," in Paris, ou le livre des cent-et-un (Brussels, 1831–34), II, 226–60. For comments on Dumas and his coachman, as

Other popular writers pointed out that coachmen were synony-mous with honesty and fidelity. Nicolas Brazier wrote that coach-men could frequently be seen returning gold-filled purses to their rightful owners and that the coachmen's reputation for honesty caused many wine merchants to adopt as their establishments' names the words *Au cocher fidèle* ("At the Faithful Coachman"). Emile de La Bédollière reported that the "cocher de fiacre is truly as faithful" as Saint Fiacre, his patron saint. The ultimate faithful and honest coach-man, perhaps, was "an old man, bent, with sickly eyes" who once took a passenger to a business meeting but refused his tip because he believed his horse had been too slow. When the client emerged from the meeting, he was surprised to see the old coachman waiting for him. "He even remained on the spot where [the client] had left him, crammed, on his seat, inert."[6]

Nothing catches the image of the suffering coachman better, however, than the portrait Gustave Flaubert painted in *Madame Bo-vary*. Although the incident described in the novel concerns a pro-vincial coachman, the type it presents is universal. The soon-to-be lovers Léon and Emma hire a cab and force the coachman to drive an entire night "without any fixed plan or direction, [wandering] about at hazard." The coachman's frustration emerges quickly: "From time to time the coachman on his box cast despairing eyes at the public houses. . . . He tried now and then [to stop], and at once exclama-tions of anger burst forth behind him. Then he lashed his perspir-ing jades afresh, but indifferent to their jolting, running up against things here and there, not caring if he did, demoralized, and almost weeping with thirst, fatigue, and depression."[7]

The public did not regard all coachmen as faithful, honest, or exploited, however. One writer reported that coachmen loved to

---

well as on Hugo and his, see A. de Bersaucourt, "Cochers de fiacre," *L'Opinion*, July 25, 1925, pp. 15–17, and Georges Montorgueil, *La Vie des boulevards* (Paris, 1896), 70–72.

6. Nicolas Brazier, "Les Cochers de Paris," in *Paris, ou le livre des cent-et-un*, XI, 181; Émile de La Bédollière, *Les Industriels, métiers et professions en France* (Paris, 1842), 166; Robert de Bonnières, "Vieux cocher," in Editions du Figaro, *Les Types de Paris* (Paris, 1889), 114–15.

7. Gustave Flaubert, *Madame Bovary*, trans. Eleanor Marx-Aveling (London, 1928), 202.

bang their whips against the cab window as a joke. A cartoonist for *Le Charivari* drew a coachman turning away a female passenger because she was not a blonde and showed another refusing to move until he finished reading his journal. Brazier wrote that any time a passenger wished to go to Bicêtre, the site of a mental hospital, he suffered the standard coachman's banter of being asked if he wished to remain there "and [the coachman] laugh[ed] this stupid laugh." One poem related the exploits of a mean coachman who loved to run down bicyclists because they caused accidents. In his novel *The Red and the Black*, Stendhal describes in a telling comparison the force of anger expressed by the Marquis de la Mole against Julien Sorel: "He began to heap Julien with atrocious insults, worthy of a cabman." A chronicler of Parisian life warned against hiring a coachman immediately after the latter had eaten: "Exposed since morning to cold, to rain, he senses very imperiously the need to revive himself, and, communicating to his horses the excitement that he himself feels, he takes to his route with an unaccustomed daring, passes private coaches, cuts into corner posts, climbs to attack the sidewalk." One popular book on horse-drawn vehicles described coachmen in this manner: "Very servile or very arrogant, little by little, their rough humor disturbs the client. When the client hires a coach, he knows how the trip will begin, but never how it will end." Another commentator opined that "the shortest road between one point and another is certainly not the cab."[8]

Foreign visitors to Paris did not fare any better than the native French. An Italian tourist at the time of the 1878 exposition wrote: "We find ourselves suddenly embarrassed. We had read in the newspapers that the coachmen of Paris pushed their presumptuousness to such a point, that they are not willing to carry fat people." As he himself was overweight, he found "the brutality of coachmen" very tiresome. A guide book to the 1878 exposition warned visitors to "turn over [to the police] the coachmen's number, and . . . not [to]

8. Victor Fournel, *Ce qu'on voit dans les rues de Paris* (Paris, 1858), 275; *Le Charivari*, September 13, 1883, p. 3; Brazier, "Les Cochers," in *Paris, ou le livre des cent-et-un*, XI, 181; *Le Cocher vélophobe* (Paris, 1896); Stendhal, [Marie Henri Beyle], *The Red and The Black*, trans. Lloyd C. Parks (New York, 1970), 436; La Bédollière, *Les Industriels*, 163; *A propos du concours hippique: Les Voitures et les ordonnances de police* (Paris, n.d., [ca. 1889]), 15; Montorgueil, *La Vie des boulevards*, 70.

suffer either insolence or illegitimate demands on their part." Another guide book, for the 1889 exposition, advised its readers that "the coachmen on the road always find some hitch, some traffic jam to make you late."[9]

Then there were the scheming coachmen. One bragged that a maid had hired him for her mistress and paid for the ride in advance. The cabbie picked up his client and drove her to her destination. Not knowing he had already been compensated, she paid him again. The coachman not only did not explain the mistake but also said he had no change for the large denomination coin she offered. He volunteered to obtain change in a nearby boutique, knowing his passenger was late for her appointment. She "lost her patience, as I hoped she would" he reported happily, and "leaving the cab while hurrying away [she] said 'keep the change.'"[10]

The most widespread popular belief about coachmen was that they were drunkards. A provincial visitor to the capital wrote that "it is impossible to imagine the degree of insolence achieved sometimes by the *cochers de cabriolet,* especially if they are drunk, which is often." The businessman who took pity on the faithful coachman who had refused to tip was convinced by the end of his ride "that this old coachman was tipsy." Besides, he ventured, "everyone knows that in Paris all old coachmen booze it up." A popular vaudeville play of the Restoration period took for granted its audience's knowledge that coachmen constantly frequented wine merchants' shops. A student of Parisian customs, doing research for a story on coachmen, obtained the total confidence of a coachman by offering him wine.[11]

9. Edmondo de Amicis, *Studies of Paris,* trans. W. W. Cady (New York, 1882), 2, 253–54; Hippolyte Gautier and Adrian Desprez, *Les Curiosités de l'exposition de 1878. Guide du visiteur* (Paris, 1878), 227; Exposition de 1889, *Guide bleu du Figaro et du Petit Journal avec 5 plans et 31 dessins* (Paris, 1889), 37.

10. Victor-Joseph-Etienne Jouy, *L'Hermite de la Chaussée-d'Antin, ou observations sur les moeurs et les usages français au commencement du XIXe siècle* (Paris, 15–18), III, 33.

11. Louis-Gabriel Montigny, *Le Provincial à Paris, esquisses des moeurs parisiennes* (Paris, 1825), II, 32–33; de Bonnières, "Vieux Cocher," in Editions du Figaro, *Les Types de Paris,* 116; Gabriel Dumerson and Nicolas Brazier, *Les Cochers, tableau grivois, mêlé de vaudeville, en un acte* (Paris, 1825); Jouy, *L'Hermite de la Chaussée-d'Antin,* III, 29.

At the negative end of the range of popular opinion, even past the schemes and drunkards, was the vision of the coachman as criminal. Public authorities assumed that the profession of coachman had "become a resource for bad fellows" and that coachmen used their coaches to receive stolen goods and to hide criminals. The ultimate criminal coachman was a murderer, the infamous Jacques Collignon, who in 1855 shot and killed one of his clients. According to accounts of this incident, on September 16, a tourist couple who had been visiting Paris with their daughter for the 1855 exposition hailed Collignon at the Place de la Concorde for a drive to the Bois de Boulogne.[12] At their destination a heated argument broke out between the cabbie and Monsieur Juge, the husband, when Collignon refused to return two francs change from a five-franc piece, claiming that the two francs were an appropriate tip. Madame Juge restrained her husband by convincing him to report the incident to the police. The following day Juge submitted a formal written complaint, together with Collignon's cab number, to the police. The police summoned Collignon, who on September 22 appeared at the police pound. There, a police official demanded that Collignon visit Juge, who was staying with friends on the rue d'Enfer, return the disputed sum, and report back to the police within twenty-four hours. Collignon asked whether he would be suspended, and the police agent's vague answer implied he would. Collignon left the police, purchased two pistols, and on September 24 called on Juge. Instead of returning the money, however, Collignon shot and killed his former passenger and also wounded Juge's wife. He then calmly left the apartment building but made no serious effort to escape, and the police, responding to the commotion the shootings had created, easily apprehended him.

According to one version of this event, Collignon was so furious at being taken advantage of that he exclaimed, "Ah! someone wants to reduce me to poverty! Well then! I shall teach the bourgeois what it means to take away the bread of a coachman!" During his questioning by the police, he stated, without any feeling of remorse, that he "had . . . definitively decided to avenge [himself] against the ex-

12. France, Conseil d'État, *Projets de décrets et rapports, 1806–1809* (Paris, 1811), report no. 29002, pp. 2–4. Pierre Bouchardon, *Crimes d'autrefois* (Paris, 1926); Théodore Labourieu, *Le Cocher Collignon* (Paris, n.d.).

ploiters who only aim to make [the workers] die of hunger." He concluded that he "preferred to die a free man than to live as a slave." Neither the police nor the court had much sympathy for Collignon's sense of outrage, so he was convicted of murder in mid-November and executed on December 6. One narrative of the crime concluded: "The memory of Collignon's act of murder, its brutality, its cynicism, has remained an indelible stain on the corporation of the [coachmen]. There is no more bloody insult for these brave men than to address them with the qualification *Collignon!* For them this name is the most coarse invective."[13]

This tale, however, does not consider the injustice a working man saw in being first deprived of his tip and then faced with the prospect of several days' suspension from work. These stories, told from the perspective of those outside the profession, conform to superficial stereotypes of coachmen. What is needed is a balancing perspective that penetrates the popular image of the coachman and offers a new assessment of this much maligned portion of the Paris population.

As a work force, the numerically significant and omnipresent coachmen had two overriding characteristics. First, the great majority of them had migrated to Paris from some rural region of France. Many were seasonal workers in the capital, though a significant portion of Parisian cabbies integrated themselves into urban life. These provincials often saw their jobs, as did café workers or female servants, as the first step toward permanent integration into the urban milieu.[14] Many coachmen settled in the city, married women with urban backgrounds, raised families, and socialized within a network of Parisian friends, including some with commercial occupations. They frequently had commercial aspirations, and for some, driving or owning a cab was a stepping stone into the commercial world. Permanent or transient, they hoped to better their social and economic situation by working in the capital.

13. Labourieu, *Le Cocher Collignon*, 260; Bouchardon, *Crimes d'autrefois*, 46–47; Labourieu, *Le Cocher Collignon*, 282.

14. McBride, *The Domestic Revolution*, 10–11; see also Louise A. Tilly and Joan W. Scott, *Women, Work, and Family* (New York, 1987), a work that contains information on the migration of women into cities throughout. For information on *garçons de café*, see De Langle, *Le Petit Monde des cafés*.

Second, coachmen were not traditional members of the working class, and it is this fact that makes them interesting and important. Some coachmen owned their own cabs, some were members of coachmen's cooperatives, and others worked for cab firms ranging in size from a few cabs to several thousand. In spite of these differences, at midcentury coachmen generally regarded themselves as members of one *corporation des cochers de Paris*. Those with no stake in ownership were not sharply divided from small-scale cab entrepreneurs, nor did they regard their interests as mutually exclusive. Small-scale entrepreneurs, single-cab owners, cooperative coachmen, and hired coachmen all shared common adversaries: the police, their customers, and the giant capitalist cab firms that were beginning to form. Ownership of a cab did not automatically lead to class consciousness. As the century wore on, especially after 1870, however, a working-class consciousness increasingly set in among the coachmen. By the 1880s a decided shift of alliances had occurred in the cab trade. Small-scale entrepreneurs united with large cab companies against a working-class socialist union of coachmen that had formed within the corporation. Over a thirty-year period, the status of cab ownership had come to divide the corporation of Parisian coachmen.

From these characteristics spring the two central concerns of this study. The first concern is to explore the factors that motivated rural men to seek the trade of coachman in Paris. What can we learn about the social integration of rural inhabitants into an urban environment by examining this trade? The second is to investigate the kinds of experiences that generated class consciousness and collective action among coachmen. These men developed self-conscious attitudes about class largely, as will be argued here, because of the economic structure of the cab industry and because of work-site experiences, but these attitudes were also tempered by concerns for their integration into the rhythms of Paris life and for the economic and social improvement such integration afforded. This conclusion begs the question of why ownership in itself became a serious dividing line among coachmen in the 1880s when it had not been so in the 1850s. To frame an adequate response to that question, one must consider the factors that generated shared attitudes and values at midcentury and the factors that eventually exposed the markedly different interests and goals of capital and labor.

In an article on the formation of the French working class, Michelle Perrot writes that in the first half of the nineteenth century class consciousness arose largely out of both the experiences of urban artisans and mutual aid societies and the fundamental impact of political events, especially the revolutions of 1830 and 1848. Not central to the formation of a self-conscious working class, economic structures became more important, however, in the second half of the century. The Great Depression of the 1880s, for example, looms too large not to have had some impact on working-class formation, but even in this period "it is by no means certain that economic factors were determinative."[15] The Great Depression, Perrot notes, produced contradictory effects. Besides the possible contribution of economic factors, she points to other elements that most historians agree were critical in the forging of a collective identity among workers. The working class defined itself by its common space (enclosed or mobile), its common enemies, its common misfortune (especially its low wages), its belief that it alone produced something of material value, and its shared culture, at the heart of which stood the family and the neighborhood.

Perrot is describing, for the most part, the formation of a collective identity among "traditional" workers—workers who produced material objects or at least acted upon them with great physical exertion. Such workers, Perrot writes, excluded from their ranks those who toiled in the domestic trades or the service sector; they regarded the work of the latter as servile or too closely allied to the bourgeoisie. Even public coachmen, who, unlike private coachmen or domestics, could not be said to have adopted bourgeois values and who were not especially servile, were looked upon with suspicion by traditional workers. Yet by the 1880s there did develop within the coachman's trade a working-class identity, working-class insti-

15. Michelle Perrot, "On the Formation of the French Working Class," in *Working-Class Formation: Nineteenth-Century Patterns in Western Europe and the United States*, ed. Ira Katznelson and Aristide R. Zolberg (Princeton, 1986), 71–110, esp. 94. This book, whose essays sum up recent literature on the problematic of working-class formation, contains two more essays on the French working class, one by William H. Sewell, Jr., on artisans and factory workers and one by Alain Cottereau on French working-class cultures, as well as essays on the German and United States working classes.

tutions, and collective action aimed against the owning class. Standing apart from working-class coachmen were the small cab owner-workers, cooperative coachmen, aspiring cab owners, and, at the other extreme, medium- to large-sized cab firms. A detailed investigation of this one trade reveals not only many similarities between coachmen and more traditional workers in the development of class attitudes and loyalties but also some significant differences. It also illuminates the factors that led a portion of the trade to remain apart from working-class institutions and activities.

There are several key elements in the process of class formation and class consciousness among coachmen, some more important than others. Of central importance is the fact that coachmen wished either to supplement other wages by driving cabs or to integrate themselves more fully into the life of Paris, which suggests that they entered the profession to improve their economic and (perhaps) social standing. The structure and development of cab trade in the nineteenth century limited the ability of coachmen to realize these goals. In addition, police and cab company rules governing the workday were fundamental in shaping coachmen's attitudes. These factors, ever present in the history of the cab trade, defined the coachman's workday, his employment, and his opportunities for social advancement and integration from the moment of his arrival in Paris. Thus, the structure of the cab trade and the rules governing its operations were as integral to the coachman's working world as the streets of Paris.

It is a basic argument of this study that the concentration of ownership and the intensification of surveillance were central to the formation of working-class consciousness and activity within the cab trade. Concentration of ownership meant that an increasing number of coachmen worked for a few large capitalist firms. The existence of such powerful companies, in turn, reduced an individual coachman's chance for ownership. Moreover, working for a large capitalist cab firm habituated many coachmen to thinking of themselves merely as workers. The intensified surveillance contributed to their sense of closed opportunities and to their growing feeling of kinship with more traditional workers. Additionally, the pressure of an economic crisis in the 1880s, an intensification of the workday during Paris expositions, and the beginnings of a revolutionary syndicalist movement were important short-term factors in the development of this working-class identity among many coachmen.

The types of clients coachmen served and the neighborhoods in which they lived also helped to define class loyalties, though never consistently. Even more, a political tradition of Republican socialism and a hearkening back to the ideals of the French Revolution, extended to the workers and not merely to the bourgeoisie, animated the coachmen in the 1880s. The primary emphasis here, however, is on the importance of the daily operations and overall structure of the workplace, the coachmen's experiences there, and their material well-being and social aspirations. What did not play an important role in the formation of class consciousness among coachmen was technological change, loss of skills, or any revolutionary experience.

The cumulative impact of economic structure, workplace, domicile, material well-being, and the hope for urban integration did not always result in a neat delineation of class boundaries, though. Not all coachmen identified themselves as workers. Concentration of ownership in the cab trade notwithstanding, the small firm remained an essential component of the cab trade. In addition, despite the highly regulated nature of their workday, coachmen always exercised a high level of "shopfloor" autonomy: they worked alone and had some control over their hours of employment. Factory workers frequently had such control as well; Perrot cites the example of leather-dressers of Gentilly (near Paris) and of nailworkers of Revin (Ardennes) who struck in 1907 because their employers tried to regulate their work schedules. Alain Cottereau points out that the image of a factory as a well-run prison rests mostly on literature produced by the bourgeoisie, modeled on its conception of the ideal factory.[16] Coachmen, however, because they were responsible for the cab's financial productivity and because their work site was the entire city of Paris, exercised a measure of autonomy and responsibility unique among French workers. This combination of opportunity, responsibility, and autonomy kept alive (sometimes barely so) hopes for social advancement.

16. *Ibid.*, 82–83; Alain Cottereau, "The Distinctiveness of Working-Class Cultures in France, 1848–1900," in *Working-Class Formation*, ed. Katznelson and Zolberg, 130–35.

Thus, such factors as concentration of ownership, surveillance, the economic crisis of the 1880s, the intensification of the workday, and the introduction of revolutionary ideas created a situation in which hard-core working-class coachmen stood at one extreme, cab entrepreneurs and large cab companies at the other. Standing somewhere in between were the coachmen for whom a measure of upward social movement, represented by the ownership of a cab or permanence in the capital, was still the major goal. The close link between the desire for some social and economic advancement and the formation of class consciousness touched all coachmen. Those for whom upward social movement remained a primary objective refused to define themselves as classic workers. Others, as opportunities for advancement diminished, cast their lot with the traditional members of the Parisian working class. The model employed here, with greater weight given to economic structures and workplace, differs from the factory model Perrot describes. The reasons are threefold: the first involves the trade itself, which is in the service sector; the second lies in the initial impulse that drove people to this occupation, the desire to improve social and economic standing; the third is the unique organization and structure of this trade. The above explanatory agents and special characteristics of the coachmen's trade are the subjects of the chapters that follow.

# I — THE STRUCTURE OF THE PARISIAN CAB INDUSTRY

Parisian coachmen worked within an unusual environment and industry. They plied their trade on all the streets and boulevards of Paris, frequently far removed from the watchful eye of cab inspectors or the police. They were also financially responsible for the cab's total receipts. Below these important surface characteristics lay the particular structure of their industry, which shaped the coachmen's social status and political action. From 1855 on, the ownership of cab firms became more and more concentrated in a few hands. Nevertheless, small cab firms and cooperative cab enterprises continued to compete with the giant capitalist companies, and the cab industry remained highly competitive throughout the nineteenth century. The cab trade attracted men with hopes of improving their material well-being and perhaps of one day becoming (cab) entrepreneurs. Concentration of ownership extinguished that hope for many, while the small firms kept it alive for others.

There were two kinds of public cabs in Paris in the nineteenth century, the *voiture de place* and the *voiture sous remise*. The voiture de place, the common Parisian cab, had two basic models, the standard four-seat vehicle and the smaller *cabriolet*. The popular and affectionate name by which this ordinary cab was known to Parisians was the *fiacre,* a name about whose origins there is some controversy. One popular account is that in 1632 a coachmaster from Amiens, Nicolas

Sauvage, established a cab company in Paris. He located his firm in the Hotel Saint Fiacre on the corner of the rue Saint Martin and the rue Montmorency and hired out his cabs from the courtyard of the hotel. In front of the hotel was a statue of Saint Fiacre, and the saint's name eventually became associated with the coachmen and their cabs, then as time passed with the cab only.[1]

Whatever the origins of its popular name, the voiture de place was the only vehicle authorized to park at municipal cab stations. Customers could engage these cabs solely at these stations, for in the nineteenth century the law generally forbade cabbies from cruising for a fare. The voiture sous remise, a fancier vehicle than the voiture de place, remained at the owner's depot, where clients had to go to rent them. The fees for voitures sous remise were always slightly higher than for voitures de place. However, the former served essentially the same function as the latter and was eventually used in the same fashion. The cab trade also supplied a vehicle known as the *voiture de grande remise*. The largest cab on the road, it was an enclosed coach with glass windows, seating as many as six people. Hired for at least a day, it was used mostly for special occasions such as weddings.

Among the important technical improvements in horse-drawn cabs was the rubber tire, which first appeared on Paris streets in 1896. By the end of that year, three hundred voitures de place had rubber tires; by 1903 six thousand voitures de place were so equipped. Some cabs had heated interiors, the heat generated by coal or briquettes. A police regulation of 1897 required that cabs with heat indicate that fact with the sign *chauffée* and that the exhaust from the fire run outside the vehicle.[2] Electronic meters to indicate clearly and uniformly the number of kilometers a vehicle had traveled, the time elapsed, and the price of the ride began to make their appearance in the 1890s; they came into general use during the following decade.[3]

---

1. See Causse, Les Fiacres de Paris, 14–15.

2. Anne Boudou, "Les Taxis parisiens de la fondation des Usines Renault aux 'Taxis de la Marne' 1898–1914" (Mémoire de maîtrise, Université de Paris X, Nanterre, 1981), 47–48.

3. Excellent discussions of meters may be found ibid., 75–97; Alfred Martin, Étude historique et statistique sur les moyens de transport dans Paris, avec plans, diagrammes et cartogrammes (Paris, 1894), 54–67; and Georges Mareschal, Les Voitures de place: Étude de la réglementation parisienne de la circulation (Dijon, 1912), 181–91.

The cost of a cab ride depended on the type of vehicle employed, whether the cab was engaged *à la course* (by the ride) or *à l'heure* (by the hour), whether it was during the day or evening, and whether the cab remained inside Paris or was engaged to travel outside the city's walls. Throughout the nineteenth century the prefect of police, the official in charge of the Paris traffic codes, kept fares for cab rides stable in order to preserve social peace. In the mid-1850s, for instance, a daytime ride in a voiture de place with two horses was one franc, fifty centimes à la course and two francs for the hour. These rates increased to two and three francs, respectively, for a nighttime trip, and all rates increased slightly for a cab ride beyond the city's walls. The cost of the voiture sous remise was generally higher for all categories of rides.[4] An attempt to reform this system in July, 1857, by basing the fare structure solely on the duration of the ride as measured by the cabbie's timepiece proved a disaster. Clients complained endlessly of faulty watches or purposely slow coachmen. In November, 1857, the police restored the old system but raised fares slightly. They continued one reform, however, permitting cab firms to charge extra fees for large packages brought into the cab and for a cab returning to Paris empty from beyond the city's fortifications.[5]

A technological change far more dramatic than meters made its appearance in Paris during the 1890s: the automobile. By the early twentieth century Paris was also served by omnibuses, trams, a circular railway line for transportation around the city and to its suburbs, a river boat service, and a metropolitan underground railway. For most of the nineteenth century, though, the omnibus was the cab's major rival for passengers. An omnibus was a rectangular closed carriage with a row of windows on each side and room for (at first)

4. For a comparative analysis of tariff rates and tariff systems, see the following: Préfet de Police, *Tarif des voitures de place* (Paris, 1842), in APP, D/B 506; Préfet de Police, *Tarif des voitures de place* (Paris, n.d. [1850]), *ibid.*; *Livret des voitures publiques: Guide des voyageurs dans Paris* (Paris, 1850), 58, and (Paris, 1857), 37; De Lizaranzu, *Nouveau Tarif et ordonnances concernant les voitures de place* (Paris, 1857); and Préfecture de Police, *Ordonnance concernant le tarif des voitures de place* (Paris, December 24, 1857), in APP, D/B 506.

5. See Préfecture de Police, *Ordonnance concernant le tarif* (December 24, 1857). Coachmen claimed that the firm's charges for baggage brought into the cab angered clients, who then refused to tip cabbies. See *Rapport à messieurs les administrateurs et à monsieur le Directeur Général de la Compagnie Impériale des Voitures de Place* (Paris, November 2, 1857), in APP, D/B 505.

twelve passengers. Omnibus service began in the capital in 1828 when the prefect of police granted to Stanislas Baudry, a transportation entrepreneur from Nantes, the exclusive right to run one hundred omnibuses along fixed routes. The starting point for Baudry's omnibuses was the rue Lancry on the right bank. From there, some would travel to the church of the Madeleine, while others traveled in the opposite direction to the Place de la Bastille. Departures were every quarter hour, and the price of a ride was initially twenty-five centimes, soon increased to thirty centimes. There were no fixed boarding points; people along the designated route and passengers within the omnibus signaled the coachman to stop. It was not long before the authorities granted other routes to additional transportation firms, and the simple omnibus with passengers riding inside was supplemented in 1853 by a model with an *impériale,* an open platform fitted on the omnibus roof with a guardrail and benches accommodating up to twelve passengers. Interior seating was first class, whereas those on the top rode second class.[6] In 1855, all existing omnibus firms merged to form a municipal omnibus service under the CGO.

Railway companies also provided their own special omnibus service to take travelers from the Gare Saint-Lazare or the Gare Montparnasse to a station in one of the several central Parisian *quartiers.* By 1900, just in time for the Paris exposition of that year, the two companies that ran steamers up and down the Seine River merged with a third to form the Compagnie Générale des Bateaux Parisiens. Ironically, however, transportation by river boat began to decline in 1900, most likely because of competition from the metropolitan underground.[7]

London had had an underground rail system since 1863, and New York had inaugurated an elevated railway system in 1868. Although discussions concerning a metropolitan railway line had begun in Paris as early as 1845, not until the 1870s did city officials begin to

6. So many secondary works have information on the omnibus that only a few useful ones are cited: Martin, *Étude historique,* 80–110; Alfred de Foville, "Les Transports: Les Voitures publiques," *L'Économiste français,* August 26, 1876, pp. 273–75; Evenson, *Paris;* Louis Lagarrigue, *Cents ans de transports en commun dans la région parisienne* (Paris, 1956); and Conservatoire National des Arts et Métiers, Centre de documentation, *Analyse historique.*

7. See Evenson, *Paris,* 79–122.

debate this issue in earnest—a debate that continued for over twenty years. Some wanted an urban railway underground; others insisted it be elevated. The city government believed the issue was a municipal matter, while the minister of public works and the prefect of the Seine Department each argued that the proposed transportation system was of national interest and should therefore belong to their respective domains. By the 1890s the grand outline of the plan had been decided. The Paris urban railway would be a local system serving the needs of Parisians. It would be an underground transportation system, with the major lines following the north-south and east-west routes of the major streets above ground. The first line of the Métro, as it was called, followed the east-west route between the Porte de Maillot and the Porte de Vincennes. Eleven kilometers long, the partially completed line was inaugurated on July 19, 1900.[8]

Cabs and cab companies, therefore, formed one part of an extensive and varied transportation system in Paris. The general rise in the population of the city throughout the nineteenth century and the improvement of the street system during the Second Empire were important stimuli for the growth of the cab industry. Employment opportunities in this trade were a major attraction for workers and entrepreneurs alike.

In the nineteenth century Paris grew in area as well as in population. In 1836, the small zone that was Paris was populated by 899,313 persons. That figure grew to 1,174,346 by 1856. In 1860, Paris formally annexed its immediate suburbs, and the population the following year for the expanded city stood at 1,696,141. By 1911, the number of inhabitants of Paris was 2,888,107.[9] Until the middle of the nineteenth century, when Emperor Napoleon III and the prefect of the Seine Department, Baron Georges Haussmann, made radical improvements in street and boulevard construction, the average Parisian found the circulation of traffic a major nuisance. Paris was a city of winding, narrow streets, with no arteries crossing the entire city in either a north-south or an east-west direction. The difficulty in reaching the center of the city hindered the development of residen-

8. *Ibid.*

9. See Louis Chevalier, "L'Évolution du peuplement," in *Paris 1960* (Paris, 1961), 37–46.

tial districts on its outskirts. Matters were further complicated when an 1842 law made Paris the national center of a radiating system of railway lines. Private railway companies constructed their lines to Paris but took no interest in the transportation system within the city. The railway terminals, moreover, were situated on the fringes of Paris rather than in its center, placing an additional burden on adjacent small streets as passengers negotiated their way to other terminals or to different parts of the city.[10]

One of Haussmann's great accomplishments was the significant improvement of the street system of Paris. He created the long-needed north-south, east-west axial crossing in the center of the city, the so-called *grande croisée*. The east-west artery extended the rue de Rivoli to the rue Saint Antoine, leading in turn to the Place de la Bastille and continuing to the Place de la Nation. In the opposite direction, the rue de Rivoli connected with the Champs Élysées. The north-south axis was formed by the present avenue du Générale Leclerc, the avenue Denfert-Rochereau, and the boulevard Saint Michel on the Left Bank. This route crossed over the Seine through the Île de la Cité and continued on the right bank over the boulevards Sébastopol and Strasbourg all the way to the Gare de L'Est. Haussmann not only constructed and extended these major avenues but also linked them to side streets, creating a fairly coherent street and boulevard system for Paris and thus accommodating an increased number of vehicles of all kinds on the streets.[11]

As the population grew throughout the nineteenth century, the number of Parisian cabs grew steadily and sometimes dramatically. A generally agreed upon estimate for the number of Parisian cabs at the time of the French Revolution is 1,000 fiacres and 800 *carosses de remise*.[12] In 1817, demographers embarked on a survey of the material condition of Paris, completed in 1819 and published in 1821, which included a tally of all public and private vehicles registered or circu-

10. See Sutcliffe, *The Autumn of Central Paris*, 28–29, and Barrie M. Ratcliffe, "Urban Space and the Siting of Railway Stations, 1830–1847," *Proceedings of the Annual Meeting of the Western Society for French History*, XVI (1988), 224–34.

11. An excellent discussion of this project is Evenson, *Paris*, 15–75.

12. See Causse, *Les Fiacres de Paris*, 53, and Alfred de Foville, *La Transformation des moyens de transports et ses consequénces économiques et sociales* (Paris, 1880), 172.

TABLE 1
Number of Cabs in Paris in 1819, by Type

| Type of vehicle | Number of registered vehicles | Average circulating in 1818 |
|---|---|---|
| Fiacres or Carrosses de place | 900 | 817 |
| Cabriolets | | 1,259 |
| interior[a] | 765 | |
| exterior[b] | 406 | |
| Carrosses de remise | 489 | |
| Cabriolets de remise | 388 | |
| Total | 2,948 | |

[a] For service inside Paris.
[b] For service outside Paris.
Source: Préfecture de la Seine, *Recherches statistiques* (Paris, 1821), I, Table 55.

lating in Paris.[13] The total number of public cabs in 1819 came to 2,948. Table 1, reproduced from the 1821 survey, breaks down this figure to show the numbers of the different types of cabs.

By midcentury, Paris was served by approximately 5,400 voitures de place and voitures sous remise of all kinds.[14] In 1900, the year of an international exposition, it had the largest number of horse-drawn cabs, 17,145 (a figure that does not include 4,272 voitures de grande remise).[15] The trend was reversed during the period from 1901 to the end of World War I. The number of horse-drawn cabs declined steadily from 10,703 in 1901 to 4,325 in 1913, and the war hastened their demise. The number of horses in Paris also kept pace with changes in population and transportation. In 1819, there were 16,000 horses in Paris. By 1892, there were 86,150 horses, 15,084 of which worked for the CGO and 11,177 for the CGV. In 1912, by contrast, the horse population of Paris had declined to 55,418, of which 9,733 belonged to the CGV and 621 to the CGO.

13. Préfecture de la Seine, *Recherches statistiques sur la ville de Paris et le département de la Seine* (Paris, 1821–60).
14. Martin, *Étude historique*, 46–47. The exact figure he gives is 5,442.
15. All data on public coaches in Paris from 1880 may be found in tables published annually by the service de la statistique municipale, Préfecture de la Seine, in *Annuaire statistique de la ville de Paris* (Paris, 1880–1919).

TABLE 2
Passengers Using Mass Transportation and the CGV, 1865, 1901

| Type of transportation | Number of passengers transported | | Augmentation | Percentage increase in passengers |
|---|---|---|---|---|
| | 1865 | 1901 | 1901 | |
| Voitures de place | 10,840,890 | 29,779,620 | 18,938,730 | 174 |
| CGO | 104,579,750 | 266,935,912 | 162,356,162 | 155 |
| Chemin de fer de ceinture | 3,664,735 | 31,398,348 | 27,733,613 | 756 |

Source: CGV, *Assemblée générale . . . du 27 avril 1903* (Paris, 1903), 26.

From 1898 on, however, the cab companies began converting from horse-drawn coaches to auto-taxis, at an average annual rate of increase for auto-taxis of about 60 percent by 1913. The number of motor cabs of all kinds ranged from 22 in 1898, the first year the *Annuaire statistique* of the city of Paris began to record these data, to slightly over 10,000 in 1913.[16] The employment opportunities for cabbies obviously remained excellent despite the decline of the horse-drawn vehicle. Drivers of horse-drawn cabs not old enough to retire often made the transition to automobiles.

A final barometer of the scope of public transportation in Paris is provided by the figures on ridership of the CGV, the largest cab firm in the capital. In presenting these data to its shareholders, the CGV, in a mood of confidence in its future, contrasted the percentage growth of the Paris population from 1861 to 1901, 48 percent, with the combined average percentage increase of passengers transported by cabs, omnibuses, and the rail line encircling Paris over these same years, 315 percent.[17] A comparison of the number of its passengers with those of the CGO and the rail line is found in Table 2.

The number of cab entrepreneurs also increased steadily in the nineteenth century. One Paris almanac records twenty-seven entre-

16. Préfecture de la Seine, *Recherches statistiques*, I, Table 55; Préfecture de la Seine, *Annuaire statistique* (1892), 586 and (1912), 726, (1898), 528, (1913), 396.
17. CGV, *Assemblée . . . du 27 Avril 1903* (Paris, 1903), 26–27.

preneurs operating public cabs in Paris in 1769.[18] By 1803, according to the most useful of all Parisian almanacs, the *Almanach de commerce de Paris,* popularly known as the *Bottin,* 45 *loueurs de carrosses* (cab entrepreneurs) provided Paris with cab service, a figure that increased to 80 by 1810 and to 161 by 1820. By 1825, the nomenclature in the *Bottin* for cab entrepreneurs had changed to *loueurs de voitures et cabriolets,* and under this heading the *Bottin* listed 141 for that year. The number rested at 145 in 1854, one year before Napoleon III created a virtual monopoly over fiacre service under the CIV.[19] The key question, though, is how many cabs each individual cab firm controlled. The data used here to answer this question—data covering specific rather than successive years and ranging from the late seventeenth to the late nineteenth century—both provide a picture of the cab trade at individual moments in time and generally characterize the industry over this period.

In its 1860 survey of Parisian industries, the Paris Chamber of Commerce reported on the number of cabs in relation to cab owners for the year 1753. Since the voitures de place were organized under the monopoly of one firm in 1753, the Compagnie des Carrosses à l'Heure, the Chamber of Commerce surveyed the voitures sous remise portion of the cab trade.[20] The data show the small-scale nature of cab ownership in the industry. According to Table 3, 13.3 percent of the owners possessed 5 to 11 cabs, 58.0 percent owned 2 to 4 cabs, and 28.3 percent had only 1.

In 1779, Louis XVI granted the Compagnie Perreau a thirty-year monopoly over the voitures de place of Paris. The voitures sous remise continued to operate freely. Eleven years later, the anti-monopolistic National Assembly of the French Revolution decreed on November 19, 1790, that the monopoly of the Compagnie Perreau would cease on January 1, 1791. The voiture de place trade was hence-

18. *Essai sur l'almanach général* (Paris, 1769). This volume has no pagination; topics are listed alphabetically.

19. Firmin-Didot, *Almanach de commerce de Paris* (Paris, 1803), 228–38; (Paris, 1810), 237; (Paris, 1820), 505–506; (Paris, 1825), 239–40; (Paris, 1854), 1007–1008.

20. Chambre de Commerce de Paris, *Statistique de l'industrie à Paris: Résultat de l'enquête faite par la Chambre de Commerce pour l'année 1860* (Paris, 1864), 977. For general information on the monopolies of the eighteenth century, see Causse, *Les Fiacres de Paris,* 23–36.

TABLE 3
Cab Ownership in 1753

| Number of cabs per owner | Number of owners |
| --- | --- |
| 5 to 11 | 8 |
| 2 to 4 | 35 |
| 1 | 17 |
| Total | 60 |

Source: Chambre de Commerce de Paris, *Statistique de l'industrie à Paris* (Paris, 1864), 977.

forth open to all entrepreneurs, provided they conformed to police regulations governing public transportation in Paris and paid a tax on each vehicle they owned. The first reliable data on the structure of the postrevolutionary cab trade date from 1855. In the three years from 1855 to 1858, the CIV merged with or acquired cab firms running all but 64 voitures de place, which remained in private hands. The CIV thus enjoyed a virtual monopoly over the Parisian voitures de place. Fortunately, the original schedule of these mergers and acquisitions has survived, also providing a survey of the cab industry in 1854, one year before the establishment of the CIV.[21] According to this document, the CIV took over 140 firms operating cabriolets or fiacres in Paris. Collectively these firms owned 687 cabriolets and 895 fiacres, a total of 1,582 voitures de place. At the time of the takeover, 32.1 percent of the firms, or 45, owned only 1 fiacre or cabriolet; 28.6 percent, or 40 owned 2 to 4 cabs; 21.4 percent, or 30, owned between 5 and 11 cabs; 5.0 percent, or 7, owned 12 to 20 cabs; 7.6 percent, or 11, owned 21 to 50 cabs; and 5.0 percent, or 7, owned 51 to 100 cabs. Thus, 87.1 percent of the Parisian cab owners taken over by the CIV operated 1 to 20 cabs, 7.6 percent operated 20 to 50 cabs, and only 5.0 percent operated 51 to 100 cabs. The 7 firms operating 51 to 100 cabs were large capitalist enterprises, but there were also many small- to medium-sized ventures.[22] The heterogeneous na-

21. ACGV, CIV, "Rachat des numéros de voitures."
22. No other source is as accurate as the CIV's inventory. However, the reader should also consult Martin, *Étude historique*, 48, and APP, B/A 444, note of Paris, December 8, 1856, no. 162.

ture of ownership in the cab trade, with small, medium, and large firms existing side by side, is a very important aspect in the development of political consciousness and union activity among the cabbies, as we shall see.

The Parisian cab trade underwent a radical transformation in 1855 when Napoleon III created the CIV, establishing a virtual monopoly over the voitures de place service. The CIV served several functions. A giant capitalist firm, it was a perfect model of the emperor's policy of economic growth through industrial concentration.[23] It also became one of the two urban transportation monopolies (the other being a monopoly of omnibus firms) he envisaged would service the influx of visitors to Paris his radical building program and the upcoming Universal Exposition in 1855 were expected to attract.[24] He began his experiment of grouping transportation firms with the omnibus service.[25] In May, 1854, the prefect of the Paris police, the official who, with the prefect of the Seine Department, was the most intimately involved with Parisian transportation, suggested that the 11 existing private omnibus firms be combined into 1 and granted a monopoly. A commission chosen by the Paris police prefect, J.-M. Pietri, to study the merger issue, the Commission Municipale, approved the measure, and long and complex negotiations ensued. The merger discussions finally ended successfully in February, 1855, and the newly formed CGO began its operations on March 1, 1855.

23. See Maurice Agulhon, *The Republican Experiment, 1848–1852,* trans. Janet Lloyd (Cambridge, Eng., 1983), 181–82, and Guy P. Palmade, *French Capitalism in the Nineteenth Century,* trans. Graeme M. Holmes (New York, 1972), 122–23.

24. For the rebuilding of Paris, see Gaillard, *Paris, la ville,* and Pinkney, *Napoleon III.*

25. A general overview of omnibus service in Paris from 1828 to 1890, very strong on statistical information though weak on analysis, may be found in Martin, *Étude historique,* 80–110. A more recent discussion of the concentration of Parisian omnibus firms is in T. C. Barker and Michael Robbins, *A History of London Transport: Passenger Travel and the Development of the Metropolis* (Rev. ed.; London, 1975), I, 69–98. This last work, though primarily concerned with London transport, has important information on the Paris merger of 1855 because this event became the model for similar developments in London. Moreover, some French businessmen who were closely associated with the Paris merger played an instrumental role in bringing about the concentration of London omnibus service and in organizing the London General Omnibus Company.

The success of this measure prompted the prefects of the police and the Seine Department to turn their attention to public cabs. By April, a new company to run most of the Parisian voitures de place had been unofficially established and on August 16, 1855, Napoleon III issued the decree officially creating the CIV. In substance, this document formally granted the Messageries Générales de France, one of France's oldest and largest stagecoach companies, 500 new fiacre numbers, or *médallions gratis*. No cab could circulate in Paris without such a number, which only the police could issue. The Messageries Générales, which transformed part of its operations to become the CIV, already possessed 1,569 numbers for voitures de place and 352 for voitures sous remise and was required to build 500 new voitures de place within three months.[26] The government also obliged it to buy out any cab owners or firms willing to sell at prices determined by government experts. (At that time a cab number for a fiacre was worth 7,500 francs and for a cabriolet 6,500 francs.) In 1862, Haussmann further required the new firm not only to continue operating its voitures sous remise but also to have in circulation by January 1, 1865, a total of 3,000 voitures de place. The city imposed a tax of 365 francs on all the vehicles the CIV was required to have in circulation, whether or not they were functioning. Cab firms outside the CIV's control, including most of the voiture sous remise portion of the cab industry and 64 voitures de place, were exempt from this tax unless they wished to park their cabs near public ceremonies and at train stations. The 1855 and 1862 agreements were clearly motivated by the emperor's desire for a rapid expansion of Parisian cab service and for increased revenue through the cab tax.[27]

Although Napoleon III established the domination of the CIV over the voitures de place, he disregarded the voitures sous remise,

26. *Statuts modifiés de la société anonyme projetée sous la dénomination de la Compagnie Impériale des Voitures de Paris* (Paris, 1855), in AN, F12 6762.

27. Two government contracts regulated the CIV: see "Traité avec M. le Préfet de Police" (MS in AN, F12 6762), which includes the "Décret Impérial du 16 août 1855"; and Préfecture du Département de la Seine, Ville de Paris, *Voitures de place et de remise. Traité* (Paris, 1862), also in AN, F12 6762. The founding and history of the CIV is covered in Nicholas Papayanis, "Un Secteur des transports parisiens: Le Fiacre, de la libre entreprise au monopole (1790–1855)," *Histoire, économie et société* (1986), 559–72, and Papayanis, "The Development of the Paris Cab Trade, 1855–1914," *Journal of Transport History* (March, 1987), 52–65.

which remained free and highly competitive in the midnineteenth century. The Paris Chamber of Commerce found that 480 entrepreneurs operated cabs in Paris in 1860, mostly voitures sous remise.[28] Of the 480 cab entrepreneurs, 39, or 8.1 percent, employed 10 or more workers; 105, or 21.9 percent, employed from 2 to 10 workers; and 336, or 70.0 percent, hired 1 worker or worked alone. The pattern is typical of the Parisian cab trade: a significant concentration of cab companies and the continued existence of the small cab firm.

In the mid-1860s the emperor began to "liberalize" his empire, and the cab industry became a convenient symbol of the new policy. Baron Haussmann, who had never been satisfied with the performance of the CIV, welcomed free trade in the cab industry, and in February, 1866, the government ended the CIV's near-monopoly over the voitures de place.[29] Officials of the CIV reacted with a determination to remain the dominant Parisian cab entrepreneur. Their first act was to change the name of the firm to the CGV. The legal pursuit to retain the monopoly went into arbitration. On March 29, 1866, three official arbitrators, two senators and a member of the Council of State, decided that the government had the right to unilaterally suppress the CIV's monopoly (according to an 1862 treaty between the firm and Haussmann, the monopoly was to remain in force until 1912) but that the city of Paris must compensate the CIV 6,473,164 francs. On August 5, 1866, the government granted the CGV the status of *société anonyme* (a legal corporation in the modern sense), which it never had as the CIV, having been organized as a limited partnership.[30]

28. Chambre de Commerce de Paris, *Statistique de l'industrie à Paris,* 977. The *Recherches statistiques* for 1860 indicates that 337 cab entrepreneurs controlled a work force of 4,205 people (4,156 men and 49 women) but provides no further information (Préfecture de la Seine, *Recherches statistiques,* VI, 644).

29. Georges Haussmann, *Mémoires du Baron Haussmann* (Paris, 1890–93), III, 322; Préfecture de la Seine, "Extrait du Registre des Procès-verbaux des Séances du Conseil Municipal de la Ville de Paris. Séance du 9 avril 1866," in AN, F12 6804, note of Paris, February 26, 1894. This latter source also contains a summary of the legal opinion, without a title, concerning the end of the CIV's monopoly once this issue went to arbitration.

30. CGV, *Statuts* (Paris, 1866). Concerning the fifty-year monopoly, see Préfecture de la Seine, *Traité,* 4–5. For the legal decision, see AN, F12 6804, note of Paris, February 26, 1894.

TABLE 4
Employees in Paris Transportation Industry,
1866, 1886

|  | 1866 | 1886 |
|---|---|---|
| Owners | 4,294 | 1,298 |
| Employees | 4,576 | 4,604 |
| Workers | 3,612 | 11,241 |
| Totals | 12,482 | 17,143 |

Source: Préfecture de la Seine, *Résultats statistiques du
dénombrement de 1886 pour la ville de Paris et le département
de la Seine* (Paris, 1887), lxiii.

Although its structure had been permanently altered by Napoleon III's previous policy, the cab industry was now open to free competition. There was a major difference between the pre- and post-1866 periods. Before the monopoly, no single firm or cluster of firms had dominated the trade, but this was no longer true after 1866. In the post-1866 period, the CGV was by far the single most important cab company in Paris. Statistics from the *Résultats statistiques de dénombrement de 1886 pour la ville de Paris et le département de la Seine,* which was published in 1887 in Paris and includes some results of a similar study for 1866, make this fact clear.[31] The 1886 survey, which shows a trend rather than specific details, totals all employees for all types of Parisian transportation (diligences, omnibuses, fiacres, *voitures de démenagement, loueurs de chevaux et voitures*) and compares the 1886 statistics with those for 1866 (see Table 4). The data document a trend toward concentration in the transportation field, a tendency confirmed by an 1896 government survey.

The French government conducted a survey of the major industries and professions in the country in 1896. The section on the cab trade lists 549 cab enterprises: 42.8 percent employed from 1 to 4 workers; 15.7 percent hired from 5 to 10; 12.8 percent, from 11 to 20; 11.7 percent, from 21 to 50; 3.1 percent, from 51 to 100; and 0.9 percent, from 101 to 200. One firm employed 2,000 to 5,000

---

31. The 1866 study, however, cannot be located in any major Parisian library and appears to be lost. Fortunately the 1886 work compares its findings with those of the earlier volume.

TABLE 5
Cabs per Company, 1900

| Type of company | Number of companies | Number of cabs |
|---|---|---|
| Large companies | 2 | 5,300 |
| Small companies | 4 | 524 |
| Large cab-leasing entrepreneurs with from 70 to 200 cabs | 9 | 1,087 |
| Cab-leasing entrepreneurs with at least 25 cabs | 42 | 1,832 |
| Small cab-leasing entrepreneurs with 1 to 3 cabs | 1,077 | 2,503 |
| Cab cooperatives | 16 | 680 |
| Totals | 1,150 | 11,932 |

Source: CGV, "Note sur l'état de l'industrie des voitures de place à Paris . . . le 24 février 1900," *Rapports divers* (Typescript in ACGV).

workers and another, the CGV, over 5,000. The 1896 survey gave no employment data for 62 establishments and listed 8 firms with a single employee. Two other studies, one public and the other private, complete this survey of the trade in the era of the horse-drawn carriage. A 1901 government investigation of the cab industry, similar to the 1896 study, recorded the number of workers per cab firm. The results were as follows: 2.1 percent of the cab firms employed no other worker; 41.0 percent employed from 1 to 4; 13.0 percent employed from 5 to 10; 13.0 percent employed from 11 to 20; 17.3 percent employed from 21 to 100; and 2.5 percent employed more than 100 workers. The survey had no information on 11.1 percent of the firms in the cab trade.[32] The second study came from Maurice Bixio, president of the CGV, who in 1900 circulated within his company a memorandum on the state of the cab trade, using as a standard of a firm's size the number of cabs it circulated (see Table 5).

These studies demonstrate that the cab trade, like any major heavy

32. Ministère du Commerce, de l'industrie, des postes, et des télégraphes, Office du Travail, *Résultats statistiques du recensement des industries et professions, 1896* (Paris, 1896), 114–15, 208, 278–79, and 232–33; Statistique générale de la France, *Résultats statistiques du recensement général de la population effectué le 24 mars 1901* (Paris, 1904–1907), I, 351.

industry, grew and concentrated throughout the nineteenth and early twentieth centuries. This trend was further confirmed when the CGV eventually absorbed the second largest Parisian cab company, the Compagnie Urbaine. At one time, the CGV alone operated half of all Parisian cabs. However, small cab firms persisted throughout this era, too. In 1896, close to 43 percent of the cab firms employed 4 or fewer coachmen and close to 59 percent employed under 10. The trend was still true five years later, when almost 56 percent of the firms surveyed engaged less than 10 people. The CGV's memorandum documented the importance of the small cab firm. It revealed that over 1,000 entrepreneurs operated anywhere from 1 to 3 cabs, and 16 cooperative societies consisted of 680 cabbies. Thus, a coachman could still hope to purchase a cab or, at minimum, save enough to purchase a share in a cooperative society.[33]

This juxtaposition of the giant capitalist cab firm with both the small-scale enterprise and the cooperative society is central to an understanding of the formation of political and class attitudes on the part of cabbies. Although some still aspired to own a cab, others had given up this dream. These attitudes were determined, at least in part, by the structure of the cab trade and the position of the cabbie in relation to the cab firms.

33. See Chap. 5.

# 2 — The Police, Company Discipline, and the Coachman's Workday

In the nineteenth century the cab industry, including the coachmen, was closely supervised by the state and highly regulated from within as well. In fact, no industry, except perhaps the mining industry, was more closely scrutinized and regulated. The purpose of the regulations was twofold. First, the government wanted to assure the delivery to the public of an essential service, transportation, and, since it touched the public so directly and intimately, deliver it in a manner that would guarantee public peace and safety. Second, both the government and the cab industry sought to create in the coachman a submissive worker.[1] Such workers would further the government's aim of social peace in the transportation sector, while the goal of the cab firms was to control a virtually unsupervised employee who could readily keep for himself some of the cab's receipts or simply not perform well.

The state and especially the large cab firms intensified their control as the nineteenth century progressed. This increasingly severe treatment could not but contribute to the coachman's growing sense that he was nothing but a wage-earner with decreased oppor-

1. See Michelle Perrot, "The Three Ages of Industrial Discipline in Nineteenth-Century France," in *Consciousness and Class Experience in Nineteenth-Century Europe*, ed. John M. Merriman (New York, 1979), 157–58.

tunities for independent action. No matter how severe the mechanisms of control, however, they could never totally eliminate an important measure of autonomy, independence, and responsibility that the coachman continued to exercise: police and company agents could not accompany him on all his rounds. This measure of freedom, however faint, kept alive a coachman's sense that he was not like other traditional wage-earners and thus preserved for him a space of social maneuverability, both real and symbolic.

In nineteenth-century Paris, the prefect of police was the virtual master of cab firms and cabbies, a tradition of government power dating from the seventeenth century.[2] At that time the royal government had already established the minimum age for a coachman (eighteen years old), a regulated tariff schedule, and the right of public authorities to tax public vehicles and to determine who could establish a cab firm. The French Revolution seemed to break the pattern of strict government control when, in January, 1791, the authorities abolished the monopoly of one cab company, the Compagnie Perreau, over the operation of fiacres in Paris. Actually, however, the revolutionary authorities ended up merely transferring control from the royal Bureau de la Régie des Carrosses to the prefecture of Paris police, an office created in March, 1800.

The basic requirement imposed by the police on cab owners was that they obtain police authorization before operating or stationing any voiture de place in Paris.[3] All authorized voitures de place prominently displayed inside and outside the cab an official number issued by the prefecture, which enabled the police to identify legitimate cabs. To obtain permission to operate and station cabs, the owners had to ensure that their coaches were solidly constructed, that they were kept in good repair, and that their horses were neither sick nor vicious.[4] Once these requirements were met, the police issued the cab

2. The definitive work on the police and government rules regulating the cab trade in the seventeenth and eighteenth centuries is Causse, *Les Fiacres de Paris*.

3. There is considerable information on the subject of police rules and cab owners throughout Martin, *Étude historique*. See also any printed edition of the police ordinances.

4. Préfecture de Police, *Collection officielle des ordonnances de police, 1800–1874* (Paris, 1844–74), V, 690–91.

owner a certificate for each cab he operated, attesting to its right to park at public cab stations and to circulate. The owner was responsible for ensuring that each of his cabbies carried this certificate on his person, as well as work sheets (*feuilles de contrôle*) to record each fare, a copy of the police rules governing coaching, and cards with the cab's number to give passengers. The police also required cab owners to keep on the streets each day the same number of cabs for which certificates had been issued. Under no circumstances could one owner transfer his rights or obligations to another.

Cab firms could employ as coachmen only those having a police-issued *bulletin de dépôt,* which indicated that they had a valid police *livret* (registration booklet) kept on file at police headquarters or at the cab firm office, depending on whether a cabbie was employed or self-employed. Owners maintained a register in which they entered the name, date of employment, date of withdrawal, and the livret number of all their coachmen. They were required to present this register to the police for inspection at any time and to bring it each month to the *fourrière* (police coach pound) for an official examination. Registers were kept on file for at least a year.

Most of the police rules applied to the conduct and driving procedures of the coachmen. As indicated above, all coachmen had to be at least eighteen years old and in possession of a livret. In 1837, the prefect of police created the post of expert-examiner to test individuals wishing to become Paris coachmen. This official, initially a contract employee working a maximum of twelve hours a week at the coach pound, examined men on their ability to drive a coach and on their knowledge of Paris streets. The prospective cabbies were required to present themselves and their cabs at the coach pound for this examination and could return indefinitely until they satisfied the expert-examiner's requirements. In 1841, the examiner became a full-time employee of the police prefecture.[5] Two major changes in this licensing system occurred in 1888: the police permitted coachmen permanent possession of their own livrets and also restructured the driving examination along more formal lines. From 1888 on, a

5. APP, D/A 259, notes of Paris, August 28, 1837 [Dossier "Expert-examinateur"], and February 22, 1842.

coachman was required to present himself before an examining commission composed of an agent of the police prefecture, representatives from the cab companies, and three other coachmen.[6] The major cab companies established apprenticeship schools that provided a month-long course to prepare cabbies for the examination. The apprentices paid anywhere from twenty-five to fifty francs for the course, depending on the era. If the candidate passed, the police issued him a license with his photograph on it. The police kept a copy of the license in their files.

The working coachman first reported to his depot, where he received his horse and cab. Once he left the company depot, he was required by law to report directly to his assigned public cab station, where clients usually hired cabs. Cruising for a fare was generally illegal, though a coachman on his way to a public cab station during hours of light traffic could stop on the street if hailed by a client. Because of this exception, as one writer noted, coachmen could never be found in cab stations when it was raining.[7] The cabbies preferred to abandon the stations to search for clients on the road. There, far from the watchful eyes of police agents, they would accept as passengers only those wanting to hire them for short rides; several single rides within an hour produced more revenue than an hour-long ride.

A long list of minor rules governed a coachman's comportment. These ranged from prohibitions against speeding (a difficult regulation to enforce in the absence of scientific instruments to determine speed), racing fellow coachmen on Paris streets, and driving while intoxicated to ones against acting rudely toward the public or cracking a whip against the coach's windows and thereby frightening passengers. The only significant difference in the police rules governing the fancier voitures sous remise was that they could not normally park at public cab stations.

Day-to-day police control over coachmen was enforced by the police surveillance system. During the Restoration the Paris police established a permanent surveillance bureau to oversee public cab sta-

6. See Martin, *Étude historique*, 246–47, for a copy of the police ordinance that established this rule.
7. Montigny, *Le Provincial à Paris*, II, 28.

tions.[8] On July 11, 1822, the Paris Municipal Council granted the prefecture of police funds to expand and regularize its cab station inspection. Starting on May 1, 1823, therefore, auxiliary inspectors surveyed each cab station, noting the physical state and exact movement of coaches in and out of the station, the cleanliness of each station, and the suitability of the cabbies. In 1826, the police apportioned 102 inspector's assistants among 68 of the 72 municipal cab stations in Paris, a system codified in 1857.[9]

The system operated in a military fashion. The authorities classed all Parisian cab stations into four geographic sectors and placed one *contrôleur ambulant* over each sector. In 1857, Paris had 139 public cab stations spread throughout twelve *arrondissements* (city wards). They contained places for slightly more than two thousand cabs. The controleur ambulant visited each station within his district to ensure order and to receive the reports of the *surveillants* (supervisors) in his charge. He forwarded the reports to the prefect of police. The surveillants performed the basic work of control in individual stations. *Cantonniers* (station men) cleaned each cab station and maintained its property.

Failure of a coachman to obey any police rule could lead to a hearing before the Disciplinary Commission or a police tribunal. The former listened to complaints against cabbies initiated by the public, whereas the latter involved cases of violations against a police ordinance. Depending on the severity of the infraction, punishment could involve a reprimand, a fine, a short suspension from driving, or even a jail sentence or the rescinding of a driver's license. For example, in 1906, 558 coachmen appeared before the Disciplinary Commission. Of these, 115 received a reprimand for some infraction of the public conduct code; 80 were suspended from work for one day, 44 for two days, 28 for three days, 10 for four days, 21 for five days, 1 for six days, and 68 for eight or more days; and 191 coachmen

8. For information on the creation of this service, see Préfecture de Police, *Compte d'administration des dépenses de la Préfecture de Police, pour l'exercice de l'année 1823* . . . (Paris, 1825), 54; Préfecture de Police, *Compte d'administration . . . pour . . . 1828* (Paris, 1830), 60–61; and the documents in APP, D/A 2, esp. notes of Paris, December 21, 1825, and June 28, 1826.

9. Préfecture de Police, *Arrêté. Service permanent de surveillance sur les stations des voitures de place* (Paris, April 10, 1857), in APP, D/B 503.

had their cases suspended.[10] Moreover, a police agent on the street could invoke a measure against the coachman known as *l'envoi en fourrière,* an expression that translates as "to send to the coach pound." This sentence was imposed if the cab lacked a proper number, if the coachman could not present his permit to circulate, or if the coach's horse was infirm. Sending a coachman and his cab to the pound ensured that the owner of the cab would pay whatever fine might be levied as a result of the infraction. The police also enforced the Loi Grammont, a measure passed in 1850 to protect animals from harsh treatment, for coachmen were frequently accused, by the Society for the Protection of Animals, of abusing their horses.[11]

When the auto-taxi appeared on the streets of Paris, it, too, was subject to a whole host of regulations. Fines were most typically levied against the automobile for excessive odor or smoke, speeding, cruising for a fare, improper numbers, or improper or insufficient lighting.

These, then, were the major rules promulgated by the police to regulate the workday of coachmen. However, coachmen had another set of regulations to contend with—regulations originating with their employers—that further circumscribed their activities. Our best sources of information for company rules and discipline are the several company employment contracts still extant and documents originating with the CIV and the CGV. Most of the examples of company control offered here are taken from the files of those two companies, but they are typical of the measures taken by other cab companies as well.

All coachmen, working for whatever firm, were required to sign contracts with their employers.[12] To work as a cabbie for the CGV,

10. This section on sanctions is based on the discussion in Mareschal, *Les Voitures de place,* 342–50, esp. 343. One writer drew up a manual to assist coachmen appearing before the police with their legal rights. See Lucien Tricot, *Les Droits des cochers* (Paris, 1896).

11. Société Protectrice des Animaux, *Lettre aux cochers de Paris par G. de M., membre de la Société Protectrice des Animaux* (Paris, 1890), and *Nouvelle lettre aux cochers de Paris, par l'administrateur de la Société Protectrice des Animaux* (Paris, 1898).

12. The following are typical coachmen's contracts: Des Berlines de Place, dites les Anciennes, *Réglement* (Paris, 1842), CGVPP, *Réglement* (Paris, 1842), CGV, *Réglement des cochers* (Paris, 1868), all in BNSR; and CIV, *Réglement* (Paris, 1857), in APP, D/B 505.

an individual first had to attend the firm's apprenticeship school for a month, for which he paid twenty-five francs, a sum forfeited if he failed the coaching examination. The companies usually incorporated the major police rules within the terms of their contracts, thereby shifting liability from themselves to the cabbie for infractions for which the police tried to hold the employer responsible.

An important part of the contract was the schedule of fines the company established for violations. To cover any fines they might incur, coachmen had to post a security deposit when they signed their contracts. In 1856, the CIV set its security deposit at one hundred francs, a rather high figure considering that a coachman's average salary that year was three or four francs per day, excluding tips. The CIV placed this deposit in an interest-bearing account and contributed the interest to its coachmen's welfare fund, as required by law. It ceased making payments, though, when the law no longer required them.[13] Companies also withheld from the coachman's daily wages a smaller deposit, one franc in 1856 and sixty centimes in 1868, to cover miscellaneous fines. Cab firms reimbursed their cabbies during the first ten days of each month for the previous month's daily security deposit but returned the major deposit only when the coachman left the company. A portion of the major deposit was retained for several months, however, to cover any "hidden" police fines imposed on the coachman after the termination of his employment.[14]

Broad as it was in scope, the company contract was merely the foundation of a comprehensive system of management by which the companies simultaneously disciplined, controlled, and reformed their coachmen. The system, entrepreneurs believed, would enhance both the character of the coachman and the profits of the cab company. The CIV made a point of reporting to its shareholders that it had established "a new disciplinary organization in regard to the coachmen." In another report, company officials deplored laziness in coachmen and "their deadly habits [that] are still far from coming under satisfactory reform." Officials believed that coachmen had problems of character and that the firm had the duty "to improve moral standards with the aid of an increase in wages honestly

13. CIV, *Réglement*, 3–5; CGV, *Réglement*, art. 11, and *Réglement des cochers*, 2.
14. CIV, *Réglement*, 5, and CGV, *Réglement des cochers*, 5–6, 2.

earned." To this end, the company decided on July 1, 1858, to sup-plement the coachman's daily salary with "a share of five per cent on the gross receipt" and believed that "such concern on the part of the Company [for its workers] ought to be appreciated by those who are its beneficiaries." This bonus, however, was denied any coachman caught embezzling or pocketing fares, a necessary injunction since the CIV reported on August 11, 1859, for instance, that 2,179 out of its 3,200 coachmen had been penalized for pocketing fares.[15]

The CIV was more successful in reducing accidents among its coachmen than in reducing fraud. It required its cabbies to pay ten centimes a day into a *caisse d'assurance mutuelle,* a mutual insurance fund to help pay for damage resulting from accidents. As a conse-quence of this program, the director of the firm reported, "I am happy to be able to say, in praise of the coachmen of our Company, that there has been a sensible amelioration in their attitude, and that their discipline is incomparably superior to what it had been for-merly." He noted with pride that coachmen even returned lost items to the police (ninety-five out of one hundred items returned to the prefecture of police in 1861 came from the CIV's coachmen), though this fact had nothing to do with the mutual insurance fund.[16]

At the heart of the CIV's systematic attempts to reform its coach-men lay its surveillance system. The company's major worry con-cerned the honesty and veracity of its cabbies' work sheets and receipts. To inhibit cheating, it employed company inspectors to spot-check cabbies' work sheets on the streets and in the depots. It also organized "a service of secret agents" and based their remunera-tion "upon the very fines that their reports generate[d]." Unknown to the coachmen and "invested in discovering frauds," these agents were expected to "hold back nothing from the Company," which considered this system "the best organization possible in matters of personnel." These company spies made life difficult for the coach-men, since the failure to report a ride or an attempt to keep a fare could result in a harsh fine. Not fully satisfied with its own agents

15. CIV, *Rapport . . . Assemblée générale du 25 mai 1857,* p. 24, in AN, F7 6763; CIV, *Assemblée générale annuelle . . . Procès-Verbal, le 13 avril 1859* (MS in ACGV), 15–16.

16. CIV, *Assemblée générale annuelle . . . Procès-Verbal, le 13 avril 1859,* 15, and CIV, *Assemblée générale du 18 mai 1861, Rapport . . .* (Paris, 1861), 5.

and spies, the CIV also expected the police agents to check cabbies' work sheets, which they did.[17]

The CGV's surveillance system basically followed the CIV's plan, except that it had a more formal structure. In the first year of its existence, 1866, the CGV established an external surveillance department to supplement its internal surveillance branch. The company initially set aside about 23,000 francs for this department to cover the expenses of twenty-four agents who would patrol fifteen designated sections of Paris. It combined these two services in 1885. Field agents, the heart of the system, operated under cover in street clothes. Since it expected to cooperate closely with the authorities, the CGV also took care to inform the police of the details of its system. It reinforced its connection with the police by frequently hiring former or retired police officials to head its surveillance department and by contributing generously to police charities. The CGV also welcomed former military men to its surveillance department, to enhance control and discipline.[18]

Two factors made the surveillance system especially successful. Agents received a salary from the company, but they also got a bonus for every cabbie for whose conviction on a rule infraction they were responsible.[19] Typically, these agents obtained information by discreetly and randomly asking disembarking passengers about their ride, then checking this information against the cabbies' work sheets. The CGV assured the loyalty and diligence of its field agents by holding out to them the possibility of promotion within the service

17. CIV, *Assemblée générale du . . . 17 avril 1860* (Paris, 1860), 6–7; [François-Joseph] Ducoux, *Notice sur la Compagnie Impériale des Voitures de Paris depuis son origine jusqu'à ce jour* (Paris, 1859), 45; CIV, *Assemblée générale . . . du 17 avril 1860*, 7.

18. ACGV, CGV, *Comité de direction*, reg. no. 1, meeting of June 23, 1868, pp. 286–87; *Conseil d'administration*, reg. no. 1, November 26, 1866, p. 33; *Comité*, reg. no. 1, October 9, 1866, pp. 21–22; *Conseil*, reg. no. 5, December 12, 1884, p. 1638; *Comité*, reg. no. 1, October 26, 1866, pp. 28–29; *Conseil*, reg. no. 5, December 19, 1884, p. 1640; *Comité*, reg. no. 11, May 17, 1899, p. 4586, and reg. no. 12, May 15, 1901, p. 4972; *Comité*, reg. no. 6, July 17, 1885, p. 2538. See also Perrot, "The Three Ages of Industrial Discipline," 158, where she points out that to exert control over the workers, employers turned to the military for retired personnel to serve as foremen.

19. ACGV, CGV, *Comité*, reg. no. 1, March 12, 1867, pp. 92–93, and January 15, 1867, p. 66.

or to the central administration and by granting pensions to its older agents.

There was a graduated schedule of fines for cabbies found to have pocketed a fare. For a first offense the cabbie would be liable for a thirty-franc fine, for the second offense sixty francs, "and the third time" it was raised to a hundred francs, "independent of legal proceedings of the common law."[20] Whether or not a cabbie was convicted played a role in determining his salary. Throughout the nineteenth century, the CGV, like all cab companies, refused to pay coachmen a straight wage for a day's work because it defined the coachman as other than a worker: "The coachman of a voiture de place is not a worker. In effect, a worker is a man who works in a workshop or in a building site, under the surveillance of a foreman, or who produces a determined number of goods or a number of hours determined beforehand."[21] The coachman, as opposed to a worker, exercised "a preponderant influence" over the sale of his product. The cab's daily receipts depended on the enterprising nature of the individual cabbie. According to the company, therefore, the coachman was "a man who must be interested in the yield of the vehicle and who must gain as much as this vehicle shall be able to produce." Cab companies in the middle of the nineteenth century, therefore, paid their coachmen low wages as an incentive to secure as many rides, and thus as many tips, as possible. In 1866, the CGV was paying its coachmen three francs per day. By the end of that year, it raised the base wage to four francs, but conditionally: only "those faithful coachmen" who "brought back to the Company the totality of their receipts" received the salary increase. The following year, the CGV established a two-tier salary system. Apprentice coachmen and cabbies convicted of embezzling, or pocketing a fare, received three francs daily; coachmen who had been with the company for at least six consecutive months and who were "faithful" earned four francs. The CGV made a final adjustment to this policy, posting a

20. *Ibid.*, reg. no. 2, November 11, 1870, p. 597.

21. CGV, "Notes et renseignements sur la question des voitures de place de Paris," in *Rapports divers* (MS in ACGV), 7–9. See also Maurice Bixio, *Note adressée à la Commission permanente du Conseil supérieur du Travail par la Chambre Syndicale des Entrepreneurs de Voitures de Place du Département de la Seine, sur la question de la possibilité de limiter les heures de travail des Cochers de Place* (Paris, 1903), 5–7.

notice in all its depots stating that any fine would lead to the reduction of the cabbie's wage from four to three francs or from three francs to two francs, fifty centimes, depending on the coachman's current wage rate.[22]

The CGV (and other companies) also employed a closely related wage scheme known as payment *à la moyenne*. The cab company posted each day a target for that day's earnings, a figure arrived at by calculating its total expenses and then establishing a reasonable profit for each cab or, more commonly, by averaging the previous day's receipts and using this figure as a guide. A coachman working à la moyenne contracted to meet the daily stated sum; whatever excess he earned in addition to his tips he could keep. Payment à la moyenne was not common in the middle of the nineteenth century, but it became more usual as the century progressed. By the 1890s it was the norm.

Entrepreneurs first used this system to discipline unproductive cabbies. Those with low receipts were forced to work à la moyenne. Some cabbies, however, welcomed the system as an opportunity to earn more money. The CGV therefore established a dual salary structure: *à la moyenne volontaire* and *à la moyenne forcée*. Occasionally, however, it assumed a more disciplinary approach to such payments, permitting only its loyal and industrious cabbies to volunteer for à la moyenne as a reward for good behavior or high productivity.[23] Eventually, it expected all its coachmen to bring in fares equal to those earned by their colleagues working à la moyenne.

A variant to working à la moyenne was to work *à la planche,* according to which a cabbie was required to meet a monthly rather than a daily target fare. In effect, he was leasing the cab from the owner. Many coachmen preferred this method to being paid à la moyenne since companies could not then arbitrarily inflate the daily target fare as coachmen charged they did. The CGV would not employ payment à la planche, however, even though it recognized that this was a more "correct [and] regular" system of letting cabs out to coachmen. Such an employment method, it argued, could work

22. ACGV, CGV, *Conseil*, reg. no. 1, November 26, 1866, pp. 33–35, and November 25, 1867, pp. 169–70; *Comité*, reg. no. 2, November 11, 1870, p. 597.

23. ACGV, CGV, *Comité*, reg. no. 4, August 9, 1878, p. 1525.

only if the cab industry consisted of a genuine year-round work force, so that coachmen would not merely lease cabs in high traffic months. The CGV concluded, thus, that since two-thirds of all Parisian coachmen were inherently nomadic, rarely staying with one firm for a year, payment à la planche would be inappropriate.[24] It is also possible that the CGV simply did not wish to see its earnings mathematically flattened out by a monthly average.

The salary system as a form of incentive, control, and discipline became more effective when the cab companies perfected the electronic meter in the early twentieth century. Cab companies were then quite happy to pay their coachmen a percentage of the cab's receipts, measured accurately by the new meters. The CGV noted that "the very successful adoption of the taximeter [*taximetre*] has made it possible to firmly establish the common interests shared by the companies and the coachmen in the receipts of the cab." Still, however, coachmen might tamper with or not activate the meters. Company agents or the police could identify this infraction if a cab's *libre* sign was on while a passenger was in the cab.[25] Moreover, a locked part of the meter, to which only the owner had a key, contained a tape recording of the cab's travels each day.

The cab company could exercise scrupulous control over its coachmen in its depots. These were highly bureaucratized, partly to encourage sound management and efficient financial operations and partly to impose another layer of discipline over the coachmen. In charge of the depot, its absolute master, was the *chef de dépôt*. He hired, fired, and fined the grooms, the coach washers, the floor sweepers, and the common laborers. Coachmen were hired at the CGV's personnel bureau in the company headquarters, but thereafter they, too, became subject to the authority of the chef de dépôt, who could fine them for infractions of company rules or forbid entry into the depot to drunken or insubordinate cabbies.[26]

Not all measures used by the CGV to control its coachmen had a Draconian flavor, however. The firm established a coachman's mu-

24. For the CGV's opinion on working à la planche, see CGV, "Notes et renseignements," in *Rapports divers*, 11.

25. ACGV, CGV, *Comité*, reg. no. 15, June 30, 1905, p. 5845, and reg. no. 14, September 16, 1904, pp. 5664–65.

26. ACGV, CGV, *Réglement sur le service des dépôts* (Paris, 1868), esp. 4.

tual aid society, which included medical service and a retirement fund. It also encouraged its coachmen to accumulate savings by establishing a company bank in which cabbies could deposit as little as fifty centimes at a time. It paid a bonus to cabbies with low absentee rates and on rare occasions paid a bonus for especially high receipts, exemplary conduct, and well-kept equipment. According to one source, a bonus of one hundred francs went to any coachman who, within a period of 365 days, worked 310 days; the company increased this bonus fifty francs if a cabbie worked 320 days and added another fifty for 330 days worked during a 365-day period. The CGV increased its payment annually for each category if the coachman repeated his record, increasing the bonus for up to nine years.[27] The company also publicly congratulated a coachman receiving a commendation from the Society for the Protection of Animals for taking good care of his horses or a commendation from the police, usually for returning lost items or money found in the cab. Occasionally, and with some publicity, the company also contributed a voluntary financial gift to a coachman injured on the job or to the widow of a coachman.[28] From 1872 on, the CGV represented its coachmen gratuitously when they appeared before the police tribunals for infractions of police rules.[29]

So successful was the CGV's socialization policy that in 1891 the firm abolished its secret field agents and reduced the work force of its surveillance department. It took special care to pension off older agents who had been in its employ for a considerable time.[30]

At the root of the attempts of the police and the cab companies to control the cabbies lay the very nature of the coachman's occupation. For the police, it was a matter of keeping social peace in the streets. The coachman sold his services directly to the public in those very streets. For the cab companies, it was a matter of controlling a

27. ACGV, CGV, *Conseil*, reg. no. 6, April 24, 1896, p. 2216; *Comité*, reg. no. 14, January 20, 1905, p. 5744, reg. no. 1, December 24, 1867, pp. 204–205, and December 31, 1867, p. 206.

28. For an example, see ACGV, CGV, *Comité*, May 17, 1868, pp. 281–82.

29. ACGV, CGV, *Conseil*, reg. no. 2, September 18, 1872, pp. 780–81.

30. *Ibid.*, reg. no. 5, February 27, 1891, pp. 1946–47. See also ACGV, CGV, *Comité*, reg. no. 1, September 8, 1868, p. 328, for an early indication of satisfaction with the CGV's socialization program.

work force that did not lend itself to control. Coachmen were entrusted with a cab firm's coaches and with the responsibility for directly handling the firm's income, but the companies, the police, and the public also harbored the notion that coachmen were generally an unsavory lot, irresponsible and nomadic in nature, almost a breed apart from other categories of workers. Only prostitutes had a lower reputation on the social ladder. Thus, coachmen were not trusted, and their conduct was carefully scrutinized. No matter how carefully they were watched, however, for the greater part of the day cabbies circulated unobserved by agents. No matter how zealously the state and the companies tried to domesticate them and treat them like factory workers, the cabbies always exercised a measure of independence not common among laborers in the nineteenth century. Coach driving was an occupation that held out possibilities for maneuverability. It was attractive to people with some social ambitions. Who, then, were the coachmen? Where did they come from, and where did they live? Were their ambitions for social advancement or social integration realistic? Finally, how accurate were the popular impressions of these workers? These and related questions are explored in the next few chapters.

# 3 — THE COACHMEN: A STATISTICAL PROFILE

No other segment of the Parisian working class has been the subject of such extensive popular mythology as have the Parisian coachmen. Typically, coachmen were seen by other Parisian social groups, including workers, as sluggards, drunkards, country bumpkins, and unreliable nomads.[1] It was not unusual for coachmen to complain that they were regarded by the general populace as no better than prostitutes, meaning not only that they were low on the social ladder but also that they, too, sold a service to the wealthier classes. For Parisians, throughout the nineteenth century, the coachman conformed to Louis Chevalier's portrait of the migrant who arrived in the big city and immediately sank into a dangerous underclass of criminals and paupers.[2]

In 1903, Georges d'Avenel, writing for the *Revue des deux mondes,* studied 4,000 coachmen working for the CGV, the largest Parisian cab company in the nineteenth and early twentieth centuries. He reported in general terms that most of these cabbies come to Paris from Savoie, Auvergne, and Limousin. Other writers have stated that most Parisian coachmen were born in Auvergne, Normandy, Li-

1. For more examples, see Maxime Du Camp, *Paris, ses organes, ses fonctions et sa vie dans la seconde moitié du XIXe siècle* (Paris, 1869–75), 235, 239.
2. Louis Chevalier, *Laboring Classes and Dangerous Classes in Paris During the First Half of the Nineteenth Century,* trans. Frank Jellinek (New York, 1973).

mousin, and Lorraine. In more recent times Chevalier, in his classic work on the formation of the Parisian population, mentioned in passing that many Parisian coachmen came from Creuse and Aveyron. Françoise Raison-Jourde focused only on the Auvergnats in Paris and pointed out that many of these provincials became coachmen.[3] What is lacking in all the published literature is a sustained and detailed look at this important segment of the Parisian work force.[4]

An in-depth investigation reveals a portrait of the coachman quite at odds with any in popular literature. The individual who settled in Paris as a coachman, unlike the drunk, the sluggard, and the bumpkin, was motivated by an intense desire for integration into the life of the capital and a significant measure of hope for social and economic improvement. (For those who worked as seasonal coachmen in Paris, a topic dealt with in the next chapter, the goal of economic betterment through supplementary wages was primary.) Every aspect of a coachman's social background, including his life-style in Paris and his network of friends and acquaintances, points to this conclusion. For the most part, Paris coachmen came from the rural provinces of France, though a significant number were native Parisians. They arrived in Paris possessing a minimal skill, the ability to read and write, and enough savings to afford the apprenticeship course and the major security deposit required of all coachmen before they could begin to work. Once employed, they earned a decent wage, albeit for a rather long workday. In Paris, they established a network of respectable friends, many of them petit bourgeois entrepreneurs. They generally married working women, which added to their income. The important point is that they had not only the motivation but also the ability, with or without a spouse's income, to

3. Georges d'Avenel, "Le Mécanisme de la vie moderne," *Revue des deux mondes*, I (1903), 595; Toussaint Loua, "Les Voitures publiques à Paris," *Journal de la Société de Statistique de Paris* (July, 1875), 191–94; E. Bernaud and L. Laloy, *Guide pratique du cocher de fiacre à Paris* (Paris, 1906), 5–6; Guy Tomel, *Petits Métiers parisiens* (Paris, 1898), 249; Louis Chevalier, *La Formation de la population parisienne au XIXe siècle* (Paris, 1950), 228 and 174 n. 1; Françoise Raison-Jourde, *La Colonie auvergnate de Paris au XIX siècle* (Paris, 1976), 206ff.

4. Anne Boudou's useful master's thesis, "Les Taxis parisiens," relies mostly on the *Annuaire statistique* from the Préfecture de la Seine, which included coachmen from 1898, d'Avenel's "Le Mécanisme de la vie moderne," and the *Recensement* of 1901.

realize savings and improve their social and economic status. Like domestic servants or waiters in Paris, coachmen used their occupation as a vehicle for adaptation, assimilation, and social mobility.[5] Thus it becomes clear that coachmen can no longer be regarded as a marginal, dangerous, or criminal portion of the Paris population. They were far more stable and productive than the popular literature would indicate.[6]

Before we turn to the subject of social status, it would be useful to have a sense of the number of coachmen in Paris during different eras of the nineteenth and early twentieth centuries. In December, 1819, the total of officially registered cochers de fiacre in Paris was precisely 1,847 and the total of cochers de cabriolet, 2,182.[7] The total of active coachmen of all types (sous remise and de fiacre) in Paris in 1860 was approximately 5,000, though undoubtedly many more were registered as coachmen with the police.[8] About 20 percent of the total number of registered coachmen actually worked at any one time. The *Annuaire statistique* provides totals of all coachmen, omnibus and eventually tram cabbies included, registered in Paris from 1871 on. The totals are inflated, therefore, if applied strictly to cabbies. They are useful, however, as a basis of comparison with other existing data, while the overall trend charts the general numerical rise and fall of the cabbie population of Paris. To illustrate, 32,653 coach-

5. McBride, *The Domestic Revolution*; De Langle, *Le Petit Monde des cafés*.

6. Recently William Sewell and Barrie Ratcliffe have challenged Chevalier's bleak vision of the degradation of migrants in French cities during the first half of the nineteenth century. See William H. Sewell, Jr., *Structure and Mobility: The Men and Women of Marseille, 1820–1870* (Cambridge, Eng., 1985), and Barrie M. Ratcliffe, "Classes laborieuses et classes dangereuses à Paris pendant la première moitié du XIXe siècle?: The Chevalier Thesis Reexamined," *French Historical Studies*, XII, no. 2 (Fall, 1991), 542–74. What we see in this chapter is that recent, more positive assessments of urban life in the first half of the nineteenth century also hold true for the coachmen in the second half of the century, as many coachmen successfully integrated themselves into urban life or merely went back and forth from country to city.

7. APP, D/A 2 ["Voitures et cabriolets"], note of Paris, December 19, 1820.

8. This figure is arrived at by combining the total number of coachmen employed by the CIV, 3,200, with the 1,733 coachmen employed in the voiture sous remise part of the cab industry. See CIV, *Assemblée générale ordinaire et extraordinaire du 18 mai 1861* (Paris, 1861), 9, and Chambre de Commerce de Paris, *Statistique de l'industrie à Paris* (1860), 977–78.

men were registered to drive in Paris in 1871, compared to 99,509 in 1900. In 1903, the police began counting only active workers in these totals; the number of registered coachmen that year was 61,600, a figure that fell to 48,557 in 1907. The totals begin to climb after 1907 to slightly above 60,000 in 1913, but these most likely included motor cab drivers.[9]

A slightly more accurate estimate of the number of working coachmen in the early twentieth century may be obtained from a comparison of information in the census of 1901 and in the *Annuaire statistique*. The statistical survey in the census includes a section indicating the provincial origin of various professions in Paris. For coachmen of any kind, it lists two separate categories, one designated "*cochers, charretiers* [carters], *livreurs* [deliverymen], etc." and the other entitled "*roulage* [haulage], *voitures publiques, cochers et charretiers*." Under the second category, which includes the voitures publiques (omnibuses as well), the census reports 9,872 people in that profession. The *Annuaire statistique,* however, states that 15,041 voitures de place were registered in Paris as of December 31, 1901. Of these, 10,455 were second-class cabs. The same publication indicates, moreover, that close to 87,000 coachmen were registered with the Paris police in 1901. If the cochers des voitures de place came from a pool of 9,872, as the census indicates, they would hardly be sufficient in number to fill the cab industry's needs. The census also reveals that 25,790 people fell into the first professional category, "cochers, charretiers, livreurs, etc." From these figures we can calculate, therefore, that the active cocher des voitures de place population in 1901 was somewhere near 26,000, a figure considerably lower than 87,000, the number given as the total population of registered coachmen in Paris.[10]

Tabulating data from the census and the *Annuaire statistique* of 1911, we can estimate the active coachman population in Paris for that year as well. The 1911 census is less complicated than the census of 1901, but it, too, has important limits. It has only one classifica-

9. Préfecture de la Seine, *Annuaire statistique* (1881), 639; (1900), 789; (1903), 414; (1907), 374; (1913), 396.

10. Statistique générale de la France, *Résultats statistiques 1901,* IV, 292–305, esp. 300–301; Préfecture de la Seine, *Annuaire statistique* (1901), 520.

tion for coachman, "cocher," but this is commingled with various other types of transportation workers. The survey indicates that approximately 29,000 coachmen migrated to Paris from other parts of France in 1911. Not all would have continued as coachmen, and the number is inflated to begin with. The same study reports that Parisian cab stations could accommodate 7,425 second-class cabs and 294 first-class ones. If we combine the two figures and assume that there were as many voitures de place as there were spaces for them and that each cab had a relay of two cabbies, then the population of active coachmen in Paris in 1911 was about 15,000. The *Annuaire statistique* records the presence in Paris in 1911 of approximately 6,000 basic cabs. Using the above formula, we can calculate the cabbie population in 1911 to total almost 12,000. A safe conclusion would put the cabbie population of Paris in 1911 somewhere between 12,000 and 15,000, considerably lower than the total pool of registered coachmen in Paris that year (nearly 61,000).[11]

Who were these cochers who drove the basic Parisian cab? A good starting point in answering that question is the geographic origins of these men. Data concerning geographic origins for the period before 1896, when the *Annuaire statistique* first began to record applicants for the coachman's driving license according to department of origin, may be obtained from the coachmen's marriage certificates. Parisian marriage certificates of the nineteenth century regularly included information on the profession, age, birthplace, and address in Paris of the bride and groom, as well as the names, addresses, and professions of the parents of the bride and groom and of the witnesses to the marriage. The certificates are grouped by arrondissement for every year.[12] Of course, many Parisian coachmen did not marry in the capital, and many never married at all. However, there is no reason to assume that they were fundamentally different in other respects from those who did.

For the parts of this chapter based on marriage certificates, 1860

11. Statistique générale de la France, *Résultats statistiques du recensement général de la population effectué le 5 Mars 1911* (Paris, 1911), I, pt. 4, pp. 100–11; Préfecture de la Seine, *Annuaire statistique* (1911), 404.

12. The marriage certificates for 1860 are housed in AP. Andrew Lincoln called my attention to the marriage certificates as a source for social analysis.

TABLE 6
Coachmen's Department of Origin, 1860

| Department of origin | Percentage marrying in 1860 |
| --- | --- |
| Savoie and Haute-Savoie | 9.8 |
| Moselle | 8.4 |
| Paris | 5.6 |
| Aveyron | 3.8 |
| Pas-de-Calais | 3.8 |
| Côte-d'Or | 3.5 |
| Orne | 3.1 |
| Seine-et-Oise | 2.8 |
| Belgium | 2.8 |
| Luxembourg | 2.8 |
| Sarthe | 2.4 |
| Doubs | 2.1 |
| Manche | 2.1 |
| Saône-et-Loire | 2.1 |

Source: AP, Régistre des mariages, 1860.

has been used as the sample year. In 1860, in Paris, there were 15,343 marriages, of which 286 were those of coachmen.[13] A majority of these coachmen, conforming to the popular stereotype, did come from the rural provinces of France. Table 6 lists the coachmen's department of origin in order of frequency and supports the common opinion that most Parisian coachmen came from the provinces. A significant number of cabbies, however, were born in Paris, an unexpected finding that requires some mention, especially since the phenomenon was true for the latter part of the century as well.[14] The

13. The professional category listed in the marriage certificates is merely cocher. However, since other types of cochers are designated as such, we can assume that the simple classification "cocher" refers to a cocher de fiacre. In addition to the 286 cochers de fiacres who were married in Paris in 1860, 28 cochers des maisons bourgeoises, 9 cochers de remise, 5 cochers d'omnibus, 1 cocher au garde mobile, 1 cocher de factage du chemin de fer du Nord, and 1 cocher au M. le Prince Napoléon also took their marriage vows.

14. See, as an example, Préfecture de la Seine, Annuaire statistique (1896), 738.

popular literature probably did not single out native-born Parisian coachmen because they had an "urban comportment" and were not so conspicuous as their country brethren.

A similar pattern emerges from the *Annuaire statistique* for the period 1896 to 1914. Table 7 lists data on the geographic origins of Parisian coachmen presenting themselves for the permit-to-drive examination from 1896 to 1914, translated into percentages. It shows that by the end of the nineteenth century the Paris region had become the primary recruiting area for Parisian cabbies. The predominantly rural parts of southern and eastern France ranked second.

From the census data for 1901 and 1911, we can determine if certain departments specialized in sending coachmen to Paris. These two surveys include a section indicating, for various professions, the number of persons who had migrated to Paris to pursue that profession. The 1901 survey, unlike the one of 1911, includes two categories of coachmen. The present analysis uses the larger category, "cochers, charretiers, livreurs," which probably includes the cochers des voitures de place, as noted earlier. Comparing the number of

TABLE 7
Department of Origin of Coachmen Taking
the Permit-to-Drive Examination, 1896–1914

| Department or country of origin | Percentage of coachmen |
| --- | --- |
| Seine | 18.6 |
| Corrèze | 8.1 |
| Aveyron | 7.6 |
| Savoie | 4.3 |
| Italy | 3.6 |
| Cantal | 3.5 |
| Creuse | 3.3 |
| Haute-Savoie | 2.0 |
| Seine-et-Oise | 1.9 |
| Alsace-Lorraine | 1.5 |

Source: Préfecture de la Seine, "Commission . . . d'examin des cochers," *Annuaire statistique* (Paris, 1896–1914).

TABLE 8
Percentage of Coachmen of the Total of
Professions Migrating to Paris, 1901, 1911

| 1901 | | 1911 | |
|---|---|---|---|
| Department | Percentage | Department | Percentage |
| Aveyron | 9.4 | Savoie | 8.0 |
| Corrèze | 8.8 | Corrèze | 7.5 |
| Savoie | 8.4 | Cantal | 7.0 |
| Cantal | 6.1 | Aveyron | 6.5 |
| Lozère | 5.5 | Côtes-du-Nord | 6.5 |
| Mayenne | 5.0 | Alpes (Basses) | 6.2 |
| Haute-Savoie | 5.0 | Haute-Savoie | 5.7 |
| Orne | 5.0 | Lozère | 5.6 |
| Côtes-du-Nord | 4.7 | Orne | 4.9 |
| Haute-Loire | 4.3 | Mayenne | 4.5 |
| Manche | 4.0 | Haute-Loire | 4.2 |
| Puy-de-Dôme | 4.0 | Lot | 4.1 |
| Jura | 3.8 | Manche | 3.8 |
| Saône | 3.8 | Nièvre | 3.7 |
| Lot | 3.7 | Jura | 3.6 |
| Doubs | 3.4 | | |

Source: Statistique générale de la France, *Résultats statistiques du recensement général de la popula-tion effectué le 24 mars 1901* (Paris, 1904–1907), IV, 292–305, and *Résultats statistiques du recense-ment général de la population effectué le 5 mars 1911* (Paris, 1911), I, pt. 4, pp. 100–11.

coachmen with the number of men in all other professions going to
Paris from each department in 1901 and in 1911 (see Table 8), we see
that a large group of Parisian cabbies originated near or in the Massif
Central, Auvergne, Limousin, and Languedoc-Roussillon. The departments of this region that appear in Table 8 are all adjacent to each
other: Creuse, Puy-de-Dôme, Haute-Loire, Lozère, Aveyron, Lot,
Corrèze, and Cantal, forming a concentrated region from which
many Parisian coachmen migrated. This area of France was heavily
agricultural. Although coachmen also came from regions with a tradition of industrial activity, such as the Puy-de-Dôme, a mixed region of industry and agriculture, and the Seine Department, agricultural roots loom large in the profile of the Parisian cabbies.

Although this study is concerned mostly with the experiences of
coachmen in Paris, some indication as to why provincials left their
homes to drive cabs in the capital is in order here. Raison-Jourde has

researched the Auvergnat colony in Paris, for many Parisian cabbies originated in the Auvergne, and suggests several important reasons. Emigration was not motivated by expectations of an exotic life in the capital or by a desire to travel. High taxes, family debts, a desire for liquidity, and, in the second half of the nineteenth century, an economic crisis in the countryside forced many provincials to set out for Paris. Moreover, there was a strong tradition of independence in the Auvergne, and the cab trade presumably appealed to those with a free spirit. In addition, the social patterns of the Auvergnats, compared to those of the Bretons for instance, strongly suggest a pronounced desire to better their social status by going to Paris. Thus, a realistic chance for upward social mobility and the opportunity to supplement rural income also appear to have served as major incentives for migration. Whatever the reason for migration, Paris offered possibilities for improved social and economic conditions not easily available outside important cities. This last reason, the chance for upward social mobility or supplementary income, is consistent with Sewell's conclusion concerning migration to Marseille: migrants' "decisions to move to Marseille were typically prompted less by the goad of poverty or unemployment in their home communities than by the lure of greater opportunities or a more interesting life in the city."[15]

Many of the wine merchants in the capital came from the Auvergne, and many coachmen hoped to join their ranks, frequently treating their trade as a rite of passage into the milieu of the *petit commerçant*. Becoming a wine retailer, as Chevalier has suggested, and then a wine merchant was one of the easiest ways to enter the Parisian commercial environment.[16] The connection between coachmen and wine merchants will be further explored when we consider the network of friends the coachmen established when they settled in Paris.

Parisian coachmen lived throughout the city but were found predominantly in those arrondissements with a heavy concentration of cab depots and cab stations or with a major cab company located there. Raison-Jourde investigated coachmen who were arrested in a

15. Raison-Jourde, *La Colonie auvergnate*, 66, 179–80, 209–10; Sewell, *Structure and Mobility*, 170.
16. Louis Chevalier, *La Formation de la population parisienne*, 227–29.

strike of 1884 and their domiciles and found that most lived in close proximity to the important cab stations of the seventh arrondissement, along the avenue de la Grande-Armée, and at the foot of the Buttes-Chaumont. Her map of the homes of strikers arrested in 1884 shows that they lived mostly in the seventh, seventeenth, eighteenth, and nineteenth arrondissements.[17] Raison-Jourde's conclusion misses the real significance of this fact. The arrondissements she identifies were not merely cab station centers but also districts with a concentration of cab depots. Since the coachmen began and ended their workday at the cab depots, it made sense for them to live nearer the depot than the station.

The 1911 population census published a list of various professions and the arrondissements in which their practitioners lived. The broad category of coachman was included in those professions, thereby permitting us to compare these data with the 1884 strike statistics. The comparison is not entirely accurate, however, since by 1911 the horse-drawn carriage trade was in decline, which may account for any shift in the living patterns of cabbies. In addition, the 1911 survey is a far more complete statistical picture than that produced by simply recording the domicile of those coachmen who took part in a strike. There is a drawback to the census, however. The 1911 census brackets together several types of transportation workers, resulting in a sample that includes more than cab coachmen. Table 9 thus indicates what percentage of the Parisian coachmen of all types lived in each arrondissement.

According to the *Annuaire statistique* of 1911, six arrondissements of the first ten in terms of cab station capacity match up with the top ten arrondissements in terms of where cabbies lived. The single largest cab company in Paris, the CGV, had five depots in the eighteenth arrondissement, three in both the nineteenth and the eleventh, two in both the seventh and the fifteenth, and one each in the ninth, tenth, fourteenth, and seventeenth arrondissements. In addition, its depot in Levallois-Perret was next to the seventeenth arrondissement, its depot in Aubervilliers was close to the eighteenth and nineteenth arrondissements, and its depot in Montrouge was near the

17. Raison-Jourde, *La Colonie auvergnate*, 205.

TABLE 9
Homes of Parisian Coachmen
by Arrondissement, 1911

| Arrondissement | Percentage living in the ward |
|:---:|:---:|
| 18 | 11.5 |
| 19 | 9.6 |
| 17 | 8.9 |
| 15 | 8.6 |
| 11 | 7.5 |
| 12 | 5.4 |
| 10 | 5.3 |
| 13 | 5.2 |
| 20 | 5.1 |
| 14 | 4.7 |
| 16 | 4.1 |
| 7 | 3.8 |
| 8 | 3.6 |
| 4 | 2.8 |
| 3 | 2.8 |
| 5 | 2.6 |
| 2 | 2.5 |
| 9 | 2.4 |
| 1 | 1.9 |
| 6 | 1.8 |

Source: Statistique générale de la France, *Résultats statistiques* (1911), II, 10–16.

fourteenth.[18] In short, cabbies tended to live near their place of work, which meant near cab depots, though the depots, too, were frequently located near areas of heavy cab usage.

A second manner of looking at the coachmen's living situation compares the percentage of coachmen in each arrondissement to all professions in that ward. This perspective simply indicates what arrondissements featured certain kinds of professions (see Table 10). From these data we see that coachmen added a significant flavor to the first four arrondissements on the list, the nineteenth, fifteenth,

18. Préfecture de la Seine, *Annuaire statistique* (1911), 403; ACGV, Plans of the Stables.

Table 10
Percentage of Coachmen Compared with All
Professions by Arrondissement, 1911

| Arrondissement | Percentage compared with other professions |
|---|---|
| 19 | 7.2 |
| 15 | 5.4 |
| 17 | 5.0 |
| 18 | 4.9 |
| 13 | 4.5 |
| 12 | 4.4 |
| 7 | 4.2 |
| 2 | 4.1 |
| 8 | 4.0 |
| 10 | 3.7 |
| 16 | 3.7 |
| 11 | 3.6 |
| 14 | 3.5 |
| 3 | 3.4 |
| 1 | 3.3 |
| 20 | 3.2 |
| 4 | 3.1 |
| 5 | 2.6 |
| 9 | 2.3 |
| 6 | 2.1 |

Source: Statistique générale de la France, *Résultats statistiques* (1911), II, 10–16.

seventeenth, and eighteenth, and perhaps to the following few. The balance were scattered throughout Paris and remained a small portion of the professions in most of the city.

Class consciousness in the coachmen is dealt with fully in Chapters 5 and 6, but a discussion of domicile raises an important consideration in that area that may be addressed here. That coachmen tended to live near their place of work also meant that they lived close to each other. Moreover, the arrondissements within which they lived often coincided with centers of labor activism. Bernard H. Moss writes that many labor militants, labor headquarters, and cafés were located in the northeast of Paris, particularly in the tenth, eleventh, nineteenth, and twentieth arrondissements.[19] Such proximity of coachmen to each other and to other kinds of workers would facilitate the communication of socialist ideas and could have been a factor in the growth of a working-class consciousness. (By working-class consciousness as applied to coachmen, I mean both a strong identification with other Parisian workers from whatever sector of the economy rather than a fraternal sense for members of their own craft and a general, though not consistent, hostility to cab owners.) Militating against such a consciousness, however, were two factors: coachmen serviced mostly middle-class clients, who treated them as hired hands, and coachmen's domiciles were spread throughout Paris and commonly touched on middle-class neighborhoods. These factors could have inspired coachmen to work for the entrée into the ranks of the middle class that a simple commercial enterprise, no matter how low the level, might confer. Domicile, therefore, could cut both ways, but in the formation of class consciousness, what loomed with more importance was economic crisis, the structure of the cab industry, and the employer's and state's control over coachmen. Living in certain arrondissements was primarily a function of establishing a close proximity between living space and working space, thereby easing the difficulty of the workday.

The next question to consider is how coachmen stood in relation to their parents' occupations. Of the 286 marriage certificates under consideration, 54.2 percent indicated that the coachman-groom's father was deceased or that his professional background was unknown. From the remaining 45.8 percent we may derive a breakdown of the fathers' professions. Leading the list, far ahead of any other category, is the classification of *cultivateur,* or farmer, constituting 32.8 percent. In second place is *propriétaire, propriétaire cultivateur* (property-owner, property-owner farmer), comprising 9.9 percent. Adding to these figures the percentages for gardener, 3.8 percent, and vine grower, 3.8 percent, the grand total for agriculture-related pursuits comes to 50.3 percent. Taking a more conservative view, we could eliminate the category propriétaire, propriétaire cultivateur from these statistics on the assumption that a percentage of the propriétaires were not

19. Bernard H. Moss, *The Origins of the French Labor Movement, 1830–1914: The Socialism of Skilled Workers* (Berkeley, 1976), 16.

Table 11

Coachmen-Grooms' Mothers by Profession, 1860

| Profession | Percentage |
|---|---|
| No profession | 32.8 |
| Farmer | 19.8 |
| Landed proprietor | 12.2 |
| Household (cook, domestic, housekeeper) | 9.2 |
| Day laborer | 5.3 |
| Shareholder | 5.3 |
| Dressmaker | 2.3 |
| Merchant | 2.3 |
| Weaver | 1.5 |
| Yarn spinner | 1.5 |
| Clerk | 0.8 |
| Coal dealer | 0.8 |
| Concierge | 0.8 |
| Washerwoman | 0.8 |
| Winemaker | 0.8 |

Source: AP, *Régistre des mariages*, 1860.

farmers. Agriculture-related professions would then compose 40.4 percent of the total professions, a rather high figure in any case. Immediately below the agricultural professions and property owners are the unskilled day laborers, comprising 6.9 percent, followed by the cochers, comprising 5.3 percent. In next place are household professions: *domestique* (domestic), 2.3 percent, *ménager* (housekeeper), 0.8 percent, and *valet de chambre* (valet), 0.8 percent, for a total of 3.9 percent. An additional 3.8 percent of the fathers did not have any profession. The absence of certain professions is striking. Coachmen's fathers, with few exceptions, did not engage in urban professions. On the 131 certificates listing a profession for the father, there were only three carpenters, one shoemaker, two merchants, an innkeeper, a customs official, and a teacher.

The pattern of professions for the coachman-groom's mother is seen in Table 11. The percentages in this table also derive from 131 certificates, or 45.8 percent, the cases in which the mother was alive at the time of the wedding and her profession known, the same number coincidentally as for the fathers. The high percentage of coachmen's mothers with no profession might simply be a reflection of the failure of official sources to recognize work done at home, taking in a boarder or sewing, for instance, as legitimate employment.

Most coachmen who drove cabs in Paris, therefore, were born in the provinces, though a not-insignificant number were born in the capital. A large percentage of their fathers were farmers. Almost half of their mothers had few or no skills, and a sizable number were involved in farming. The coachman's profession, a low, entry-level urban occupation, was a means to supplement rural wages in the off-season or at times of more serious unemployment. It was additionally a conduit for assimilation into the urban world.

The occupational status of the women these coachmen married is strong evidence that the coachman's trade constituted a means both for integration into urban life and for achieving upward social mobility. In discussing the marriage patterns of female domestics in Paris, Theresa M. McBride points to two possible models. In one, marriages are seen as combining social or occupational groups; rural people of one social or occupational category marry urban people of a similar status. In the second model, marriage can represent a step up or down the social ladder, depending on the occupational or social status of the marriage partner. In both models the person raised in the country marrying someone settled in the city has taken the significant step of integration into the world of artisans and shopkeepers, into the world of the city.[20] If we apply these two models to coachmen's marriages, the occupations and the geographic origins of the women coachmen married support the contention that coachmen were becoming integrated into the life of Paris. For the most part, these women pursued entry-level urban occupations on a par with the trade of coachman.

Table 12 lists, in order of frequency, the occupations most brides engaged in. These figures are based on 285 out of 286 certificates for which the bride's profession is known. What is notable about the brides' occupational categories is the data revealed by aggregating the household professions. According to the table, these consist of cook, 35.1 percent; maid, 12.3 percent; domestic, 6.7 percent; and linen maid, 5.3 percent. Two other household professions, house-

20. McBride, *The Domestic Revolution*, 90.

Table 12

Coachmen's Brides' Professions, 1860

| Profession | Percentage |
|---|---|
| Cook | 35.1 |
| Dressmaker | 12.6 |
| Maid | 12.3 |
| Domestic | 6.7 |
| Linen Maid | 5.3 |
| Laundress | 4.6 |
| Day laborer | 4.2 |
| No profession | 3.9 |
| Milliner | 1.1 |
| Property owner | 1.1 |
| Landlord | 1.1 |

Source: AP, *Régistre des mariages*, 1860.

keeper, 0.4 percent, and servant, 0.7 percent, were too insignificant to be included in the table. The total for all household professions is 60.5 percent; considered with the professions of day laborer and laundress, these data indicate that coachmen's brides had distinctly low-level urban professional status.

The geographic origins and professions of the brides' parents are similar in many respects to those of the grooms' families. The data are different, however, in several significant details. Table 13 compares the geographic areas from which brides originated with similar information for the coachmen. The data for the brides are based on 283 identifiable provinces. As this table indicates, the brides, as well as the grooms, were essentially from the rural provinces of France. What is different about the brides, however, is that the largest single block of them were born in Paris, indicating a slightly greater degree of urban integration. Perhaps marrying a woman with a decidedly urban background represented a small measure of upward social mobility. It certainly represented a major step toward integration into urban life.

The profile for the mother of the coachman's bride is very similar to that of the coachman's mother but the brides' fathers differ from the grooms' fathers in some subtle respects. Table 14 gives the professional status of the brides' fathers and mothers. We can identify a profession for 49.0 percent of the brides' fathers and for 45.5 percent of the mothers. The composition of the fathers' portion of the table

TABLE 13

Geographic Area of Origin, Brides and Coachmen-Grooms, 1860

| Bride's department or country | Percentage | Coachman's department or country | Percentage |
|---|---|---|---|
| Paris | 6.7 | Savoie and Haute-Savoie | 9.8 |
| Moselle | 5.7 | Moselle | 8.4 |
| Savoie and Haute-Savoie | 5.7 | Paris | 5.6 |
| Côte-d'Or | 3.2 | Aveyron | 3.8 |
| Haute-Saône | 3.2 | Pas-de-Calais | 3.8 |
| Jura | 2.8 | Côte-d'Or | 3.5 |
| Manche | 2.8 | Orne | 3.1 |
| Doubs | 2.5 | Seine-et-Oise | 2.8 |
| Haut-Rhin | 2.5 | Belgium | 2.8 |
| Seine-et-Oise | 2.5 | Luxembourg | 2.8 |
| Belgium | 2.5 | Sarthe | 2.4 |
| Luxembourg | 2.5 | Manche | 2.1 |
| Aveyron | 2.1 | | |
| Orne | 2.1 | | |
| Seine | 2.1 | | |
| Yonne | 2.1 | | |
| Aisne | 1.8 | | |
| Sarthe | 1.8 | | |
| Somme | 1.8 | | |

Source: AP, *Régistre des mariages,* 1860.

TABLE 14

Professions of Brides' Parents, 1860

| Fathers' professions | Percentage | Mothers' professions | Percentage |
|---|---|---|---|
| Farmer | 17.9 | No profession | 50.8 |
| Property owner | 13.5 | Farmer, gardener | 13.1 |
|    *propriètaire* | 11.4 | Property owner | 11.5 |
|    *rentier* | 2.1 |    *propriètaire* | 6.9 |
| Day laborer | 10.7 |    *rentière* | 4.6 |
| Carpenter | 5.0 | Household | 8.4 |
| Mason | 5.0 | Day laborer | 7.7 |
| Weaver | 3.6 | Laundress | 1.5 |
| No profession | 3.6 | | |
| Shoeing smith | 2.9 | | |
| Gardener | 2.1 | | |
| Vine grower | 2.1 | | |

Source: AP, *Régistre des mariages,* 1860.

changes slightly if we combine a few professions, some not in the table because of their small percentages. The agricultural classification remains in first place, but by adding the related categories of gardener, at 2.1 percent, and vine grower, also at 2.1 percent, we increase the percentage of fathers engaged in agriculture-related pursuits to 22.1 percent. We can also create a category entitled "transportation industry" to include coachman/coachman-owner (1.4 percent), blacksmith (2.9 percent), horsegroom (0.7 percent), and coachmaker (1.4 percent). The total for these professions is 6.4 percent, putting this category in fourth place, just behind day laborer. These data show that there were very many farmers among the brides' fathers but more skilled professions were represented here than among the coachmen's fathers. The breakdown of professions for the mothers of both brides and grooms is virtually the same. Thus, the coachmen's brides and the brides' fathers seem to have had more experience with urban skills and occupations than the coachmen or their families.

A discussion about brides and grooms leads to the question of where they might have met. Part of the answer is found in the marriage certificate itself, which documents where the bride and groom were living just before their marriage. This information does not necessarily reveal where they first met, but in the absence of other evidence, some interpretations are suggested by the data. At the time of the wedding ceremony, 44.9 percent of the newlyweds lived in the same arrondissement, 42.5 percent lived in the same house, and 5.3 percent resided on the same street. Only 7.4 percent lived in different arrondissements before they married. The marriage certificates do not indicate whether those living in the same building lived together or separately before the marriage. An important study of women suggests, however, that cohabitation among working-class men and women in cities was common.[21] The above figures do show that over 90 percent of the engaged couples lived in the same neighborhood, if not in the same house or on the same street. Those who did not know each other from the provinces or were not introduced by mutual acquaintances probably met in cafés, bistros, or wine merchants' shops. Many may have encountered each other on the stairs of their apartment buildings or on a common street.

21. Tilly and Scott, *Women, Work, and Family*, 38–39.

The occupational status of the witnesses to these marriages tells us something about the coachman's network of friends. In his study of marriage patterns among workers in Marseille, William Sewell notes that the bride and groom frequently had as witnesses friends and acquaintances of a higher social status than themselves. According to Sewell, this tendency, whether conscious or not, helped enhance the wedding couple's own social standing within their community. Such witnesses might also, however, be a reliable measure of the level of the prestige of the groom's occupation.[22] If so, the same would hold true for the bride's occupation, as well. Thus, the witnesses reflect the real or the hoped-for social network of the bridal couple.

In Paris in 1860, each coachman's marriage typically was witnessed by four people, sometimes only three. The marriage certificate specifies their professions and addresses but not always with which partner they were associated. Unlike rural weddings, where one witness to the ceremony may have been a village notable, whether a personal friend of the bride or groom or not, urban weddings were generally free of such customs. The choice of witnesses thus provides an excellent barometer of the couples' friends, with one exception: a coachman may have invited his employer to witness the marriage. This possibility is suggested by the percentage of *loueur des voitures* (cab entrepreneurs or subcontractors) who served as witnesses. Whether they were friends or simply the urban equivalent of rural notables, their presence reveals something of the nature of the milieu in which the coachmen functioned. Table 15 identifies the leading professions of witnesses at coachmen's weddings and indicates that coachmen were more deeply integrated into urban life than the brides' backgrounds suggest. Its calculations are based on 1,113 witnesses with identifiable professions out of a total of 1,117 witnesses.

That the highest percentage of witnesses were coachmen, and by a wide margin over the second category, seems quite appropriate. Coachmen's closest friends were fellow cabbies. Usually working a fourteen-hour day, they congregated several times during the workday, and friendships naturally developed. Drivers for large and small cab firms reported to their depots an hour before taking their cabs

22. Sewell, *Structure and Mobility*, 76.

TABLE 15
Professions of Witnesses at Coachmen's
Weddings, 1860

| Profession | Percentage |
| --- | --- |
| Coachman | 18.1 |
| Merchant | 9.3 |
| wine merchant | 5.6 |
| others | 3.7 |
| Clerk (*employé*) | 7.2 |
| Household (domestic, valet, cook) | 7.0 |
| Property owner | 5.0 |
| *propriètaire* | 2.0 |
| *rentier* | 3.0 |
| Transportation (excluding | |
| coachmen) | 4.4 |
| *loueur de voiture* | 1.5 |
| others | 2.9 |
| Concierge | 3.7 |
| Carpenter, furniture-maker | 3.4 |
| Merchant's agent (*representant de* | |
| *commerce*) | 3.0 |
| Shoemaker | 2.7 |
| Tailor | 2.7 |
| Police related | 2.3 |

Source: AP, *Régistre des mariages*, 1860.

out. They usually surreptitiously tipped a horse groom to get a healthy animal and a well-built coach and then inspected their equipment, for once outside the depot, they were liable for any damages to it. During this hour the cabbies mingled with each other. Their next meeting point would be the public cab station since the law required them to wait for their clients there. The first two men on line were obliged to wait with their cabs, ready to ride at a moment's notice, but the rest could leave their cabs and assemble for conversation, food, or drinks within or near the station. They could also socialize when they returned to the depot at the end of the workday to hand in their work sheets and their equipment. From the percentage of wine merchants as witnesses in Table 15, we can deduce that coachmen frequently met in their off-hours at these wine merchants' shops. In addition, coachmen shared a sense of common enmity against the police, the public, and their employers, as is apparent in the complaints, hopes, and frustrations they voiced in the columns of the many newspapers devoted exclusively to the coachman's trade.[23]

Another profession on the list with a rather high percentage also seems naturally to belong there. Considering that over 60 percent of coachmen's brides engaged in a household profession, it is not surprising that witnesses similarly engaged occupy place number four.

One striking feature of the table is the absence of any clearly identifiable rural profession. The category "landlord" consists of propriétaire, at 2.0 percent, and rentier (stockholder or person of property), at 3.0 percent. Such a person may have been a rural property holder, but it is just as likely, given the rest of the table, that he was an urban one. Only three decidedly rural occupations, farmer, gardener, and vine grower, are among the professions documented, and these account for only 0.9 percent of the witnesses' professions. Once in an urban setting, coachmen and their brides appear to have sought friends from their new environment.

The integration of the coachman into city life is confirmed by the appearance of the occupation employé, or clerk, on the list. This term could refer to a clerk in a department store, in an office, or in a cab company, for instance. The CIV alone had 70 employés working at its headquarters and another 64 in its depots. Male clerks, from department stores or other establishments, frequented cafés and restaurants in central Paris in the evenings, and female clerks tended to take Sunday walks in local parks, where they mixed with people of other occupations.[24] It would not have been surprising if they had mingled with coachmen. No matter where the clerk worked or socialized, however, the profession was an urban one and a small but decided step ahead of the coachman's trade on the social scale. The significant number of employés that coachmen or their brides had for friends indicates a start in their own rise up the social hierarchy.

Examining the coachmen's connection with wine merchants, who

23. For example, see Le Cocher, from no. 1, January 20, 1864, to no. 34, December 20, 1864.

24. Chambre de Commerce de Paris, Statistique de l'industrie à Paris: Résultat de l'enquête faite par la Chambre de Commerce pour l'année 1860 (Paris, 1864), 1060–62; Theresa M. McBride, "A Women's World: Department Stores and the Evolution of Women's Employment, 1870–1920," French Historical Studies (Fall, 1978), 680.

made up 5.6 percent of the witnesses, strengthens this projection. Contact between coachmen and wine merchants should not be surprising, for like any other Parisian workers, coachmen drank wine with their meals. In petitioning the CIV for higher wages in 1857, they placed their "indispensable refreshment" second only to food as their single greatest daily expense.[25] This item, they claimed, perhaps exaggerating a bit, required a daily expenditure of ninety centimes. Whatever the exact figure, coachmen certainly visited wine merchants' shops frequently to buy wine. Later in the century, when the police documented the events of the coachmen's strikes during the universal expositions in Paris, they frequently noted that coachmen used the back rooms of wine merchants' shops as meeting places.[26] Such a tradition did not materialize overnight; it reflected the already close ties between coachmen and wine merchants—ties that existed for an important socioprofessional reason as well. Raison-Jourde reports that the profession of coachman was frequently a rite of passage to a commercial pursuit, quite often that of wine merchant. Chevalier writes that one of the easiest ways to enter the commercial milieu, a step up the social ladder for peasants and sons of peasants in Paris, was to become a retailer of cheap wine (débitant de boissons); the next step was to become a wine merchant. President Maurice Bixio of the CGV confirmed the connection between wine merchants and coachmen when he reported to the Ministry of Labor that his firm's cabbies improved their economic and social standing most typically by becoming wine merchants. Without identifying his statistical evidence, he noted that 16,000 wine merchants in the Seine Department had formerly been coachmen.[27] Another reason coachmen may have associated with wine merchants, therefore, was their vision of a rise up the urban hierarchy.

There is another explanation for the presence of certain witnesses at the weddings: the bride and groom most obviously came to know

25. Rapport à messieurs les administrateurs et à monsieur le Directeur Général de la Compagnie Impériale des Voitures de Paris, in APP, D/B 505.

26. See APP, B/A 178–79, for the strikes from 1878 to 1891 and APP, B/A 1365–67, for the strikes from 1892 to 1900.

27. Raison-Jourde, La Colonie auvergnate, 209–10; Chevalier, La Formation de la population parisienne, 227–29; Maurice Bixio, Note adressée à la Commission permanente, 4.

TABLE 16
Professions of Relatives of Coachmen
and Brides, 1860

| Profession | Percentage |
| --- | --- |
| Coachman | 14.9 |
| Merchant | 7.2 |
| wine merchant | 5.1 |
| others | 2.1 |
| Transportation | 6.0 |
| Household | 5.7 |
| Clerk | 5.4 |
| Property owner | 4.1 |
| propriètaire | 1.9 |
| rentier | 2.2 |
| Shoemaker | 3.2 |
| Concierge | 2.5 |
| Tailor | 2.5 |
| Cabinetmaker | 1.9 |
| Day laborer | 1.9 |

Source: AP, *Régistre des mariages*, 1860.

their witnesses through family association. Almost 28 percent of the witnesses were related to one or the other of the newlyweds. A survey of the professions of these relatives adds weight to the assertion that provincial coachmen were a segment of the Parisian working class approaching a greater integration in the urban milieu. Listed in Table 16 are the leading professions practiced by relatives of the coachman or his bride—professions that correspond fairly well to those in Table 15. Clear-cut urban professions dominate the list. As 316 of the witnesses indicate, either the coachman or his bride already had a relative with a tradition of urban employment. There is thus an obvious network leading from an entry-level job to a petit bourgeois profession. These two tables reinforce the impression that coachmen, far from being nomads in the urban setting, constituted a social group integrating itself into the working-class life of Paris and poised at the edge of the next higher class in the social hierarchy.

One profession listed in Table 15 requires special comment. Police professionals or employees (a police agent, an inspector, an employee at the prefecture, gendarmes, Paris guards and sergeants, a blacksmith at gendarme headquarters, and bailiffs) accounted for 2.3 percent of the witnesses at the marriages, occupying twelfth place on Table 15. Their presence is unexpected considering the enmity coachmen usually evinced for the police. Throughout the history of the corporation of Parisian coachmen, cabbies complained of vexatious police driving codes that curtailed their "freedom of trade" and of the zealousness of police agents in giving out fines.[28] Moreover, coachmen as a group ranked high among all French workers arrested in any given year for certain types of crimes. A writer observed in 1824 that the police correctional tribunal, which was especially occupied with the cases of the "inferior classes" (identified as rag pickers, secondhand clothes dealers, and coachmen) who were involved in "open-air frauds" or "fights in cafés" (*guinguettes*), had taken on increased importance over the last several years.[29]

The Ministry of Justice maintained statistics on the number of persons from the major occupational categories arrested for crimes against public order, crimes against public decency, and crimes against property. The relationship between coachmen and these arrest records may be illustrated by taking as sample years 1855, 1860, and 1865.[30] In 1855, there were 20,360 arrests in all of France for the above crimes, 15,686 in Paris. Coachmen accounted for 736 of these and were fifth on a list of 63 professions tabulated. In 1860, the arrests totaled 20,497, of which 17,819 were in Paris. Coachmen were sixth on a list of 147 professions involved. In 1865, coachmen ranked fourteenth out of 147 professions (303 coachmen of 25,516 arrested in France; 22,928 in Paris). Scott Haine has tabulated statistics for drunken and disorderly cases heard before the police correctional tri-

28. See, for example, the many reports summing up this complaint during the strikes of 1878 and 1889, which are covered extensively in APP, B/A 178 and 179. See, too, *La Lanterne des cochers de Paris*, nos. 1–10, 1880.

29. From a letter quoted in Victor-Joseph-Etienne Jouy and A. Jay, *Les Hermites en liberté, pour faire suite aux hermites en prison, et aux observations sur les moeurs et les usages français au commencement de XIXe siècle*, (6th ed.; Paris, 1824), II, 35–36.

30. For this information, see Ministère de la Justice, *Compte général de l'administration de la justice criminelle en France pendant l'année 1855* (Paris, 1856), 272–73; *Compte général . . . pendant l'année 1860* (Paris, 1862), 266–67; *Compte général . . . pendant l'année 1865* (Paris, 1867), 272–73. See also Horace Say, *Études sur l'administration de Paris et du département de la Seine* (Paris, 1846), 460–63, in which Say, too, notes the large number of coachmen being arrested for crimes in Paris in the 1840s.

bunal for 1873, 1880, and part of 1890. Although his statistics are drawn from later in the century, his conclusions add weight to the above data. Haine discovered that coachmen were numbered among the primary professionals arrested for drunken and disorderly conduct in the decades of the 1870s, 1880s, and 1890s and that over 90 percent of those coachmen arrested were convicted of their crimes.[31] That they were more visible than most other workers and that they were subject to a plethora of rules and regulations undoubtedly contributed to the high incidence of arrests among coachmen. Additionally, plainclothes police agents regularly followed and spied on coachmen, supplementing the surveillance of uniformed police agents and adding, no doubt, to the number of arrests. Police employees turning up as witnesses to coachmen's weddings lends some credence to the general impression that coachmen themselves often served as police spies. Too, some coachmen, perhaps because of frequent and amicable contact with police, became friends with their "natural enemy." The presence of police agents at a coachman's wedding may also have raised the social prestige of the gathering, as did other professionals on the list.

So far, the discussion of the coachmen's status has focused on marriage patterns and friends, but the question of their wages is central to the discussion as well. Although coachmen may have aspired to improve their social status by working at this trade in Paris, if their wages were low, such aspirations would have been unrealistic and quickly scrapped. They were not. Yet cabbies never ceased complaining that they were underpaid for their arduous workday. How much did cabbies earn in the nineteenth century? Parisian workers' salaries and their relation to the cost of living are difficult to analyze, as Jacques Rougerie has demonstrated, because we lack consistent data on wages and occupations throughout the nineteenth century.[32] The exact daily wage of the major industrial occupations is known for specific years, but the cabbie's wage is more difficult to ascertain. None of the standard government or other contemporary sources took much interest in cabbies' salaries, and their reasoning is made

31. Scott Haine to Nicholas Papayanis, March 23, 1982 (from Dept. of History, American University, Washington, D.C.).

32. Jacques Rougerie, "Remarques sur l'histoire des salaires à Paris au XIXe siècle," *Le Mouvement social* (April–June, 1968), 71–108.

explicit in one government report.[33] The Office du Travail wrote in 1893 that there were too few transportation firms for it to include them in its survey and that it preferred "to limit [its] inquiry to manufacturing industries." This assessment was not altogether accurate since by 1893 the CGV employed over 5,000 workers, most of them cabbies. Moreover, the report continued, "all the workers who belong to this category [transportation] are manual laborers, for the occupation of carter or of cabbie cannot be counted among those which require a long apprenticeship."[34] The Office du Travail was reflecting a bias in favor of industrial, as opposed to transportation, workers.

We are not completely in the dark about wages, however. Some secondary and official sources and certainly cab company reports indicate the cabbies' wages for different periods throughout the nineteenth century.[35] The average tip cabbies received can never be known for certain, though, and there were wage differentials between new and seasoned cabbies. Reasonable estimates of tips are possible, with the caveat that cabbies understated them and cab companies and guidebooks overstated them.

In his seminal study of Parisian wages during the nineteenth century, Rougerie indicates that from the early to the midnineteenth century, nominal wages for workers stagnated or decreased as the cost of living and the quality of life stagnated as well.[36] These three

33. See, for example, the following, none of which includes salaries for cabbies: Statistique de la France, *Prix et salaires à diverses époques* (Strasbourg, 1864); Bureau de la statistique générale, *Statistique annuelle*, 1882–89; Statistique générale de la France, *Salaires et coût de l'existence à diverses époques, jusqu'en 1910* (Paris, 1911); Ministère du Commerce, de l'industrie, des postes et des télégraphes, Office du Travail, *Salaires et durée du travail dans l'industrie française* (Paris, 1893–97); Emile Chevalier, *Les Salaires au XIXe siècle* (Paris, 1887); Agricol Perdiguier, *Statistiques du salaire des ouvriers: En réponse à M. Thiers et autres économistes de la même école* (Paris, 1849); Alfred de Foville, "Statistiques des salaires en France, de 1853 à 1871," *Journal de la Société de Statistique de Paris* (February, 1875), 36–46.

34. Ministère du Commerce, *Salaires et durée du travail*, I, 437.

35. See, for instance, Louis Landouzy, Henri Labbé, and Marcel Labbé, *Enquête sur l'alimentation d'une centaine d'ouvriers et d'employès parisiens* (Paris, 1905); Annales de la Chambre des Deputés (nouvelle série), *Commission d'enquête parlementaire sur la situation des ouvriers de l'industrie et de l'agriculture en France et sur la crise industrielle à Paris*, XII, session ordinaire de 1884 (Paris, 1885), 360–61; and CGV, *Assemblée générale ordinaire du 29 avril 1875, rapport* (Paris, 1875), Table 7.

36. Rougerie, "Remarques sur l'histoire des salaires," 71–108.

indices showed a strong increase throughout the years of the Second Empire, lasting into the 1880s, though not so uniform in all professions as during the empire. From the 1880s to 1900, Rougerie finds a strong, though irregular, increase in nominal wages, a lowering of the cost of living, a marked unemployment crisis, and stagnation or a decrease in the quality of life. The only changes in the early years of the twentieth century were an increase in the cost of living and a decline in the quality of life for workers.

Cabbies' wages remained stable up to the midnineteenth century. One large, well-known cab company of the first quarter of the century, the EGC, paid its cabbies monthly, at the rate of 2 francs per day for a twelve-hour workday. The company never failed to mention that this wage was independent of tips. Company contracts, which the coachmen signed on entering the firm, specified that cabbies could not request more than a 10 percent tip from a client. The 10 percent gratuity was regarded as customary, but a tip could be as low as 5 percent. The firm reported in 1829 that on weekdays each cab could earn an average of 18 to 24 francs, depending on when it was in service, during the day or during the evening. The average daily earnings increased slightly on Sundays and holidays. If a cabbie received tips of 10 centimes per franc, his earnings could increase by 1.8 to 2.4 francs per day. He might, therefore, earn between 3.8 and 4.4 francs a day. Such estimates must be made cautiously, however, as the average daily earnings for each cab were based on projections, not on actual financial reports.[37]

Two financial reports of one company, the CGVPP, for 1842 and 1843 and the prospectus of another cab company, Des Confortables, provide more accurate information by which to judge the general range of tips for coachmen.[38] In the period covering 1841 and 1842, the daily earnings of a voiture de place belonging to the CGVPP averaged 13 francs, 68 centimes. For the period covering 1842 and

37. EGC, *Tarif du prix de location des voitures de l'Entreprise Générale des Citadins* (Paris, 1829), 6, in BNSR. See also EGC, *Réglement ou contrat mutuel* (Paris, 1828), EGC, *Société Camille, Gorre, Daux et Cie.* (Paris, 1828), and EGC, *Réglement* (Paris, 1830), all in BNSR.

38. Société en commandite pour l'exploitation des Confortables, Voitures et Cabriolets sous Remise, [*Prospectus*] (Paris, 1838); CGVPP, *Rapport fait à l'assemblée générale des actionnaires, du 1er avril 1842* (Paris, 1842); and CGVPP, *Rapport du gérant à l'assemblée du 1er avril 1843* (Paris, 1843).

1843, this average dropped to 11 francs, 70 centimes. A cabbie working for this firm might have earned 1 franc, 36 centimes per day in tips in 1841 and 1842 and 1 franc, 17 centimes per day in 1842 and 1843. In 1838, the prospectus of the firm Des Confortables projected that each of its cabs would earn from 13 to 15 francs daily, figures close to the earnings of the CGVPP in 1842. The slightly higher figures might reflect both an optimistic projection designed to attract shareholders and the fact that it ran voitures sous remise rather than the voitures de place that the CGVPP did. If the figures of Des Confortables were more realistic than those of EGC twenty years earlier, then a cabbie working for Des Confortables would augment his daily wage by approximately 1.5 francs, rather than by the 1.8 to 2.4 francs of the EGC figures.

Des Confortables proposed to pay its cabbies 2 francs per day. Another firm, operating the larger cab known as a *Berline,* also paid its men 2 francs daily. The CGVPP paid its coachmen 3 francs daily in 1842, a wage it still paid in the early 1850s. The CIV also remunerated its cabbies 3 francs daily throughout its history from 1855 to 1866.[39]

We may conclude that in the 1840s and up to the end of the Second Empire coachmen could earn a straight wage of 3 francs per day. To this we can add another franc and a half in tips, bringing the ideal wage to approximately 4 francs, 50 centimes per day. Before the 1840s coachmen had earned 2 francs daily and might bring in an additional franc in tips.

By 1870, the cabbies of the CGV were earning a fixed wage of 4 francs per day. By the summer of that year, the firm, in response to a collective request by its coachmen, agreed to raise this wage to 5 francs for its seasoned cabbies. If this firm is a standard for the industry, which we may fairly assume, then the base wage of cabbies in the decade of the 1870s ranged from 4 to 5 francs, to which an additional 2 francs in tips may be added. By 1885, the base wage had risen to 5 to 6 francs. A survey of workers' wages in 1905 reported

39. Les Berlines de Place, dites Les Anciennes, *Règlement* (Paris, 1842), 3, CGVPP, *Règlement* (Paris, n.d., [*ca.* 1850]), 1–2, all in BNSR; CIV, *Règlement du service des cochers* (Paris, n.d. [1856]), 3, in APP, D/B 505; Chambre de Commerce de Paris, *Statistique de l'industrie à Paris* (Paris, 1864), 977–78.

that cabbies were still earning 6 francs, and a 1912 study indicated that the salary of coachmen varied from 4 to 6 francs per day.[40] How did a cabbie's salary compare with the salaries of other Parisian workers? In 1830, when the average cabbie could earn, with tips, 3 francs, 50 centimes, a cotton spinner earned 2 francs, 25 centimes; a weaver, 1 franc, 50 centimes; a cabinetmaker, 4 francs, 50 centimes; a blacksmith, 5 francs; a day laborer, 2 francs; a roofer, 4 francs; a stonecutter, 3 francs, 50 centimes; and a locksmith, 3 francs, 65 centimes. A statistical study of 1875 compared the daily wages of forty-seven different Parisian workers' professions for the years 1853 and 1871.[41] In 1853, they ranged from a low of 1 franc, 75 centimes for shoemakers and 2 francs for haircutters to a high of 5 francs for bakers, carpenters, stonecutters, and metal turners. The average daily wage was 3 francs, 82 centimes. Coachmen, who in 1853 earned a flat wage of 3 francs, with tips could earn 4 francs, 50 centimes per day. In 1871, the daily wages of these same professions ranged from a low of 3 francs for haircutters and 3 francs, 50 centimes for shoemakers to a high of 6 francs, 60 centimes for bakers and 6 francs for carpenters, stonecutters, and metal turners. The average was approximately 5 francs per day. Cabbies in 1871 earned a basic wage of 4 francs and could make as much as 6 francs with tips.

One more comparison between the wages of cabbies and the pay of other workers in the capital is in order. The Parisian cabbie had an easy alternative to driving a cab, if the salary warranted it: driving an omnibus. In 1848, Parisian omnibus coachmen earned 3 francs, 50 centimes per day, 50 centimes more than cabbies earned without tips. By 1863, the salary scale of the coachmen of the CGO, which had had a monopoly over Parisian omnibus service since 1855, was regulated in the following manner: coachmen with up to one year of service earned 4 francs per day; those with one to two years, 4 francs, 25 centimes; two to three years, 4 francs, 50 centimes; and more than

40. ACGV, CGV, *Conseil*, reg. no. 2, February 28, 1870, p. 417, and *Comité*, reg. no. 2, June 24, 1870, p. 567; Annales de la Chambre des Députés (nouvelle série), *Commission d'enquête parlementaire*, 360; Landouzy, Labbé, and Labbé, *Enquête sur l'alimentation*, 24, and Mareschal, *Les Voitures de place*, 192–93, 193 n. 1.

41. Rougerie, "Remarques sur l'histoire des salaires," 78 n. 15; Alfred de Foville, "Statistiques des salaires en France, de 1853 à 1871," *Journal de la Société de Statistique de Paris* (February, 1875), 39–40.

three years, 5 francs daily. Coachmen could also earn a bonus of 50 centimes on their basic wage if they worked 12 out of 15 days or 24 days each month. These wages were for a fifteen-hour workday of which twelve hours and twenty minutes were spent conducting the omnibus. By 1895, omnibus coachmen earned 6 francs, 50 centimes daily for slightly more than eleven hours of driving.[42] On the one hand, then, omnibus coachmen earned slightly more than cabbies in straight wages during the nineteenth century. They were also guaranteed steadier employment as municipal services expanded to meet the transportation needs of an expanding Parisian population. On the other hand, cabbies could earn a higher income than omnibus coachmen through tips and by operating their cabs for longer periods of time.

Coachmen were thus among neither the lowest nor the highest paid workers but fell somewhere in between. With their tips, though, they might earn as much as the highest paid Parisian worker. Coachmen, like most other workers in the city, had another source of income: they married working women. As Louise Tilly and Joan Scott have shown, working women's wages were an important part of "the family wage economy."[43] Although the wife may at some point have had to quit working full-time to raise a family, the addition of her income, no matter how low, certainly increased for a time the coachman's family income.

A study of the indigent population of Paris supports the view that coachmen were relatively well-off members of the Parisian working class. Paris had a total population in 1856 of 1,151,978. Male heads of households who were indigent totaled 15,310.[44] Of these, 142, or less than 1 percent of the total, were coachmen (see Table 17). Of the approximately 5,000 cochers de fiacre and cochers sous remise working in Paris at midcentury, 3 percent were indigent.

42. CGO, *Salaires et condition des conducteurs et des cochers des omnibus de Paris* (Paris, 1865), 1–2, 5–6, and *Condition des employés et ouvriers. Institutions créées par la Compagnie* (Paris, 1867), 2–3; Ministère du Commerce, *Salaires et durée du travail*, III, 415.

43. Tilly and Scott, *Women, Work, and Family*, 104–45.

44. Records for the entire first half of the nineteenth century indicate that coachmen were consistently low on the list of the indigent male heads-of-household population.

TABLE 17
Indigent Males in Paris in 1856

| Profession | Total number | Percentage of total (rounded) |
|---|---|---|
| Day laborer | 6,251 | 41 |
| Errand boy | 1,797 | 12 |
| Building-trade worker | 1,793 | 12 |
| No profession | 1,358 | 9 |
| Porter | 1,115 | 7 |
| Shoemaker | 940 | 6 |
| Retail merchant | 705 | 5 |
| Tailor | 574 | 4 |
| Rag-picker | 201 | 1 |
| Former clerk and writer | 197 | 1 |
| Coachman | 142 | 1 |
| Domestic | 111 | 1 |
| Total | 15,310 | |

Source: Administration générale de l'assistance publique à Paris, *Renseignement statistiques sur la population indigente de Paris* (Paris, 1862), 60–61.

The designation "coachmen" in Table 17 applies to all Parisian coachmen, a total significantly higher than 5,000, though how much higher is impossible to determine. Certainly the number of indigent coachmen in relation to all cochers de fiacre and cochers sous remise was considerably lower than 3 percent.

The figures of this table should not be surprising, given what we know about coachmen. To be a coachman in the first place, an individual had to arrive in Paris with some savings, since coachmen were required to pay a substantial security deposit before commencing employment with a cab company. In times of unemployment, moreover, coachmen could return to the countryside and a network of family and friends. Finally, the wages coachmen earned put them in a relatively good position vis-à-vis other Parisian workers. The image of the coachman as a nomadic, frequently drunk worker is not borne out by the statistical profile constructed so far. It is simply a myth.

In the matter of wages, even if coachmen were doing relatively well, they would certainly not admit that fact to their employers. Thus in 1857 coachmen petitioned the CIV to increase their wages from 3 to 5 francs per day and drew up a detailed list of their earnings and expenses to support their appeal.[45] This list cannot be accepted at face value or uncritically, for the petitioners probably exaggerated their expenses and minimized their earnings to make their case stronger. The petition concludes, for example, that coachmen earned 936 francs annually, while their expenses totaled 1,700 francs. No one could afford to remain a coachman, to say nothing of improving one's economic status, were this claim accurate. Coachmen arrived at this imbalance, for one, by maintaining that because of the new police rule permitting cab firms to charge for baggage brought into the cab, Parisians had ceased tipping cabbies, a highly unlikely scenario, and, for another, by inflating totals for some expenditures, such as clothing. Nevertheless, these claims probably resonated truth and should not be dismissed out of hand. An examination of the document itself permits us a somewhat deeper entry into the world of Paris coachmen.

According to the petition, coachmen averaged 312 days of work each year, a total based on the assertion that cabbies regularly rested from work 3 days each month and lost an additional 14 days as a result of police infractions. Their official CIV daily wage was 3 francs, and their workday, the petition stated, was eighteen hours. On the debit side, the petition averred that coachmen spent 1 franc, 20 centimes each day for three meals and for drink, 30 centimes each in tips to horse grooms and coach washers, and 20 centimes to cab station handymen. Fines and accidents annually cost them 18 francs and fare beaters 10 francs. There is no reason to doubt these expenses. Data on clothing and laundry bills, however, because difficult to verify, were susceptible to overstatement, though the items claimed as expenses are quite realistic. The CIV's cabbies maintained that the uniform purchased from the firm, valued at 162 francs, was so poorly manufactured they had to replace it each year. They also reminded CIV officials that, in addition to the uniform, their job required during a typical year three shirts (15 francs), four handkerchiefs (4 francs), six pairs of socks (50 centimes per pair), four white ties (4 francs), two pairs of underpants (4 francs), one linen vest (5 francs), one hat

45. *Rapport*, in APP, D/B 505, Paris, November 2, 1857.

(3 francs, 75 centimes), two pairs of shoes (18 francs), one pair of wool-lined gloves (3 francs), and one horse whip (5 francs). Their weekly laundry bill totaled 75 centimes. The cabbies also claimed an annual heating bill of 25 francs for wood and a lighting bill of 5 francs for candles.

The final item provides a glimpse into their housing arrangements. Cabbies asserted that rent for living quarters, their largest single expense, ranged from 12 to 20 francs per month for a single room, a mean aggregate of 160 francs annually. No mention is made of sharing the rent with other cabbies or of wives and children. Coachmen could also live in furnished rooms the CIV provided on several of its properties. For the most part these were rejected, the cabbies declared, because the rooms were subject to frequent robberies.

For substantial data on the hours coachmen worked, we must go to a highly biased but quite useful source. In 1903, Bixio, head of a cab employers' association, the Chambre Syndicale des Entrepreneurs de Voitures de Place du Départment de la Seine, as well as CGV president, addressed a written affidavit to a government commission gathering testimony on whether to limit the coachmen's workday to twelve hours. Bixio opposed the limitation and offered statistical evidence to demonstrate that such a reform would be both impractical and unpopular with coachmen. Although his statistics apply to a large cab firm, there is no reason to assume that single-cab owners or drivers employed by small firms had significantly different work patterns. Bixio's data, compiled for a six-month period in 1903, revealed a wide range of starting and quitting times and of total workday hours for his firm's cabbies. This information demonstrated, he believed, that coachmen preferred elastic work patterns and hours. He noted, moreover, that a typical sixteen-hour workday consisted of only seven hours of actual work, four hours of cruising for a fare, and five hours of rest. He described the typical coachman rather contemptuously: "[He] loafs about just as easily with his coach as without it. . . . It is evident that a coachman who is not married has no inclination to return to his lodgings before the hour of retiring." He further opined that many coachmen would use their leisure time only to "distract themselves in wine merchants' shops" so they might as well be working.[46]

46. Bixio, *Note adressée à la Commission permanente*, 14–15, 16.

Table 18
Hours CGV's Coachmen Spent Outside
Firm's Depots, January 15, 1903

| Hours | Number of coachmen | Percentage of coachmen |
|---|---|---|
| 12 or less | 436 | 21 |
| 13 | 417 | 20 |
| 14 | 428 | 20 |
| 15 | 329 | 15 |
| 16 | 321 | 15 |
| 17 | 151 | 7 |
| 18 or more | 42 | 2 |
| Total | 2,124 | |

Source: Maurice Bixio, *Note adressée à la Commission permanente* (Paris, 1903), 19.

Bixio does not consider the taxing nature of driving a coach or whether cabbies worked such long hours just to earn a living wage, nor does he offer any information on how he arrived at an average workday of sixteen hours. His data on total hours and starting and quitting times seem highly reliable, however, for he based them on depot chiefs' computations of the work sheets of the entire CGV cabbie population. Tables 18, 19, and 20 record the information Bixio presented for January 15, 1903. He confused the results of Table 18, the number of hours spent outside the depot, with the causes of a long workday: 80 percent of the CGV's cabbies remained outside longer than twelve hours because of habit, he concluded. As for the data in Tables 19 and 20, Bixio believed they demonstrated that coachmen preferred flexible hours and therefore could not be treated by authorities as ordinary workers.[47] These tables certainly do show that coachmen worked long and flexible hours, but they also suggest that cabbies devised strategies to maximize their income. That 80 percent of the CGV's coachmen began their workday between 7 and 10 A.M. undoubtedly reflects their experience that heavy cab usage began between those hours. That 52 percent quit work between 8 and 11 P.M. and 32 percent between 12 P.M. and 2 A.M. probably indicates decreased cab usage after those times. Family men may have preferred to start their shift early in order to return home

47. *Ibid.*, 21–22.

TABLE 19
CGV Cabbies' Starting Times, January 15, 1903

| Starting time | Number of coachmen | Percentage of coachmen |
|---|---|---|
| 5–6 A.M. | 21 | 1 |
| 6–7 A.M. | 157 | 7 |
| 7–8 A.M. | 472 | 22 |
| 8–9 A.M. | 784 | 37 |
| 9–10 A.M. | 454 | 21 |
| 10–11 A.M. | 184 | 9 |
| 11 A.M.–3 P.M. | 52 | 2 |
| Total | 2,124 | |

Source: Bixio, *Note adressée à la Commission permanente*, 20.

TABLE 20
CGV Cabbies' Quitting Times, January 15, 1903

| Quitting time | Number of coachmen | Percentage of coachmen |
|---|---|---|
| 5–6 P.M. | 3 | 0.1 |
| 6–7 P.M. | 15 | 0.7 |
| 7–8 P.M. | 145 | 7.0 |
| 8–9 P.M. | 385 | 18.0 |
| 9–10 P.M. | 462 | 22.0 |
| 10–11 P.M. | 245 | 12.0 |
| 11–12 P.M. | 158 | 7.0 |
| 12 P.M.–1 A.M. | 328 | 15.0 |
| 1–2 A.M. | 351 | 17.0 |
| 2–3 A.M. | 31 | 1.0 |
| 3–4 A.M. | 1 | 0.1 |
| Total | 2,124 | |

Source: Bixio, *Note adressée à la Commission permanente*, 20.

at a reasonable hour. Unmarried men may have kept late social hours and begun work slightly later. The data clearly demonstrate that all coachmen worked long hours, whether with clients in the coach or cruising the Paris streets for passengers, as they sought a living wage and perhaps even savings. The data do not warrant a negative characterization.

The coachman lived in a world with a well-defined social pecking order. The cocher de voitures sous remise believed he was socially superior to the cocher de fiacres. The *cocher d'omnibus* and the *cocher de tramways* looked down on both of them, and the *cocher de maison bourgeois* felt himself to be above the entire lot. According to the self-imposed standards of the corporation of Parisian coachmen, therefore, no one would disagree that a coachman working for the imperial family was at the top of the profession. As chance would have it, in 1860 just such a coachman went to the city hall of the seventh arrondissement to marry. Jean-Baptiste Bouteiller, age thirty-two, residing at 5, rue de l'Université, listed as his profession "cocher chez M. Prince Napoleon." He was originally from Ille-et-Vilaine. His father was dead and his mother a farmer. His bride was Augustine Papoint, twenty-eight years old and a native of the Mayenne. In Paris she worked as a maid and lived not far from Jean-Baptiste, at number 48, rue des Saints Pères. Her father was also deceased, and her mother engaged in no profession. The groom's witnesses were his forty-five-year-old cousin, a domestic, residing at number 37, rue Louis le Grand, and a friend, Jean-Baptiste Aliget, a concierge to Prince Jérome at 33, Palais Royal. The bride's witnesses were the owner of her apartment building and a friend, a domestic, who resided at 30, rue du Faubourg Montmartre. Here was the ultimate Parisian coachman, only dissimilar from other Parisian coachmen in the nature of his employer and the fact that one of his witnesses, the concierge, was a royal concierge. He had come from the country and apparently done well. Other cabbies, one can conclude, were on the same road to a successful integration in the Parisian social milieu.

This daguerreotype is one of the earliest photographic images of a Paris coachman.
*Courtesy Bibliothèque Nationale*

A Second Empire *cocher de fiacre, ca.* 1860.
*Courtesy Bibliothèque Nationale*

Paris coachmen debate the strike of 1878 during a meeting at the Cirque Fernando on the Boulevard Rochechouart.

*Courtesy Bibliothèque Nationale*

6 LES PETITS MÉTIERS DE PARIS
Un Cocher de Fiacre C.

A coachman waits for a client outside a Paris park. The coach, a *calèche,* is equipped with rubber tires, a wide dashboard, and a taximeter. *Ca.* 1905.

A coachman as Parisians liked to imagine him: outside a café, drink in hand, and looking jovial. His covered *fiacre* is fitted with a taximeter, rubber tires, and a sign (*chauffée*) indicating its interior compartment is heated. *Ca.* 1905.

Courtesy Bibliothèque Nationale

The first women "coachmen," Mesdames Dufaut and Charnier, as they were photographed on Paris streets in 1907.

*Courtesy Bibliothèque Nationale*

This type of coach, constructed between 1890 and 1900, was known as a *petite voiture,* or *calèche.* It belonged to the Compagnie Générale des Voitures à Paris and was standing before the Place Saint-Sulpice when this photograph was taken.

*Photograph by Eugène Atget. Courtesy Bibliothèque Nationale*

A coachman waits for a client in the Bois de Boulogne, 1910.
*Photograph by Eugène Atget. Courtesy Bibliothèque Nationale*

An example of the first electrically powered *fiacre, ca.* 1904.
*Courtesy Bibliothèque Nationale*

A *fiacre* of the Compagnie Générale des Voitures à Paris, 1910. Its tires are inflatable.
*Photograph by Eugène Atget. Courtesy Bibliothèque Nationale*

A *fiacre* with iron-fitted wheels, 1898.
*Photograph by Eugène Atget. Courtesy Bibliothèque Nationale*

—Cocher, cocher, mais puisque votre voiture est libre . . .
—Zut! J'aime pas les blondes.

—Driver, driver, since your cab is available . . .
—Damn! I don't go for blondes.

—Eh bien, mais, cocher, quand partons-nous.
—Que diable! le temps de finir mon feuilleton; le mouvement de la voiture m'em-
  pêche de lire.

—Say cabbie, when are we leaving?
—What the devil! As soon as I finish this story. Motion interferes with my reading.

These drawings are taken from a page of cartoons published in *Le Charivari*, September 13, 1883. The collection was entitled "Coachmen and the Bourgeois: Recollections from the Battlefield."

# 4 — The Cabbies of the CGV

The coachmen featured so far were a heterogeneous group. The data on which Chapter 3 was based, with the exception of information on working hours, are representative of the total pool of Parisian coachmen during the nineteenth and early twentieth centuries. They do not indicate, however, whether these coachmen of voitures de place or voitures sous remise worked for small or large cab firms, were members of cab cooperatives, or were owners themselves of single cabs. Fortunately, personnel files of over 500 cabbies who worked for the CGV in the years following the Paris Commune up to World War I have been located and allow us thus to study a homogeneous group of coachmen.[1] Of these files, 491 are complete and can be used as a statistical sample. Each file contains, among other items, a photograph of the coachman, his name, former profession, date of birth, and birthplace. In addition, for each cabbie there is a one-sheet report on his marital and family status, his domicile, and its proximity to his depot. The information about marital and family status and domicile is not a fixed variable for each cabbie, however, since the number of years covered by the report (referred to as the apartment report) varies from one cabbie to another. Each file also contains several evaluation sheets, the number fluctuating

1. ACGV.

from cabbie to cabbie, that were filled out periodically by a depot chief, who also recorded each cabbie's dates of entry into and departure from a cab depot, as well as the dates of entry into and departure from the company. Such information facilitates an evaluation of the employment history of each coachman.

These data are valuable but before being analyzed require a few qualifications. Every coachman whose file has survived made the transition from horse-drawn cab to automobile. These files are extant in part because each cabbie they document had a record of longevity with the CGV. They represent, therefore, a select group of Parisian coachmen. The files survived partly by accident, having been commingled with the more than 20,000 files of auto-taxi drivers in the CGV's archives. With some qualification, then, they may be treated as a random sample of Parisian coachmen who worked for the CGV.

That the CGV files identify a particular kind of coachman—the coachman who worked for a giant capitalist cab firm—does not mean that his background differed from the background of cabbies working for smaller firms. In some ways the data include information similar to that given in Chapter 3, for a period thirty years later, but they also provide different kinds of information, not available from the marriage certificates or other sources noted in Chapter 3. We learn the kinds of occupations men had before becoming coachmen, their employment records, their performance on the job, and something about their characters as seen through the eyes of the CGV. Thus, there are possibilities for comparison and for a fuller portrait of the coachmen.

The greatest percentage of CGV cabbies came from virtually the same departments as the general coachman population of Paris, with one major difference: the largest single group were from the Seine Department (see Table 21). In respect to birthplace, coachmen in the latter part of the nineteenth century share similar backgrounds with those in midcentury. Most Parisian coachmen still grew up in the rural provinces of France or in an agricultural country such as Italy. Moreover, coachmen working for a large capitalist firm came from the same rural parts of France from which those working for smaller firms came. From the latter half of the nineteenth century on, however, the Seine Department, contrary to popular contemporary opin-

TABLE 21
Departments of Origin of CGV Coachmen,
*ca.* 1880–1914

| Department (or country) | Percentage of total coachmen |
|---|---|
| Seine | 16.5 |
| Corrèze | 16.1 |
| Aveyron | 7.7 |
| Italy | 4.5 |
| Cantal | 2.9 |
| Creuse | 2.9 |
| Savoie | 2.2 |
| Puy-de-Dôme | 1.8 |
| Haute-Savoie | 1.6 |
| Maine-et-Loire | 1.6 |
| Allier | 1.4 |
| Cher | 1.4 |
| Lot | 1.4 |

Source: ACGV, personnel files of coachmen.

ion, provided the largest single block of Parisian coachmen. Thus, by the end of the nineteenth century, the occupation of coachman had apparently acquired a significant degree of attraction for urban dwellers.

These data also support the contention that cabbies tended to live near their place of work. Apartment reports do not represent a fixed variable, however, because the number of years covered varied from cabbie to cabbie. Nor do the reports cover the total number of years an individual was employed by the CGV, rather only a small fraction of the cabbies' time with the firm. To make statistical sense of this information, therefore, all reports are grouped according to the number of years they cover, ranging from one to eighteen. On each report a depot chief has recorded a coachman's address and the depot out of which he worked while at that address. The proximity of work to living quarters can be measured by using a simple scale based on whether work and domicile were in the same arrondissement, were in adjoining arrondissements, or were separated by one or more arrondissements. Reports covering one year comprise the largest percentage of the CGV sample, 14.9 percent. Coachmen in this sample, however, had an average of only 1.1 apartments, not a significant enough number to arrive at any conclusion about domicile and workplace. Apartment reports covering a fourteen-year period make up the second highest percentage of the sample, 9.8 percent. The coachmen in this group had an average of 3.2 apartments during that period. Of these, 44.4 percent lived and worked out of a depot in the same arrondissement, and 36.3 percent lived and worked in adjoining arrondissements. Only 18.7 percent lived and worked in nonadjoining arrondissements.

Based on these data and those of Chapter 3, we can conclude that coachmen sought to keep the distance between their living space and their work space as short as possible. Coachmen on the morning shift reported to their depots by 6 A.M. Coachmen concluding an evening shift returned to their depots after 12:30 A.M. In both instances, it would have been a hardship to live far from the depot, which was the first and last point a coachman visited during his workday. Many coachmen did live near municipal cab stations, but living near a depot was more convenient; it was even more convenient for the cabbie if the depot and the municipal cab station were close to each other. Coachmen with their own cabs or members of cooperative societies might be willing to live a little farther from a depot to upgrade the social status of their domiciles, but even owners, especially owners of only one cab who competed with the cabbies of large firms, might seek to shorten the distance between their depots and their apartments. The conclusion drawn here with respect to work and domicile, however, applies properly to the working-class cabbies of a large cab firm.

The inquiry in Chapter 3 into the socioprofessional status of the general population of coachmen was based on data that include the professions of the coachman's parents, of his bride and of her parents, and of the witnesses at his marriage. The marriage certificates do not reveal, however, whether the coachman-groom himself had a former profession. Since the data in the CGV files do contain this information, it is possible to determine whether the CGV recruited novices, hired seasoned men, or drew its coachmen from any other specific occupational pool.

The former professions, if any, of the CGV's coachmen were also the subject of a 1903 internal CGV memorandum and of a sociological study published that same year in the *Revue des deux mondes*.[2] These serve as ideal points of comparison with the CGV's personnel files and also reflect a contemporary impression of the CGV's coachmen. The internal memorandum concluded that among the firm's 3,000 coachmen there were some "very curious . . . and particularly varied" former professions. It listed 31 of these, among them jeweler, barber, teacher, doctor, optician, and music professor. Also on the list were professions that might more obviously lead to the occupation of coachman: farmer, domestic, horse groom, and cab entrepreneur.

The more serious, and more complete, study that appeared in the *Revue des deux mondes* investigated 4,000 cabbies working for the CGV. Emphasizing the rich cross-section of former professions of coachmen, it concluded that the Parisian coachman "did not constitute a homogeneous type."[3] Among the former professions, the author, Georges d'Avenel, found an ex-priest, 2 teachers, 3 businessmen, about 60 commercial employees, and 12 police officers and soldiers. He also found 30 noble names. Despite the unusual occupations, however, d'Avenel found that most Parisian coachmen came from the manual trades: 700 food industry workers and 350 from the building trades, the steel industry, and the textile trade. One very large block of Parisian coachmen, 1,400 in number, were former domestics, and another large body, 1,300, were seasonal agricultural workers who drove cabs in Paris during the off-months.

The personnel files of the CGV do not contradict the general impression that coachmen had engaged in diverse former professions. Among the sample of nearly 500 coachmen were individuals who had been butchers and masons and at least one former wood carver, a wine steward, a women's tailor, a barber, and a lithographer. Missing from the CGV files is any mention of the exotic professions or backgrounds described in the d'Avenel study and in the CGV internal memorandum, doctors, teachers, or nobles, for instance—missing, no doubt, because the personnel files represented

2. CGV, "Rapports divers," November, 1903 (Typescript in ACGV), and d'Avenel, "Le Mécanisme de la vie moderne," 580–610.

3. D'Avenel, "Le Mécanisme de la vie moderne," 595.

career coachmen. The d'Avenel study reported on the coachmen of the CGV during a one-year period, which would include a broader range than just career coachmen, and the CGV's internal memorandum was more concerned with picturesque details than with painting a true portrait of its average coachman. A teacher or another professional or skilled worker, temporarily unemployed or seeking to supplement his wages, may have worked briefly as a Parisian cabbie. Such an employee of the CGV would have attracted the attention of CGV officials or of someone investigating the company's personnel, since he would make good, colorful copy. He might appear in a one-year study or a company brochure but would be unlikely to appear among the files of long-term employees.

The conclusion that coachmen were a heterogeneous group, however, is not accurate; the CGV's memorandum and d'Avenel's study are somewhat misleading. The backgrounds of the coachmen studied point to significant similarities and common patterns, as evidenced in an analysis of the former professions engaged in by the CGV's cabbies. Table 22 lists the leading former professions and the percentage of the CGV's cabbies that engaged in them. The list is extremely rich and suggestive. Given the large number of rural departments from which Parisian coachmen migrated, it is not surprising that the occupation of farmer is first on the list of former professions. This ranking also accords with the seasonal nature of the employment of so many of the CGV's coachmen, as d'Avenel notes and as supported by the personnel files.[4] As for the second occupation on the list, that of coachman, it was not unusual for experienced cabbies to be hired by the CGV. Coachmen frequently changed employers or may have experimented with other occupations and, having failed at them, returned to that of coachman.

A revelation does, however, emerge from this list. Thus far we have discussed the profession of coachman as a possible rite of passage into the lower ranks of commercial activity. The high percentage of the CGV's cabbies who had been rural farm workers strongly supports this contention, especially in tandem with the marriage and friendship patterns of Parisian coachmen. But the list indicates that the profession of coachman was itself a step up in the eyes of urban

4. *Ibid.*

TABLE 22
Former Professions of CGV Coachmen,
*ca.* 1880–1914

| Former profession | Percentage of coachmen |
|---|---|
| Farmer | 16.1 |
| Coachman | 14.3 |
| Deliveryman | 9.4 |
| Horse groom | 5.1 |
| Wine merchant's assistant | 4.1 |
| Café assistant | 2.9 |
| Carter | 2.6 |
| Shop-boy | 2.4 |
| Milkman's assistant | 2.0 |
| Lorry driver | 1.8 |
| Private coachman | 1.8 |
| Mason | 1.6 |
| Valet | 1.4 |

Source: ACGV, personnel files of coachmen.

workers who were lower on the social scale than the cabbies: deliverymen, horse grooms, wine merchants' assistants, café assistants, shopboys, milkmen's assistants, and valets all earned less than coachmen. Their occupations, moreover, brought them into close contact with coachmen, whom they could observe and in whose steps they might wish to follow. Horse grooms and coachmen were in daily contact, and in the hierarchy of the depot the horse groom was a clear step below the cabbie. Coachmen spent much of their time in wine merchants' shops and cafés and probably came into contact with young assistants who would be attracted to a more independent and better paying job. Deliverymen were already in a trade similar to that of the coachmen. The transition from one occupation to the other was neither dramatic nor difficult. Valets and other domestics were most frequently categorized by contemporary Parisians as belonging to the same stratum of the work force as coachmen. Chapter 3 reported that domestics and coachmen had frequent contact. That valets might have wanted to free themselves from the restraints of domestic service and turn to the coachman's freer occupation should not be surprising.

Carters, lorry drivers, and private coachmen were on a par with cabbies, though some private coachmen regarded themselves as superior to the common cabbie. Their entrance into the profession was a lateral, perhaps even a downward, move but not unusual given the similarity between the occupations. Unemployment or a desire for independence may have led them to try earning a living as a coachman. One profession that, at first glance, seems out of place in Table 22 is mason, a semiskilled and fairly respected trade far removed from the world of horses and cabs. Why would a mason choose to become a cabbie? Perhaps for the same reasons the agricultural worker had, that his own work was seasonal. A mason could work as a coachman when inclement weather forced building projects to stop. Harsh weather conditions affected cabbies, too, but only by causing them discomfort on the job; bad weather never put cabbies out of work. In addition, the building trades are always among the first in an industrial economy to reflect a downward trend in the economic cycle. Masons may have shifted to the cab trade for the same economic reasons that forced many rural workers off the farms and into the city.

Despite the influx of men from various other professions, the CGV reported that its 3,000 coachmen constituted a "generally stable" labor force and produced statistics to support this assertion (see Table 23).[5] It boasted, too, that 111 of its cabbies, or 3.7 percent, had been with the firm for twenty to twenty-five years; 52, or 1.7 percent, had been with the firm for twenty-five to thirty years; and 62, or 2.1 percent, had been with the firm for more than thirty years.

D'Avenel concludes from his sampling of 4,000 cabbies that 600 had less than one year's experience with the CGV, 1,800 had worked from one to five years, and 700 had been with the firm from six to ten years.[6] Only 250 cabbies, according to him, had been with the CGV for more than twenty years. Old coachmen were rare in any case, he wrote. Only 200 out of the 4,000 sampled were more than sixty years old, 600 were from fifty to sixty years of age, 1,000 were less than thirty, and 1,300 fell between the ages of thirty and forty. D'Avenel reported that many cabbies became cab subcontractors or

5. CGV, "Rapports divers," 3–4.
6. D'Avenel, "Le Mécanisme de la vie moderne," 594.

TABLE 23
Tenure of CGV Coachmen,
as of November 18, 1903

| Years with CGV | Number of cabbies | Percentage of total cabbies |
|---|---|---|
| 1 | 745 | 26.9 |
| 2 | 289 | 10.4 |
| 3 | 265 | 9.6 |
| 4 | 221 | 8.0 |
| 5 | 172 | 6.2 |
| 6 | 137 | 4.9 |
| 7 | 136 | 4.9 |
| 8 | 127 | 4.6 |
| 9 | 108 | 3.9 |
| 10 | 96 | 3.5 |
| 11 | 75 | 2.7 |
| 12 | 74 | 2.7 |
| 13 | 72 | 2.6 |
| 14 | 45 | 1.6 |
| 15 | 41 | 1.5 |
| 16 | 44 | 1.6 |
| 17 | 37 | 1.3 |
| 18 | 33 | 1.2 |
| 19 | 31 | 1.1 |
| 20 | 32 | 1.2 |

Source: CGV, "Rapports divers" (Typescript in
ACGV, November 18, 1903), 3–4.

went to work for other firms and that those coachmen who could save money preferred to enter more sedentary occupations, that of wine merchant the most popular.

The CGV's personnel files add considerable precision to the above information. They reveal that the average entry age of cabbies joining the CGV was twenty-nine, the standard deviation being 8.6 years. The average retirement age was fifty-nine, also with a standard deviation of 8.6 years. The average number of years a cabbie spent with the CGV was thirty, with a standard deviation of 8.2 years. This information, especially the retirement data, must be interpreted conservatively, however, since these CGV personnel files survived because of the longevity of their subjects' tenure.

There are some data on the entire employment record of CGV cabbies. From these we may confidently draw some general conclusions because the cabbies' long affiliation with the CGV provided enough time for employment patterns to emerge and because these conclusions concern a characteristically stable coachman population. Since depot chiefs recorded each cabbie's entry and departure date at a particular depot, it is possible to calculate accurately the amount of time a coachman was absent from work for any extended period. The average length of time coachmen drove their cabs on the streets of Paris for the CGV was 57.9 percent of the time between their first and last stints of employment. Their average unemployment time was 42.1 percent. In some instances a leave was for a few days only, with or without the company's permission; in others it lasted several years. D'Avenel explains that many Parisian coachmen were seasonal workers, for example, farm workers, who came to Paris between the planting and harvesting seasons. Thus, Savoyards and Limousins arrived in October and left at the end of May. Some Auvergnats passed the winter, others the spring, in Paris. Italians, he wrote, spent nearly the entire year in Paris, going home only for two months in the summer.[7]

The minutes of the CGV's Executive Committee confirm the seasonal employment record of many cabbies.[8] So does Bixio, who observed that all coachmen with a peasant background fell into two informal categories: permanent employees, who remained on the payroll for fifteen or twenty years, and seasonal coachmen, commonly referred to as *moissonneurs* (harvesters or reapers), who worked in Paris three or four months, returning to their native rural department during harvest time. This designation had a double meaning: "They [the cabbies] arrived in Paris during the busy cab season to gather their harvest" and then left "to gather their own harvest in their native region."[9]

A significant number of Parisian coachmen were seasonal workers. A study of 676 instances in which depot chiefs recorded, as they

7. *Ibid.*, 595.
8. ACGV, CGV, *Comité*, reg. no. 1, August 25, 1868, p. 321. See also Gérard Collomb, "Nouveaux Citadins ou ruraux émigrés? Les Amicales de Savoyards à Levallois-Perret," *Ethnologie française* (April–June, 1980), 185–90.
9. Bixio, *Note adressée à la Commission permanente*, 2–3.

TABLE 24
Paris Coachmen's Reasons for Leaving
Employment, *ca.* 1880–1914

| Reasons | Percentage of total |
|---|---|
| Returned to the country | 21.4 |
| Mobilized or military service | 20.7 |
| Sick | 18.3 |
| Accident | 8.3 |
| Switched to automobile | 4.9 |
| Vacation | 4.3 |
| Left for another company | 3.6 |
| Found a better job | 1.2 |

Source: ACGV, personnel files of coachmen.

often did, on a coachman's evaluation sheet the reason he left the company reveals the pattern shown in Table 24. We should not conclude, as did their contemporaries, that because many coachmen were seasonal employees, they were necessarily nomadic and unstable. Most seasonal workers toiled diligently to supplement farm income. Moreover, they returned regularly to the CGV, providing further evidence of stability in their work patterns.

As the table shows, the coachman's trade was frequently dangerous and certainly difficult: over 18 percent of the instances in which cabbies did not work were due to illness and 8 percent to accidents. If considered together, these two reasons would account for more than 26 percent of the times coachmen left their jobs and would move to first position in Table 24. Were so many instances of illness legitimate? Cabbies might simply have reported in sick to obtain relief from a long and arduous workday. The CGV anticipated the possibility of faked illness, however, and ruled that cabbies claiming to be ill had to visit a company doctor to have their ill health verified. Thus, illness was legitimately a major reason for time off.

Before we consider the performance and character evaluations from the CGV's personnel files, a word is in order concerning the apparent inconsistency between the seasonal nature of the occupation for a great many cabbies and the finding that for many the trade of Parisian coachmen facilitated permanent integration into the life of

Paris or provided a conduit to a commercial pursuit. The data in this chapter confirm that many Parisian coachmen had a rural or agricultural background and retained that connection over the years. This finding is not, however, inconsistent with the conclusion that an important segment of the cabbies were becoming integrated into the Parisian milieu. Both conclusions are valid and exist side by side. The single largest block of the CGV's cabbies, for instance, were born in the Seine Department; they would not be among those regularly returning to the provinces. Too, the self-selected nature of the data used in this chapter and the depot chiefs' vagueness in giving reasons for, or their silence with respect to, cabbies' departures prevent us from gaining an accurate sense of how many CGV cabbies left the company and successfully or unsuccessfully attempted commercial pursuits. Moreover, many coachmen leaving the CGV may have done so to work for other cab firms, and those who had married urban women would remain in the capital. In addition, most likely only the smallest percentage of cabbies coveting their own enterprises and a step up the social ladder was successful in achieving this goal. From this perspective, the notion that the coachman's trade represented an integration into the urban milieu and the first step toward something better is borne out by the information in the CGV's files.

Not only did the CGV record the employment incidence of its coachmen, but it also evaluated performance and character. Periodically for each coachman, depot chiefs filled out evaluation sheets that usually contained eight categories: (1) horsemanship, (2) receipts, (3) attitude toward the public, (4) care of coach, (5) care of personal property (primarily the uniform), (6) attitude toward superiors, (7) character, and (8) excessive drinking. Typically, the depot chief wrote one or, at most, two words summarizing his opinion of the coachman in each category. Because depot chiefs were the coachmen's immediate superiors, essential to the CGV's disciplinary authority over the cabbies, and a decided step above the cabbies in social status, one would expect them to share many of the negative opinions about coachmen commonly held by Parisians. That the collective conclusions of their evaluation sheets do not conform to the general stereotype of Paris coachmen provides a measure of confidence that the opinions on the evaluation sheets reflect a certain degree of accuracy and objectivity.

On reading the evaluation sheets, we can see emerging a pattern in the choice of words, which enables us to devise a numerical code to represent the judgments of the officials. Thus, with regard to the first seven categories, the scale appears to be as follows: 4, very bad; 5, bad; 6, mediocre; 7, passable; 8, good; 9, very good. As for whether a coachman drank heavily, the scale is: 1, no; 2, yes; 3, sometimes. If we first calculate for each question and for all coachmen the frequency of each value in the scale, we can then translate the result into a percentage of the total responses. The number of times there was no response is recorded as well, but that figure is not included in the final calculations. There are well over two thousand responses each for all but category 2, the receipts category, which was often not on the evaluation sheet or simply not filled out. For this category there are slightly more than two hundred responses. The numerical results for the first seven categories are presented in Table 25, at the end of which is a representation of the global results for each category, expressed as a mean.

Some results do not conform to the general public's perception of coachmen in the nineteenth century. Indeed, for most categories the results obtained were unanticipated. In horsemanship, for example, we might assume that coachmen would be fairly proficient, since many of them, having rural or farming backgrounds, were familiar with farm animals, all of them had to attend an apprenticeship program, and those in this sample had been affiliated with the CGV for an average of thirty years, actively conducting coaches on Paris streets for 58 percent of that time. It is surprising, therefore, that close to 70 percent of the evaluations in category 1 were no better than passable, only 30 percent of the coachmen rated as good or very good. Driving a coach was not a very complex professional skill, yet coachmen, at least in the eyes of the CGV, seem not to have mastered it fully. This rating perhaps explains why nineteenth-century Parisians frequently complained about the performance of coachmen, why the Society for the Protection of Animals monitored them so carefully, and why coachmen were not highly regarded by other, more skilled workers.

Coachmen also rated poorly, with an even lower mean score than for horsemanship, in the care-of-coach category. Like horsemanship, this category evaluated the cabbie's skill, since caring for the coach

TABLE 25
Numerical Results of Evaluation Sheets, *ca.* 1880–1914

| Category 1 Horsemanship | | | Category 2 Receipts | | |
|---|---|---|---|---|---|
| Judgment | Frequency | Percentage | Judgment | Frequency | Percentage |
| Missing ones | 14 | | Missing ones | 2,470 | |
| Very bad | 33 | 1.2 | Very bad | 1 | 0.5 |
| Bad | 210 | 7.9 | Bad | 8 | 3.8 |
| Mediocre | 427 | 16.0 | Mediocre | 10 | 4.7 |
| Passable | 1,192 | 44.7 | Passable | 65 | 30.7 |
| Good | 776 | 29.1 | Good | 123 | 58.0 |
| Very good | 30 | 1.1 | Very good | 5 | 2.4 |

| Category 3 Attitude Toward Public | | | Category 4 Care of Coach | | |
|---|---|---|---|---|---|
| Judgment | Frequency | Percentage | Judgment | Frequency | Percentage |
| Missing ones | 447 | | Missing ones | 12 | |
| Very bad | 1 | 0.0 | Very bad | 293 | 11.0 |
| Bad | 7 | 0.3 | Bad | 243 | 9.1 |
| Mediocre | 26 | 1.2 | Mediocre | 45 | 1.7 |
| Passable | 155 | 6.9 | Passable | 1,037 | 38.8 |
| Good | 2,031 | 90.9 | Good | 1,024 | 38.4 |
| Very good | 15 | 0.7 | Very good | 28 | 1.0 |

| Category 5 Care of Personal Property | | | Category 6 Attitude Toward Superiors | | |
|---|---|---|---|---|---|
| Judgment | Frequency | Percentage | Judgment | Frequency | Percentage |
| Missing ones | 5 | | Missing ones | 5 | |
| Very bad | 2 | 0.1 | Very bad | 2 | 0.1 |
| Bad | 124 | 4.6 | Bad | 84 | 3.1 |
| Mediocre | 95 | 3.5 | Mediocre | 61 | 2.3 |
| Passable | 962 | 35.9 | Passable | 558 | 20.8 |
| Good | 1,459 | 54.5 | Good | 1,949 | 72.8 |
| Very good | 35 | 1.3 | Very good | 23 | 0.8 |

| Category 7 Character | | | Category 8 Excessive Drinking | | |
|---|---|---|---|---|---|
| Judgment | Frequency | Percentage | Judgment | Frequency | Percentage |
| Missing ones | 7 | | Missing ones | 3 | |
| Very bad | 6 | 0.2 | No | 2,647 | 98.8 |
| Mediocre | 89 | 3.3 | Yes | 6 | 0.2 |
| Passable | 632 | 23.6 | Sometimes | 26 | 1.0 |
| Good | 1,666 | 62.3 | | | |
| Very good | 8 | 0.3 | | | |

TABLE 25 (continued)
Results of Table Expressed as a Mean

|  | N | Mean | Standard deviation |
|---|---|---|---|
| Horsemanship | 2,668 | 6.958 | 0.959 |
| Receipts | 212 | 7.490 | 0.823 |
| Attitude toward public | 2,235 | 7.902 | 0.385 |
| Care of coach | 2,670 | 6.876 | 1.333 |
| Care of personal property | 2,677 | 7.440 | 0.794 |
| Attitude toward superiors | 2,677 | 7.657 | 0.696 |
| Character | 2,675 | 7.383 | 0.975 |
| Excessive drinking | 2,679 | 1.021 | 0.201 |

Source: ACGV, personnel files of coachmen.

also involved hitching and harnessing the horse to the coach and repairing the harness if it broke. Only 39 percent of the time did cabbies receive a rating of good or very good in the care of their coach, compared to 59 percent ranging from very bad to passable. These results may mean that the coachman had little loyalty to the CGV and cared minimally about company equipment, but this possibility should perhaps be discounted because coachmen were financially liable for company equipment once it left the depot. Coachmen rated far better with the care of their personal property, as 56 percent of the evaluations were good to very good, 36 percent were passable, and only 8 percent were very bad, bad, or mediocre.

With respect to the coachman's attitude toward the public (category 3) and toward his superiors (category 6), results of the evaluations were also unexpected. Along with category 7, these judge the areas of character and personality. Popular literature portrayed coachmen as dangerous and rude characters, and for their part, cabbies never tired of complaining about the abuses they suffered at the hands of difficult customers. Why, then, would 92 percent of the cabbies sampled receive evaluations indicating that their attitude toward the public was good or very good? Unpleasant or hostile incidents were evidently not the norm, though they were precisely the ones likely to be remembered and written about. Most cab rides were apparently uneventful for all participants. An additional factor in ensuring that the coachman was polite to his customers was that his salary, counting tips, depended on good relations with them. As for category 6, concerning the cabbie's attitude toward his superiors, the high evaluations, 74 percent good or very good and 21 percent passable, can be explained by the fact that a cabbie's job depended on his superior's judgment of his total performance, including his attitude toward the superior filling out the evaluation sheet. In addition, as other evidence has indicated, coachmen were for the most part hardworking, serious, family men, who would tend to be deferential toward their employers. Only the common prejudice against coachmen prevalent in the nineteenth century requires one to explain these findings.

The depot chiefs' estimation of the overall character of the coachmen was lower than their rating of the cabbies' attitude toward superiors or the public. According to the last section of Table 25, the mean response in this category was 7.383 with a standard deviation of 0.975, compared to a mean response of 7.902 with a standard deviation of 0.385 in category 3 and a mean response of 7.657 with a standard deviation of 0.696 for category 6. The minimum and maximum values for all categories were 4 and 9, respectively. The evaluation section of Table 25 demonstrates that depot chiefs rated the character of cabbies as bad, very bad, or mediocre 14 percent of the time, as passable 24 percent of the time, and as good or very good 63 percent of the time. This is not a negative finding, though the rating for overall character is slightly lower than the ratings for categories 3 and 6. Several factors could account for this discrepancy. Although coachmen were generally decent and hard-working Parisians, they might not be polished and courteous. The strenuousness of their occupation could make them irritable, and a depot chief had to deal with all his cabbies' moods, good and bad. He also had to account for their productivity, and a significant amount of tension could easily develop in this matter between the cabbie and his immediate supervisor. These factors and the general reputation of the cabbies would account for a lower character rating.

As for receipts, the depot chief was interested in whether the cabbie successfully met the company's daily target rates. Depot chiefs estimated that cabbies had good to very good receipts 60 percent of the time, that they had passable receipts 31 percent of the time, and very bad, bad, or mediocre receipts only 9 percent of the time. On the whole, this is a favorable estimation of the coachmen's productivity.

The evaluations of the coachmen's drinking tendencies are the most startling. Contemporary lore held that, at best, coachmen drank a great deal; at worst, they were outright drunkards. Even coachmen themselves, as we saw in Chapter 3, estimated that they expended a significant share of their income on drink. Yet nearly 99 percent of the evaluations reported that coachmen did not drink excessively. What is the significance of this finding? These evaluations indicate that coachmen, despite the common stereotype and popular opinion to the contrary, did not appear to drink more than the general population and that their performance on the job was not impaired by the amount of alcohol they consumed.

The final brush strokes in the composite portrait of the CGV's coachman concern his marital and family status. This information is contained within the apartment reports and is not standardized for the entire sample. Statistics on this topic, computed for any year, support the conclusion that coachmen, whether seasonal or integrated into the Paris scene, were stable and productive members of the work force. The data demonstrate that the largest percentage of the CGV's coachmen were family men. Of the coachmen whose apartment reports covered five years (6.7 percent of the total sample), 81.8 percent were married, none had been divorced, 9.1 percent were single, 6.1 percent were widowed, and 3.0 percent had remarried. They had an average of 1.2 children. Of the coachmen whose apartment reports covered ten years (6.3 percent of the sample), 77.4 percent were married, 3.2 percent were divorced, and 19.4 percent were single; they had an average of 1.4 children. Apartment reports spanning fourteen years (9.8 percent of the sample) show 87.5 percent married, 2.1 percent single, 6.3 percent widowed, 2.1 percent remarried after a divorce, and 2.0 percent remarried after being widowed and an average of 1.1 children.

In 1903, Maurice Bixio presented data on the marital status and children of CGV cabbies that may be compared with the above statistics (see Tables 26 and 27). His findings show a smaller percentage

TABLE 26
Marital Status of CGV Coachmen,
January 1, 1903

| Marital status | | Percentage |
|---|---|---|
| Married | 2,059 | 65.0 |
| Widowed | 56 | 2.0 |
| Divorced | 5 | 0.2 |
| Single | 1,071 | 34.0 |
| Total | 3,191 | |

Source: Bixio, *Note adressée à la Commission permanente*, 23.

TABLE 27
Number of Children of CGV Cabbies,
January 1, 1903

| Number of Children | | Coachmen |
|---|---|---|
| 1 | | 524 |
| 2 | | 240 |
| 3 | | 119 |
| 4 | | 52 |
| 5 | | 17 |
| 6 | | 8 |
| 7 | | 2 |
| 8 | | 1 |
| 9 | | 1 |
| 10 | | 1 |
| 11 | | 1 |
| 14 | | 1 |
| Totals | 1,768 | 967 |

Source: Bixio, *Notre adressée à la Commission permanente*, 23.

of the CGV's cabbies married and a correspondingly higher percentage single. Bixio's sample, the entire cabbie population of the CGV for one year, includes seasonal as well as full-time coachmen, old and young alike, whereas the family reports are a random sample of (probably) permanent CGV cabbies over a long period of time. None of Bixio's data contradict the impression that a large portion of the CGV's cabbies were hard-working family men, for they show that significantly more than half were or had been married and nearly half had at least one child.

The data in this chapter confirm an important rural-agrarian factor in the coachman's background, though the CGV's personnel files indicate that by the end of the nineteenth century the Paris region had become an important place of origin for Parisian coachmen. Perhaps by this time earlier generations of coachmen had settled permanently in the capital and had created a tradition of coaching within the family. Or perhaps an increasing number of native Parisians saw the coaching profession as a means of advancement. Whatever the reason, the corporation of Parisian coachmen included a large block of native-born Parisians, working alongside their provincial comrades.

Whatever their origins, most of the coachmen lived near their depots, many were seasonal workers, and the majority were married and family men. The coachman's profession, far from being the province of drunkards and shiftless nomads, served as a means for assimilation into an urban environment and as a vehicle for advancement into the ranks of the petit bourgeoisie.

# 5 — Unions and Newspapers
## in the Corporation of Parisian Coachmen

Coachmen did not remain passive in the face of their hardships. They founded mutual aid societies, trade unions, cooperatives, and newspapers to defend and promote their interests. Considering their low status in the work force, the great number of their organizations and newspapers appears remarkable, especially compared with those of the better known industrial workers. Between 1846 and 1914, coachmen or their sympathizers published over twenty newspapers or periodicals devoted exclusively to the coachman's trade.[1] In most instances these publications were not mere trade sheets but an integral part of coachmen's defensive mechanisms. Their editors were either pioneers in organizing coachmen or individuals providing services to them. During this same period of time, the midnineteenth to early twentieth century, coachmen formed three major trade associations and a host of smaller ones. In short, they were well organized and had a long tradition and an extensive network of journals to protect their interests. So large a number of publications and the existence of several unions are indicative, however, of a fundamental difficulty that beset coachmen over these

---

1. See Bibliography. There is no way to determine if this list is complete, since so many of these titles are not listed in any public catalog and only the diligence and generous assistance of several librarians in the Salle des Periodiques of the BN helped to locate so many unknown publications.

years. Many of the unions and newspapers represented rival factions of the corporation of Parisian coachmen. Below the surface of the corporation lay enormous contradictions and rivalries that go a long way toward explaining why this trade was relatively powerless in the economic marketplace.

The disharmony within the cab trade, not clear-cut at first, revolved around cab ownership and related issues that divided cab entrepreneurs from cabbies who drove for others. Up until 1879, cab entrepreneurs and cabbies did not regard their interests as mutually exclusive. They both blamed the police and the large cab companies, especially a firm like the CGV, for their difficulties. A fraternal sense of cooperation, with corporate language and values, guided the two groups, though differences in policies and attitudes surfaced occasionally.[2] During the 1880s, however, with the growing working-class consciousness of many cabbies, especially in those working for the largest firms, the economic crisis of the 1880s, and the rise of the revolutionary syndicalist movement, outright hostility and rivalry set in. The key issue, apparent from the coachmen's publications, was ownership. Because the newspapers and trade unions were more often than not led or directed by coachmen or former coachmen, they stayed very close to rank-and-file sentiment. Their ideological output and collective action, which are the focus of this chapter, are thus accurate barometers of the political and class attitudes within the corporation of Parisian coachmen.

There is evidence in the *Bottin* and in the police archives that some coachmen had organized during the Restoration.[3] It was the policy of the *Bottin* to include the names and addresses of the major Parisian and provincial commercial establishments. For 1821, it listed 157 loueurs de voitures et cabriolets who had apparently formed an

2. See William H. Sewell, Jr., *Work and Revolution in France: The Language of Labor from the Old Regime to 1848* (Cambridge, Eng., 1980); Yves Lequin, *Les Ouvriers de la région lyonnaise (1848–1914)* (Lyon, 1977); and Berlanstein, *Working People of Paris.*

3. *Almanach du commerce de Paris* (Paris, 1821), 474–76, and APP, D/A 262, *A monsieur le Conseiller d'État, Préfet de Police* (Paris, n.d. [1823]). See also D/A 2, *Mémoire adressé à son excellence le ministre-d'état, préfet de police* (Paris, n.d. [1817]). The latter is a petition presented by an association, Les Entrepreneurs-Loueurs des Voitures de Paris, des Communes Rurales et des Départemens Voisins, expressly formed to contest recent cab parking fees.

association among themselves. Immediately following their names, the *Bottin* listed their "delegates" and a treasurer and a secretary. It also recorded an address for a "headquarters," 13, cour de la Sainte Chapelle. The police archives of the same period contain a petition from the Loueurs de Voitures et Cabriolets de Remise de la Ville de Paris, which may or may not have been the above organization, lobbying for the needs of their industry. No details exist concerning the early cabbies' association(s), but it is apparent that the small owners and cab-leasing entrepreneurs had banded together to represent themselves and their interests in some fashion.

The public record is silent as to other coachmen's institutions until 1846. In that year the first known publication devoted exclusively to coachmen came into being. A sheet entitled *Le Fiacre,* actually a prospectus for a journal, appeared on July 3, 1846. *Le Fiacre* was succeeded the following month by *Le Cocher,* which published until December of 1846. Monsieur Palouzié, an administrator of *Le Fiacre* and an important director of *Le Cocher,* provided continuity between the two publications.

*Le Fiacre* appeared only once, but it established the tone that many cabbies' newspapers shared until the 1880s. It appealed essentially to working-class coachmen, those cabbies who did not own their own cabs, but it also aimed to attract a broader readership, including cab owners. *Le Fiacre* stated editorially that cab owners should be solicitous "of the honest workers that they employ." Expressing the hope that owners would help to distribute the journal, it added: "We shall be happy with their cooperation, and they can rest assured that all our efforts shall make us worthy of the sympathy that some among them have already had the goodness to bear witness to."[4]

Neither *Le Fiacre* nor *Le Cocher* had any intention of challenging the system of cab ownership; both aimed to ameliorate the average coachman's condition. To this end, *Le Fiacre* formulated a demand that was also adopted by future coachmen's journals, whether reformist, socialist, or owner-oriented in nature—the demand that cabbies be granted and assured the full protection of *le droit commun* (common law). It did not use the expression "le droit commun," which became a catchphrase later on, but it meant this protection

4. *Le Fiacre: Journal des cochers,* July 3, 1846.

when it demanded that the police cease their excesses against coachmen and begin treating them impartially. When coachmen employed this expression, they did not mean rights under an English system of law. They meant instead a general right that applied to all citizens and that they believed they did not enjoy. *Le Fiacre*'s demand implied that coachmen were more closely scrutinized and heavily regulated than any other group of Parisian workers and that the police, through their control of the driving code, exercised virtual dictatorial power over coachmen both on the streets and in the police courts. Beginning with *Le Cocher,* coachmen and cab enterprises expressed their common desire that the government abolish most regulations over the cab trade, save for elementary rules of the road, claiming such regulations constituted a violation of the common law. What is interesting is that this demand was shared by ordinary coachmen and owners alike and served to unite the two groups against the police in the midnineteenth century.

*Le Fiacre* also wished to establish and maintain good relations with the public. It proposed to run a column that would list, from the police record, the names of all coachmen who had returned to the authorities objects found in their cabs, considering such a list "a noble reward for such acts." As a service to the public, another column would announce feast days, the best itinerary to follow by cab for outings outside Paris, and the names of good but inexpensive Paris restaurants. The journal also proposed to review new inventions and machines, the work of the Academy of Sciences, the outcome of important court cases, and the world of fashion and plays and to run a series on the history of the monuments of Paris.

*Le Cocher* incorporated these ideas but went further, founding an important institutional support for coachmen. It would later become common for coachmen's newspapers, especially during periods when unions were lacking, to organize a legal department at their editorial offices to provide free legal aid to cabbies who subscribed to the newspaper. *Le Cocher* established the model for this service. Its first issue announced the formation of a *bureau spéciale de défense* to be headed by Palouzié.[5] The offices of the bureau spéciale were in the

5. *Le Cocher: Journal des annonces, de la littérature, de l'industrie, des sciences et des arts*, August 2, 1846, p. 1.

headquarters of *Le Cocher,* the Maison Bidault, at 4, rue de la Jussienne, in the centrally located second arrondissement. The primary function of this new office was to provide a verbal defense at simple police tribunals on behalf of coachmen apprehended for violations of traffic or parking codes. The bureau spéciale also furnished a written defense for any coachman appearing before the coach pound.

For the most part, *Le Cocher* made no distinction between owner-cabbies and plain coachmen. It demanded on behalf of the entire profession a defense "against the abuses of unrestrained repression," documenting in its pages the paramount complaints of all Parisian coachmen, the small owner-operator as well as the mere cabbie. At the top of its list of grievances were the various police controls, especially the *mise à pied,* the suspension of a coachman from work for an infraction of the driving code. Demanding the abolition of this punishment, the newspaper noted: "The mise à pied is an especially formidable measure in that it prevents the coachman, while he is waiting to re-enter the work force, from giving bread to his family. It gives him the option to die of hunger or to steal." *Le Cocher* also wanted the authorities to abolish the *feuille de travail,* the coachman's work sheet, because many coachmen, it argued, simply could not write well. This demand apparently was not entertained by the owners, however, for the work sheet was one method by which they and the police could verify a cab's fares. *Le Cocher's* position on the many other rules and regulations promulgated by the police was that coachmen be placed "under the empire of the common law." Expanding its vision beyond this tenet, *Le Cocher* wrote that coachmen were "a part of the Charter" and that "we wish the Charter, the whole Charter, nothing more, nothing less than the Charter," the constitution of France set up during the July Monarchy.[6] Thus, long before the lines were drawn between coachmen challenging the wage system and those championing the ownership of cabs, the articulate coachmen of 1846 rallied around the claim that they were not receiving the protections and guarantees granted other workers and citizens since 1789. They argued against the enormous, unchecked power of the police to create administrative rules that shackled coachmen and

6. *Ibid.,* August 2, 1846, p. 1, August 16, 1846, p. 1, August 30, 1846, p. 1, August 16, 1846, p. 2, October 4, 1846, p. 2.

owners alike. Coachmen indicated they would be happy simply to share in all the legalities of the July Monarchy and claimed no more at this juncture. Small owners and hired coachmen saw themselves as members of the same corporation, doing the same kind of work, and experiencing the same hardships. The issue of ownership had not yet driven a major wedge between them.

Coachmen next appear as actors on the historical stage briefly during the 1848 revolution. At that time several workers' delegations representing coachmen demanded, either from their employers or from the Luxembourg Commission, an increase in their wages (to three francs for cabbies and to four francs for omnibus coachmen), the reduction of all police fines, and the shortening of their workday.[7] In September, 1849, coachmen of the voitures de place struck when employers reduced salaries and dismissed several workers. Beyond these two incidents, there is no further information about coachmen's organizations in this period. The lack of evidence of unions or newspapers during the Second Republic, though, does not indicate conclusively that none existed.

During the Second Empire, however, evidence of coachmen's organizational activities surfaced, from within the CIV. On November 2, 1857, coachmen working for that company petitioned its chief administrator, complaining about the inadequacy of their wages to cover their expenses. The petition, whose contents were noted in Chapter 3, consists of sixteen printed pages of claims concerning wages and expenses, with an exact accounting of the yearly budget of a typical coachman.[8] Signed by eight coachmen, each representing a different depot of the CIV, it was submitted by an agent of these delegates, who also signed his name and who in all probability drew up the petition. The document is important in this context because it reveals that the coachmen of the CIV managed to form some kind of organization to represent their interests. Regrettably, no further information is available on this association. Did these delegates come together only to protest an immediate issue, or did the coachmen of the CIV have a more permanent association in and around the depots

---

7. See Rémi Gossez, *Les Ouvriers de Paris: L'Organisation, 1848–1851* (Paris, 1967), 116–17.

8. A copy of this document is in APP, D/B 505, and in BHVP, Actualité, Série 125.

of their company? There is no way of knowing. What is significant, though, is that despite the efforts of the CIV to prevent it, an association of coachmen in eight depots did briefly come into existence.

Coachmen's newspapers were more in evidence during the Second Empire than were coachmen's associations. Three newspapers addressed themselves to cabbies: *Le Cocher,* published from January, 1864 to January, 1865; *L'Union des cochers,* from February to June, 1865; and *Le Cocher français,* from February, 1869, to June, 1870. The first two publications indicate that the line of demarcation between owners or independents and those who were simply coachmen had become slightly sharper. *Le Cocher* was clearly procabbie, whereas *L'Union des cochers* was a vehicle for owners. The language in both newspapers retained a corporate flavor, however, and there was still a sense of the common interests shared by these two groups. Coachmen and cab entrepreneurs were just beginning to define issues in a mutually exclusive fashion, though they continued to believe they could cooperate on essential matters. Both newspapers frequently appealed for collaboration. Entrepreneurs, the few remaining owners of voiture de place numbers, and operators of the voitures sous remise all regarded themselves in this period as victims of the large cab firm, the CIV, a perspective that constituted an important link between them and the coachmen. The third coachmen's publication during the Second Empire, *Le Cocher français,* was a trade or professional journal, containing mostly announcements for jobs and advertisements.

*Le Cocher,* the first of these three publications, reflects a transitional stage in the development of working-class consciousness among ordinary coachmen. The newspaper, founded in 1864 by Casimir Chapuy, regarded itself as heir to the 1846 *Le Cocher,* though it was more openly pro–working class.[9] It did not, however, break completely with the small owners or give up the use of corporate language, thus creating some contradictions and restraint in its agenda. On one issue it was very forceful: the 1864 *Le Cocher* was unequivocally opposed to the monopoly of the CIV, a position also espoused by those owners of the voitures de place outside the control of the CIV and by the many firms that owned voitures sous remise.

9. *Le Cocher: Organe de tous les cochers et charretiers de France,* January 20, 1864, p. 1.

*Le Cocher* expressed the greatest sympathy for the ordinary cabbie in its editorial comments but refrained from drawing the conclusion that the interests of the small cab operators might be at odds with those of ordinary coachmen. In one article, Chapuy drew a profile of just such an ordinary coachman, who was, he wrote, the most recognizable worker in Paris and the person who rendered the greatest service in the capital. The coachman also worked the longest hours and earned the least money. Chapuy concluded: "In Paris the man who is the most persecuted, the most ridiculed, the most vilified, the most hated, the most criticized, the most defamed, the most outraged, the most insulted, that man is the humble servant of everyone, it is the coachman, always the coachman." The basic goal of *Le Cocher* was to provide a forum for these unfortunate workers, who up until the present, Chapuy wrote, had not yet united. Since at that time the cab entrepreneurs already had their own association, the Union des Loueurs, as well as cooperative societies, this appeal for the unity among coachmen implied a class division based on ownership. *Le Cocher* acknowledged as much: "Some people . . . think that our newspaper must be . . . inimical to the owners, to the managers, to the heads of all administrations [of firms]."[10] It hastened to add that this assessment was not true, that "it understood that the interest of one is the interest of the other and it proposes to facilitate harmony between the master and the coachman." Such a disclaimer was a defensive reaction, a carryover of corporate discourse that no longer accurately reflected the situation. In some of its programs, *Le Cocher* came very close to a class-conscious position and a working-class discourse, though it avoided breaking openly with the independent operators and using working-class terminology.

In one program *Le Cocher* called for salary reform in the cab trade, advocating that owners pay their coachmen a fixed wage without any reference to tips.[11] A straight wage, independent of tips or of a percentage of the cab's total receipts, eventually became the quintessential demand of the working-class coachman. *Le Cocher* argued that a worker's salary should never be uncertain or dependent on someone else's generosity. "It must be certain, positive, assured, determined." The paper further argued that the daily wage should be

10. *Ibid.*, January 30, 1864, p. 1, January 20, 1864, p. 1.
11. *Ibid.*, January 30, 1864, pp. 2–3.

five francs, rejecting the CIV's argument that coachmen already received five francs each day because two francs in tips supplemented their three-franc wage.

This proposal elicited an immediate response from the Union des Loueurs, which neatly summed up the essential difference between cab entrepreneurs and coachmen. In a letter that appeared in *Le Cocher,* Mouton, director of the Union des Loueurs, stated that tips had always been a feature of the cab trade, providing an important means of control over the coachmen. Cabbies would become lazy and unproductive, he wrote, if they were guaranteed a decent daily wage, and owners would consider a higher daily wage only if there were surer methods of control. Mouton also criticized *Le Cocher* for being too proworker. Another official of the Union des Loueurs repeated the charge in a second letter to *Le Cocher.* He predicted that *Le Cocher's* strong proworker bias would be its ruin. Despite disagreeing with them, *Le Cocher* printed both these critiques that implied cab owners and ordinary coachmen should continue to cooperate. For all his talk about cooperation, though, Mouton was not above pointing out that the Union des Loueurs had an employment bureau and that owners could replace any cabbies from a pool of unemployed Parisians.[12] Cab entrepreneurs were quick to identify and defend their essential interests, despite their talk of corporate values.

On one issue, however, both coachmen and entrepreneurs agreed. They joined in attacking the monopoly of the CIV. *Le Cocher* went to the heart of the matter when, in demanding the suppression of the CIV's monopoly, it claimed that such a monopoly violated the principle of freedom of industry recognized during the French Revolution and established by the Le Chapelier Law of 1791.[13] Other industries, it editorialized, were free, and the principle should apply as well to the cab trade. The newspaper rejected, among other things, the government's argument that the number of cabs on the road had to be limited because Paris did not have enough cab stations to accommodate cabs freely entering the marketplace. The number of cabs on New York and London streets, *Le Cocher* pointed out, was un-

12. *Ibid.,* March 20, 1864, pp. 1–2, March 31, 1864, p. 1, March 20, 1864, pp. 1–2.

13. For this article, see *ibid.,* February 29, 1864, p. 1, and also March 10, 1864, p. 1.

restricted, and no one there complained about insufficient parking space. The newspaper's arguments combined statements of principle with commonsense suggestions. Streets, it stated, were part of the public domain and belonged to everyone. As for cab stations, "under the administration of liberty they would belong to the first occupant on a first come, first served basis." The excess cabs should be held *sous remise*, under the owner's roof. The newspaper noted, in concluding, that its call for "freedom of industry" did not apply to police driving regulations. These it accepted as necessary for the public safety. *Le Cocher's* attack on the monopoly of the CIV was echoed by the small cab entrepreneurs, who were adversely affected by the CIV's competitive advantage. The ordinary coachman resented the impersonality of the CIV and the sense of relative powerlessness he felt before such a formidable employer. An open cab industry also gave ordinary coachmen the opportunity to become cab entrepreneurs some day, and because of this aspiration many of them remained wedded to the goals and interests of the small owners.

Cab owners and ordinary coachmen also joined forces in challenging the CIV's payment system but for different reasons. *Le Cocher* attacked payment à la moyenne as unfair because depot chiefs arbitrarily set high target rates; because a daily average was not so accurate a reflection of productivity as a monthly or yearly average; because the condition of horses and cabs varied too greatly to give all coachmen an equal chance at the daily target rate; and, finally, because the system the CIV supported implied that coachmen were either lazy or dishonest.[14] So oppressive was this system, *Le Cocher* wrote, that several coachmen had been driven to suicide. *L'Union des cochers*, the journal of the small cab entrepreneurs, opposed payment à la moyenne because it increased the CIV's competitive advantage by making many of the large firm's cabbies put in long hours to meet the high tariff figures.[15] Small-time cab owners were reluctant to inflict long hours on coachmen with whom they were personally familiar or on themselves if they drove their own cabs, but that is what they had to do to remain competitive.

At one point in its short history, *Le Cocher* made a bold recom-

14. See *ibid.*, February 29, 1864, p. 1, March 10, 1864, p. 1, and March 20, 1864, p. 1.

15. *Ibid.*, March 10, 1864, p. 1; *L'Union des cochers: Journal des loueurs, conducteurs, palefreniers, piqueurs*, May 21, 1865, pp. 1–2.

mendation for a union of all Parisian coachmen. From the perspective of a corporate rather than a working-class position, it proposed in 1865 the formation of a mutual aid society (*une caisse de secours et vieillesse*).[16] Noting that currently there were three such societies for coachmen, the Société de Cochers de la Ville de Paris, the Société Saint-Honoré, and the Société de Saint Eugenie, *Le Cocher* suggested that having three different organizations created divisiveness within the cab trade. One union for all coachmen would place itself under government control and participate in humanitarian work. It would extend medical aid and retirement benefits to members and death benefits to members' widows. All persons who drove horse-drawn vehicles for a living could become members. Participants would pay yearly dues according to a regular schedule. *Le Cocher* proposed a fee of thirty-six francs for those forty years old and below, forty-eight francs for coachmen forty to fifty years old, and sixty francs for coachmen over fifty, to be paid in monthly installments. On the surface this plan seemed like a proposal for the unity of labor. However, owners and ordinary coachmen alike could be members of this union; corporate rather than working-class ideals would be paramount. This reform was not realized, but individual coachmen's mutual aid societies, associations that provided their members with financial support in times of illness or retirement, remained a feature of the horse-drawn-cab industry. Obtaining their funds from members' dues and, depending on their legal classification, from the government, the mutual aid societies in Paris in 1887 numbered four.[17] When some ordinary coachmen did form a genuine workers' trade union in 1877, several years passed before it was purged completely of the aims and language of mutual aid or cooperative societies.

*Le Cocher* folded in January, 1865, when its owner-editor Casimir Chapuy died, but the corporation of Parisian coachmen did not lack other spokesmen. Owners of small cab firms united in several co-

16. This proposal can be found scattered throughout the pages of *Le Cocher: Organe de tous*; see especially p. 1 of the following issues of the newspaper for 1865: April 20, May 1, 20, June 1, July 20, August 1, and September 20. What follows is a composite of the information in all these issues.

17. Joseph Barberet, *Le Travail en France: Monographies professionnelles* (Paris, 1887), IV, 319–20. For an in-depth look at the structure and services of one mutual aid society, see Bernaud and Laloy, *Guide pratique*, 214–31.

operative societies and in a trade association. *L'Union des cochers,* the journal representing their interests, entered the field almost at the moment *Le Cocher* went out of existence. Founded in February, 1865, it claimed to speak for all coachmen because both cab entrepreneurs and ordinary coachmen continued to share common enemies in the police, the public, and the CIV and frequently demanded similar reforms. The entrepreneurs, however, were not confused as to the nature of their interests; at the heart of their cause were both the desire to preserve and protect their small, privately owned businesses against the competition of a large company and the belief that ordinary cabbies should aspire to ownership themselves. Their misconceptions were that ordinary cabbies and owners would continue to cooperate and that most coachmen could become owners someday. With the increasing concentration of capital in the cab trade, the position of ownership was becoming more difficult to attain, and many cabbies eventually joined a working-class union against all owners.

*L'Union des cochers* announced in its first issue that it had no affiliation with the recently defunct *Le Cocher,* distinguishing itself from that decidedly proworker newspaper.[18] Nevertheless, it hoped to appeal to all coachmen, regarding ordinary coachmen as either partners on the road or potential cab entrepreneurs. Many of its articles complained about police fines and jail sentences for ordinary cabbies.[19] The paper opposed payment à la moyenne, police surveillance over cabbies, the CIV monopoly, and a workday that exceeded thirteen hours. It even supported the demands for wages of six francs per day made in June, 1865, by strikers against the CIV. Cab entrepreneurs did not necessarily favor a relatively high fixed wage for coachmen, but they would do anything "to struggle against the successive encroachments of the firm Ducoux and Company." (François-Joseph Ducoux was the owner of the CIV.) This hostility also explains why *L'Union des cochers* constantly urged the union of ordinary cabbies and independents in one association that could more effectively counter the CIV and the government as well. One issue of the newspaper asked rhetorically why cabbies tolerated their bad working conditions; an industry-wide union, it noted, could obtain

18. *L'Union des cochers,* February 15, 1865, p. 1.
19. See, for example, *ibid.,* April 30, 1865, p. 1.

reforms and improve "the profession of the coachmen." On another occasion it stated that "the Chambre Syndicale thus would one day create an alliance between the masters and the coachmen which would permit an equitable balancing of interests so as to arrive at a fair and just regulation of salaries and wages, and a more rational means of establishing the length of the work-day."[20]

Small cab entrepreneurs already had a protective trade association, the Union des Loueurs de Voitures sous Remise de Paris having been formed in the late winter of 1862 and definitively constituted on March 1, 1863.[21] (It may or may not have been a direct descendant of the cab entrepreneurs' association of the Restoration period.) In December, 1862, this union presented to Napoleon III, sending copies to the empress, to the minister of the interior, and to the prefects of the Seine Department and of the police, a petition that was a distillation of the major aspirations and complaints of the cab entrepreneurs. The small entrepreneur believed his major enemy to be the CIV, not his own coachmen. The memorandum to the emperor asked that the government transfer to the cab entrepreneurs the 500 numbers it had given to the CIV for voitures sous remise and henceforth permit the CIV to operate only voitures de place. The Union des Loueurs de Voitures sous Remise de Paris claimed for itself the privilege of operating all Parisian voitures sous remise, pointing out that the CIV had already concentrated on the ordinary voitures de place to the detriment of its own voiture sous remise service. Technically, the union noted, the government permitted free trade in the voiture sous remise portion of the cab trade, which was composed of many small entrepreneurs, analogous to the craft and small workshop structure of preindustrial manufacturing. The emperor's regime had, however, granted the CIV special privileges in this sector, placing the owners of small cab firms at a competitive disadvantage. Only the CIV, for example, could station its voitures sous remise on public roads during special holidays or near public monuments, theaters, or tram stations without special restrictions. The petition pointed out that the small cab owners were members of the Union des Loueurs,

20. *Ibid.*, May 21, 1865, pp. 1–2, June 18, 1865, p. 1, February 15, 1865, p. 1, March 31, 1865, p. 1.

21. For what follows, see Union des Loueurs de Voitures sous Remise de Paris, *Mémoires présentés à sa majesté l'Empereur* (Evreux, 1863), in BN, 8°V.54.

which, in turn, was represented by a syndicate with the right to speak for the entire association. It declared that eight hundred cab entrepreneurs possessed among themselves 2,043 numbers for voitures sous remise. A transfer of all voiture sous remise numbers would be easy to accomplish, since the government had only to assign the numbers to the Union des Loueurs, which would then distribute them to its members.

The government did not grant this request, and the CIV maintained its monopoly over the voitures de place and its special rights with regard to the voitures sous remise for another three years. In 1866, Napoleon III ended the monopoly and terminated the CIV's legal advantages in the cab trade.

Until that time, cab operators and ordinary coachmen had felt relatively unified, but the situation began to change, albeit slowly. Although a significant degree of concentration of capital remained and the small cab entrepreneur was never eliminated, the underlying structure of the cab industry was certainly altered after the termination of the CIV's monopoly. On top of this came a severe economic crisis in France in the 1880s, which triggered a growth of radicalism among many Parisian workers and a defensive reaction by owners, large and small. What had set the stage for this crisis, though, was the period before the 1880s, when cab operators and ordinary coachmen started perceiving fundamental and irreconcilable differences and began to grow apart.

In 1872, during the Third Republic, ordinary coachmen attempted for the first time to form a protective association, though the result was short-lived. On May 2, 1872, two unidentified coachmen sent a letter to Joseph Barberet, a republican journalist, for publication in his "Bulletin du travail."[22] They proudly announced that they had formed a *chambre syndicale,* a trade union, and that as a result of its formation and existence for several months their employers no longer regarded them as domestics but rather "at the level of other organized workers' corporations." The official name of the new union was the Société Cooperative des Cochers. Its members, only 8 in number, claimed that the means of production, in this case the horse and cab, should belong to the producers, that is, the coachmen.

22. See Barberet, *Le Travail en France,* IV, 244–45.

Despite this socialist language, the union was organized as a cooperative society and preserved the concept of private property, albeit with a Proudhonian flavor. For reasons neither explained nor noted in the public record, the Société Cooperative des Cochers soon split into two rival camps and, as a consequence, became defunct.

The following year saw the establishment of several more cooperative societies, but none made an attempt to unite all Parisian coachmen. In addition, there existed for a few months in 1876 another coachmen's publication, Le Moniteur des cochers, which promoted the organization of all Parisian coachmen into cooperatives, but this plan, too, came to nothing.[23] Finally, in 1877 a genuine trade union of ordinary coachmen was organized.

The Chambre Syndicale des Cochers de Paris was formed on December 28, 1876, and definitively constituted on January 1, 1877. Its headquarters was in number 14, rue de Rocroi, in the tenth arrondissement, a ward in which many coachmen lived and worked. It had 602 members and a treasury of 11,396 francs.[24] The immediate impulse for its establishment was the impending Paris Universal Exposition of 1878. Coachmen remembered the last such exposition, in 1867, when cab firms had greatly overworked them to take advantage of the influx of visitors. Coachmen were determined not to permit this injustice to happen again. Many also saw the exposition as an opportunity to promote their cherished demands, which they could back up with a strike, if necessary.

In January, 1877, the first secretary of the Chambre Syndicale des Cochers de Paris, Michel Moritz, addressed a circular to the entire corporation of Parisian cabbies announcing the aims of the new union. It demanded that (1) coachmen should be permitted to park anywhere in Paris so long as they did not impede circulation or violate private property rights; (2) the government should permit "the freedom to work" in the cab trade, meaning that coachmen and their clients should determine the fare for a cab ride; and (3) the cab companies should pay the coachmen à la planche, whereby the expected daily receipts were determined by averaging the cab's monthly re-

---

23. Le Moniteur des cochers: Journal indépendant des intérêts du cocher de Paris, June 22, 1876, pp. 1–2, June 29, 1876, p. 1, and June 22, 1876, to November 2, 1876.

24. Joseph Barberet, "Bulletin du travail," Le Rappel, January 5, 1877, p. 3; Barberet, Le Travail en France, IV, 245; APP, B/A 1442, "Chambres syndicales ouvrières, minute."

ceipts, the excess to be kept by the coachman. This last objective caused a split of opinion within the union, for many ordinary coachmen preferred a fixed wage, *travail à la feuille,* not dependent on tips or determined by posted daily rates. They hoped the union would agitate only to have basic wages raised. Another group wished instead to share in the cab's total receipts. These two groups coexisted in the union, and in the cab trade, well into the 1880s.

The Chambre Syndicale des Cochers de Paris was organized like a classic workers' craft union.[25] It was headed by an elected secretary and cosecretary. Three commissions oversaw its daily operations: a financial commission, an inventory commission, and a control commission. Members paid monthly dues and could participate in union meetings only if their dues were paid. Failure to attend a union meeting was punishable with a fifty-centime fine. The union also had a lawyer on its staff to defend the cabbies in the police and traffic courts.[26]

Such trade unions were then technically illegal and the Chambre Syndicale des Cochers de Paris joined with other Parisian chambres syndicales in petitioning the government to legalize them. When members of all Parisian chambres syndicales gathered on March 14, 1878, at the École de Jacob on the rue Berthe in the eighteenth arrondissement, the coachmen's chambre syndicale was among those that heard Barberet deliver the keynote address calling for a grand union of all workers' groups and for the government to sanction trade unions. A second such meeting, this one at the Salle Petrelle, was held in April, 1878, and once again a coachmen's delegation was present. In November, 1878, *Le Rappel* published in toto a petition for the legalization of trade unions that had been passed by a general assembly of Parisian chambres syndicales.[27] A relatively modest proposal, it demanded the abrogation of the Le Chapelier Law, which had outlawed restrictive trade associations, and insisted on the right

25. See *Le Rappel,* which was very sympathetic to coachmen and throughout its history reported on their activities. For what follows, see also *Le Fouet: Journal des cochers.*

26. *Le Rappel,* August 4, 1880, p. 3; *Le Prolétaire: Journal républicain des ouvriers démocrates socialistes,* January 15, 1879, p. 3; *Le Rappel,* April 15, 1879, p. 3.

27. "Bulletin du travail," *Le Rappel,* March 15, 1878, p. 3; *Le Rappel,* April 13, 1878, p. 3, April 10, 1878, p. 3; "Bulletin du travail," *Le Rappel,* November 22, 1878, p. 3.

of any chambre syndicale, whether composed of owners or workers, to organize without the prior authorization of the government. The proposed unions, the petition continued, would have as their goal "the study and the defense of the general interests of their profession." They would have funds both to aid their members in times of unemployment, illness, or old age and to establish workers' cooperatives. The appeal also suggested a concept reminiscent of trade guilds, that chambres syndicales in the same industry, representing both workers and owners, should have the right to establish wage rates for manual labor, hours, and apprenticeship agreements, all accords having the force of a contract legally binding on both workers and owners. Finally, the chambres syndicales agreed to deposit with the government their charters and the names of their members. Of the chambres syndicales at the meeting, the coachmen's association was among the large majority that accepted the proposal without qualifications.

In this first phase of its history, the Chambre Syndicale des Cochers still embraced the values of corporatism. In May, 1879, a delegation from the union met with the Syndicat des Loueurs de Voitures, the association of owners, in hopes of cooperating to effect reforms within the cab industry. On another occasion, the Chambre Syndicale des Cochers called a general meeting of "the entire corporation of the coachmen of the voitures de place and de remise" to discuss common concerns. The union also established an annual banquet-dance to which were invited all coachmen, both owners and ordinary cabbies, and their wives and children. Even more reflective of the residual corporate attitude was the union's proposal for a mutual aid fund that would be independent of the union's fund. In its plan, published in *Le Rappel,* the Chambre Syndicale des Cochers, noting that it had obtained positive results with its own retirement fund and that it was concerned with the well-being of the "entire corporation," proposed to establish "a treasury for mutual aid having as its goal to help us at times of illness." It believed this proposed institution would be able "to give the greatest moral support and material benefits to our corporation."[28] The Chambre Syndicale des Cochers con-

28. *Le Fouet,* June 2, 1879, p. 2; "Bulletin du travail," *Le Rappel,* September 25, 1878, p. 3; *Le Rappel,* September 2, 1879, p. 2, September 19, 1880, p. 3, and November 21, 1879, p. 3.

vened a general assembly of the entire corporation of Parisian coachmen to consider the formation of the new institution. Regrettably, there is no information on the outcome, though the union's intent was clear.

Although it maintained its ties with the community of owners, the Chambre Syndicale des Cochers adopted at times a decidedly working-class position. Its first statutes declared that the union had been formed "in order that there no longer be a needy future as a result of the infirmities of old age." The union's first voice, the newspaper *Le Fouet,* in an article about salaries, concluded that such help would never come from the owners: "One third for labor, two thirds for capital. Such is the logic of those who know how to dispense with material work." This journal, which published only eight issues, championed Joseph Barberet not because he was a republican but because he defended the interests of the working class. Another hero of the Chambre Syndicale des Cochers was François-Vincent Raspail, a chemist, a participant on the side of the people in the revolutions of 1830 and 1848, and the editor of *Ami du peuple.* When Raspail died in 1878, the Chambre Syndicale des Cochers collected money to buy a wreath for his tomb, and members of the union journeyed to the Père-Lachaise Cemetery to hear their leaders praise the revolutionary for his support of the "laboring classes." [29]

Union secretary Moritz recommended Barberet's book, *La Bataille des intérêts,* and concluded that the workers' ancestors had passed from slavery to the bondage of the modern wage system. "This last phase of the proletariat," he wrote, "will stir the light, which will gradually penetrate the thick mass of workers, seemingly in decline, and soon perhaps the people shall cause the dawn of liberty to shine: then all people [shall be] equal in means, and true justice shall no longer be relative." On another occasion, Moritz addressed his article "Aux prolétaires" and admonished the coachmen to read *Le Fouet* to prepare for their liberation. *Le Fouet* once advised that "since the association of capitalists is necessary in order to exploit the labor of the coachmen, it is elementary that the association of coachmen is

29. "Bulletin du travail," *Le Rappel,* April 15, 1878, p. 3; *Le Fouet,* May 12, 1879, p. 3; "Bulletin du travail," *Le Rappel,* February 11, 1878, p. 3, February 22, 1878, p. 3, and March 9, 1878, pp. 3–4.

absolutely necessary to resist, in a realistic manner and by all legal means, this exploitation."[30]

A union official of this era, Joseph Godefroy, who was secretary of the Chambre Syndicale des Cochers de Paris in 1881, clearly reflects the union's ambivalence toward the small-scale owner. In a rare autobiographical statement, Godefroy, writing in *La Lanterne des cochers de Paris,* a journal he had founded and edited, noted that he had "practiced the trade [of coachman] without interruption since 1848." Barberet, the only contemporary commentator to publish material on Godefroy, stated that the latter's decision to publish *La Lanterne* immediately followed the strike of coachmen against the CGV in the summer of 1878. The journal, which appeared once a week in the form of a brochure, was intended for coachmen and had a duration of ten issues. Barberet wrote that Godefroy was also the owner of *Le Fouet,* the weekly newspaper that replaced *La Lanterne* and that first appeared on May 12, 1879.[31] A search of Parisian libraries and archives has failed to uncover any mention of Godefroy's name, and in the absence of data on date and place of birth or death, we must remain content with his articles.

These writings reveal a brief profile. Joseph Godefroy began driving a cab in 1848, when he had to have been at least eighteen years old, though he may have been older. He thus began working as a coachman when French workers were still captive to an artisanal or craft-union mentality. Over the years that followed, many coachmen, including Godefroy, would begin the evolution to a working-class consciousness. We next hear of him in the fall of 1878, when he single-handedly published nine out of ten issues of *La Lanterne.* A colleague, A. Dulucq, wrote the second issue, though neither the men nor the record indicates why. Godefroy then edited eight issues of *Le Fouet* from May 12 to July 7, 1879. Both publications served as vehicles for his opinions about the general social status of coachmen and for his poetry, but for the most part these journals focused on practical professional aims. We observe another side of Godefroy, however, in October, 1879, when he attended the socialist congress

---

30. M. Moritz, "Bibliographie," *Le Fouet,* June 23, 1879, p. 2; *Le Fouet,* June 30, 1879, pp. 2, 1.

31. *La Lanterne des cochers de Paris,* no. 1, n.d. [1878], 4; Barberet, *Le Travail en France,* IV, 274–85.

of Marseille as a delegate of the Chambre Syndicale des Cochers de Paris. There he addressed the assemblage, speaking on women's rights, the duties of the chambres syndicales, war, the state, and socialism. Following this congress, Godefroy returned to driving a cab and continued to organize the coachmen of Paris. By 1881, he had become secretary of the Chambre Syndicale des Cochers. He resigned this position in October, 1881, when he became active in a cooperative society of coachmen. The public record then becomes silent on his activities.

Like his union in 1881, Godefroy was a transitional figure. A charter member of the Chambre Syndicale des Cochers, he was first active as an organizer and a journalist.[32] In his journalistic work, he focused on the many abuses coachmen suffered at the hands of the authorities and the public. In this respect, he echoed the sentiments of the entire profession, since all coachmen found police rules troublesome and the public a hard taskmaster.[33] Police driving ordinances, he believed, created a separate legal system for coachmen, denying them the equal protection of the law enjoyed by other French citizens. There is here an implicit demand that the liberties gained by the French Revolution and presumably enshrined in the Third Republic be extended to coachmen. Criminals, he wrote, at least had the right to a defense before their tribunals, whereas coachmen did not. Worse still, Godefroy wrote in another article, the police, and the public as well, treated coachmen as if they were no better than prostitutes: "On the one hand, you are under the yoke of the police; on the other, you put yourself under the domination of the public. These two powers treat you as slaves."[34]

As a journalist, Godefroy was content to censure abuses, to propose legal changes within the context of republican institutions, and to demand on behalf of coachmen the full protection of the law. Such was not the case, however, when he attended the October, 1879,

32. For examples of Godefroy's and the union's organizing activities, see p. 3 of the following issues: *Le Fouet*, June 9, 1879, and *Le Rappel*, May 19, June 2, June 8, 15, 23, 1881.

33. On the police, see Godefroy, *Le Fouet*, June 9, 1879, p. 4, May 12, 1879, pp. 3–4, June 2, 1879, p. 3, May 19, 1879, p. 4, and June 30, 1879, p. 2.

34. Joseph Godefroy, "La Différence des agents," *Le Fouet*, May 12, 1879, pp. 3–4, and "L'État du cocher," *Le Fouet*, May 19, 1879, p. 4.

meeting of the socialist labor congress of Marseille. There, he expressed a socialist, though not Marxist, viewpoint on social and political issues.

The Congrès Ouvrier Socialiste de France met in Marseille from October 20 to 31, 1879, the third national French workers' congress to meet since the end of the Paris Commune.[35] The first two had convened in Paris in October, 1876, and in Lyon in January and February, 1878, respectively. The Paris congress had dealt exclusively with economic issues, but the Lyon gathering, though basically moderate in tone, expressed some strong collectivist notions. It forcefully suggested that all French labor unions federate and that the government abolish all laws restricting the right to associate.[36] The congress of Marseille went a step further; the collectivist tendency prevailed over mutualist reformism.

At this congress, Godefroy expressed positions that approximated an amalgam of reformism, republicanism, socialism, and even some utopianism. In the final vote of the congress, he associated himself with the collectivists.[37] Earlier he stood out among his colleagues for having delivered an impassioned plea for equality between the sexes in the workplace. His political discourse at Marseille reflected an instinctive sense of fairness and of general equality rather than a thoroughgoing or systematic socialist or collectivist ideal. In one speech to the congress, Godefroy explained why he had become a "revolutionary," by which he meant a socialist: "I am a revolutionary because all that I perceive as injustice agitates me."[38] His socialism was appropriate to a man who had begun his career in a world still imbued with corporative, mutualist values; it also corresponded to the leadership needs of a union with an ideologically heterogeneous membership.

Despite Godefroy's progressive aims and his commitment to the working class, he never abandoned a corporate viewpoint or launched an outright attack against private property. He disdained large-scale

35. *Séances du Congrès Ouvrier Socialiste de France, troisième session, tenue à Marseille du 20 au 31 octobre 1879* (Marseille, 1879).

36. See Robert Brécy, *Le Mouvement syndical en France, 1871–1921: Essai bibliographique* (Paris, 1963), 2–3.

37. See *Séances du Congrès de Marseille*, 716–17, 814.

38. *Ibid.*, 194–96, 802–805, 668–70.

ownership of private property but found small-scale guild or cooperative ownership of property to be quite compatible with his moderate republican socialism. In *Le Fouet* he propounded notions that
would seem incompatible with a working-class union. It was not
uncommon for coachmen in this period to suggest improvements in
the cab trade that would benefit primarily the owners or the public,
and Godefroy was no exception. This sense of cooperation with the
owners grew out of a time when the owner and the cabbie shared
similar values, aspirations, and burdens. On one occasion Godefroy
invited cab owners and drivers to a general meeting to hear a member of the municipal council discuss plans to abolish special police
agents for traffic. Godefroy was pleased that the gathering produced
a consensus among them: they agreed to form a commission of ten
members, five owners and five drivers, to present the corporation's
demands to the prefect of police. The demands included (1) the application to coachmen of the "common protection" principle, (2) the
suppression of surveillance by special police agents, (3) the establishment by the government of an *école de dressage et d'aptitude des cochers,*
and (4) the abolition of the drivers' *bulletin d'entrée,* a certificate issued
to a coachman by a cab entrepreneur, containing a coachman's cab
number and a description of the driver, that cabbies carried while
working, and the issuance to coachmen of a permanent livret, or
license.[39]

From July to October, 1881, Godefroy led a campaign to form a
cooperative society of coachmen in which he officially involved the
Chambre Syndicale des Cochers, another instance of the coexistence
of his corporative values and his moderate socialism. Indeed, corporate ideas were quite compatible with his version of socialism. Believing that a cooperative society would enhance coachmen's material
situation, Godefroy invited ordinary cabbies to pool their resources
so they could free themselves "with or without recourse to the capitalists." In another appeal for membership, he wrote that "the chambre syndicale, through its council, has taken the initiative to form a
real cooperative society in order to free the entire corporation of the
infamous exploitation of which we are always victims."[40] He added

39. *Le Rappel,* January 20, 1881, p. 2, February 18, 1881, p. 3.
40. *Ibid.,* July 8, 1881, p. 3, August 11, 1881, p. 3.

tellingly that the union wished "to render coachmen owners of their coaches in the shortest time possible." His projected society seemingly established, Godefroy resigned from the Chambre Syndicale des Cochers in October, 1881, no doubt to direct the new cooperative, a fitting move for a man with one foot in the corporate world and the other in a trade union.

The organization Godefroy left was having problems. For its efforts in the 1878 strike, the Chambre Syndicale des Cochers de Paris had obtained next to nothing. As a result, once the strike was over, coachmen became indifferent to the union, forcing its liquidation in 1882.[41] Information on coachmen's associations between 1882 and 1884 is too sketchy to permit a systematic treatment. It is clear, however, that these were the last years of confusion concerning the class interests of coachmen's associations. Between the dissolution of the Chambre Syndicale des Cochers in 1882 and its re-formation in 1884, a newspaper and an association briefly became focal points for Parisian coachmen. The first issue of La Gazette des cochers, a pro-owner publication, appeared in August, 1883, and its last in February, 1884. The paper preached cooperation between owners and coachmen as a possible and worthy goal. In November 1883, the Gazette organized the Chambre Syndicale et Association Mutuelle des Cochers de Paris to provide medical aid and retirement benefits to its members.[42] It also encouraged the formation of coachmen's cooperative societies, thereby limiting its appeal to only those cabbies with enough capital to join a cooperative.[43]

On March 21, 1884, the Le Chapelier Law outlawing restrictive economic or trade associations was abrogated, thereby legalizing trade unions. That same year, coachmen revived the Chambre Syndicale des Cochers de Paris. The record is completely silent on the reason behind the formation of this union, though we may surmise what happened. In 1884, coachmen working for a major competitor of the CGV, the Compagnie Urbaine, struck to protest the firm's high daily moyenne. This strike probably stimulated the reestablishment of the union, as preparations for a strike in 1879 had roused cabbies to unionize. The secretary of the new union was Dulucq, the

41. La Gazette des cochers, October 11, 1883, pp. 3–4.
42. For the bylaws of this organization, see ibid., November 29, 1883, pp. 3–4.
43. Ibid., December 20, 1883, pp. 2–3, December 28, 1883, p. 1.

cabbie who had edited the second issue of Godefroy's *La Lanterne*. He had been a charter member of the Chambre Syndicale et Association Mutuelle des Cochers de Paris but quit on December 26, 1883, soon after he had joined, when he realized that his associates were infused with a spirit of capitalism and that the new organization excluded most of the Parisian cabbies. His own perspective was decidedly pro–working class. He warned that workers who join cooperative societies "constitute, as a group, a minor bourgeoisie" and "retard the advent of social justice."[44]

Between 1884 and 1887 the newly revived Chambre Syndicale des Cochers de Paris, according to the fragmentary evidence available, agitated in favor of moderate reforms of the police driving code and cooperation with cab owners to obtain relief from public authorities.[45] In 1887, Dulucq and the union parted company when the coachmen accused him of stealing money from the union's treasury. He was exonerated but resigned nonetheless. The next, and last, time he was heard from was in the columns of a cab owners' newspaper, where he attacked the Chambre Syndicale des Cochers.[46]

The year 1887 marked a decisive new chapter in the union's history. From then on, it would move resolutely, though not always consistently, into the ranks of the working-class unions of Paris. The decisive factors in converting the coachmen's union into a decidedly working-class organization were the continued concentration of ownership in a segment of the cab trade, the rise of the revolutionary syndicalist movement, the upcoming Paris Universal Exposition of 1889, and the severe economic crisis in France in the late 1880s.

The economic crisis in France was both an industrial and an

44. *Ibid.*, November 22, 1883, pp. 1–2, November 29, 1883, p. 2, December 28, 1883, p. 1, December 20, 1883, pp. 2–3, December 28, 1883, p. 1.

45. For example, see *Le Cocher: Organe des intérêts professionnels des cochers de la Seine*, November 13, 1884, p. 3, November 27, 1884, p. 1; *Le Rappel*, November 26, 1884, p. 4; and *Le Brancardier: Organe des cochers*, November 27, 1884, p. 1.

46. *Réveil des cochers: Organe des cochers indépendants*, December 19, 1897, pp. 1–2; see also *Le Rappel*, October 12, 1887, p. 3. Incomplete evidence also reveals that Dulucq had had a polemic with the original Chambre Syndicale des Cochers de Paris in 1879. He hinted at its contents when he called upon the coachmen to reject violence and the current leadership of the Chambre Syndicale, to establish unity, and to employ only "just and legitimate means" to attain any goals. See the three extant issues of *Feuille des cochers de place de Paris*, May 3, 1879, to May 17, 1879, esp. May 10, 1879, p. 1.

agrarian one.[47] From 1820 to 1870, industrial growth had climbed steadily at a rate of more than 2.0 percent annually. A serious decline in the rate of increase of industrial production began in the years from 1850 to 1860, reached its height after 1870, and lasted until the final years of the nineteenth century. According to one economic historian, the growth rate from 1870 to 1896 was 1.6 percent. From 1906 on, French industry experienced a period of rapid industrialization that lasted until 1929. The growth rate from 1906 to 1913, for example, depending on which economic historian one consults, was anywhere from 4.4 to 5.2 percent. The key developments underlying the growth of a working-class consciousness among coachmen occurred during the years 1875 to 1895, when "a more and more pronounced downward curve" and the deceleration in industrial growth that began in the 1850s and 1860s "reached [its] greatest intensity." Prices for all industrial goods declined significantly over these years. If 1880 is used as a base of 100, then by 1889 the curve for prices stood at 89, rising to approximately 91 by 1890, but falling to a small margin over 81 by 1896. Not surprising, unemployment also reached a peak during the 1880s. Among the several conjunctural crises of unemployment in these years, 1873, 1876, 1883 to 1886, 1900, 1907 and 1908, 1913, no other was more serious than the "great depression" from 1882 to 1886. Of 800,000 workers in the building trades industry in 1886, for example, 80,000 to 100,000 were without work; 20,000 workers, or 20 percent of the work force, in the metallurgical industry were unemployed, as were 30,000 to 50,000 miners and quarry workers. In 1886, 10 percent of all industrial workers were unemployed. Paris, with the industrial cities in the southern Loire Valley and the department of the Nord, was especially hard hit; 200,000 were without work there in 1883.[48]

A direct correlation between these figures and the increasing

47. See André Armengaud, in *Histoire économie et sociale de la France*, ed. Fernand Braudel and Ernest Labrousse (Paris, 1979), IV, pt. 1, pp. 93–113, 117–36, and François Caron, *An Economic History of Modern France*, trans. Barbara Bray (New York, 1979), 29–30. Both these works contain excellent bibliographies for further readings on the economic crisis.

48. Caron, *An Economic History*, 30, 29; Maurice Lévy-Leboyer, in *Histoire économie et sociale de la France*, ed. Braudel and Labrousse, IV, pt. 1, p. 133; Michelle Perrot, *ibid.*, IV, pt. 1, p. 485.

radicalization among ordinary coachmen is not apparent until the agricultural crisis during these same years is taken into account.[49] The years that saw a decline in industrial prices also witnessed a significant decrease in the rural population. In 1881, France had 24,576,000 rural inhabitants, a figure that had decreased to 22,096,000 by 1911; the rural population had gone from 65 to 56 percent of the total population. Conversely, the urban population grew from 13,097,000 in 1881 to 17,509,000 in 1911. It is true that the rural birth rate was lower over this period, but this reduction was more than offset by a corresponding decrease in rural mortality rates. The decrease in the rural population was actually due to a national movement of inhabitants from the countryside to the city, brought about by a progressive decline of rural industry, by a lowering of agricultural prices because of competition from other countries, and especially by the agricultural crisis caused by the phylloxera epidemic in the 1880s. Although rural inhabitants moved to cities all over France, the department of the Seine and its principal city, Paris, grew at a faster rate than the rest of the country. In 1881, this department had 7.5 percent of the total French population; by 1911 that figure had grown to 10.0 percent.

Like all Parisian workers, perhaps even more so, given the large number of them with rural origins, Parisian coachmen felt the effects of this crisis. It is not unreasonable to assume that many migrants going to Paris from the countryside tried to get jobs as coachmen. They did so at a moment favorable to the development of a radical political consciousness. They stood little chance of becoming owners because of the economic crisis and because of the concentration of ownership within a significant portion of the cab trade. It is small wonder, then, that in this period the Chambre Syndicale des Cochers joined with other Parisian workers in uniting against capitalists.

An immediate and short-term reaction to the economic crisis was the popularity among many coachmen of General Georges Boulanger and of his short-lived movement to revise the constitution of the Third Republic.[50] Boulanger, who lived from 1837 to 1891, was a

49. For the discussion that follows, see Armengaud, in *Histoire économie et sociale de la France*, ed. Braudel and Labrousse, IV, pt. 1, pp. 101–104.
50. The discussion of General Boulanger and the coachmen is based on Philip

very popular minister of war between January and December, 1886. The combination of his popularity with the general populace and his own political ambitions caused Opportunist politicians in power to block him from further advancement in his career. The general thereupon launched a nationwide campaign to revise the constitution and topple the Opportunists. He stood for by-elections to the legislative chamber in January, 1889, and defeated the official candidate by over eighty thousand votes. His followers urged him to attempt a coup against the state, but he hesitated and eventually became frightened, retreating into exile with his mistress. He committed suicide in 1891 when she died of tuberculosis. With that, the Boulangist movement came to an end.

Boulanger, who appeared as an alternative to the government of the Third Republic, was especially popular with specific segments of the Paris population. Philip Nord has written that the Boulangist "movement's rank-and-file activists were heavily recruited among shopkeepers, accountants, *marchands de vin* and the like," who reacted to the profound dislocation in their lives brought about by the double phenomenon of Haussmannization and the economic crisis of the 1880s. They saw Boulanger as a savior. With the shopkeepers were a significant number of coachmen. In the seventeenth arrondissement the police identified seventy-eight persons as belonging to a committee in support of Boulanger. Of these, according to Nord's research, the police listed the profession for sixty, and coachmen accounted for fifteen people, or 25 per cent of the membership. Nord indicates that the presence of a major omnibus depot in the seventeenth arrondissement partly accounts for this number. There may, however, be additional reasons for the attraction of coachmen to Boulanger. The seventeenth arrondissement was also home to a major cab depot belonging to the CGV and was the third most populous in coachmen, a further explanation for the number of cabbies in the movement. Nord also notes the especially close connection between "*marchands de vins* so numerous in the auvergnat community of

---

G. Nord, *Paris Shopkeepers and the Politics of Resentment* (Princeton, 1986), 302–50. For a recent treatment of the Boulanger phenomenon, see William D. Irvine, *The Boulanger Affair Reconsidered: Royalism, Boulangism, and the Origins of the Radical Right in France* (New York, 1989).

Paris" and General Boulanger.[51] The firm ties among the marchands de vin, the Auvergnat community of Paris, and the coachmen might also account for some of the coachmen joining the ranks of the Boulangists.

Whatever the weight given to these different reasons, it is quite likely that many of the coachmen in the Boulangist movement drove cabs, as opposed to omnibuses, and that many were cab owners or aspiring cab entrepreneurs. This interpretation fits well with Nord's point that Boulanger attracted not only shopkeepers but the working class as well. The Boulangists' overall appeal was to the little people, workers and shopkeepers alike, who worked hard for their earnings and perceived the established powers of the capitalist and political elite as aligned against them. Coachmen, whether owners or not, would find such a movement attractive.

Another event galvanized the coachmen of Paris even more than did General Boulanger: Paris was host to an international exposition in 1889. Coachmen had already had the experience of overwork during previous international expositions in 1855, 1867, and 1878. In 1878, for example, the CGV set such a high daily moyenne to be met during the exposition that coachmen could not take advantage of the event to increase their wages. Consequently, they struck in August, 1878. In response, the CGV simply hired other coachmen from the large pool of unemployed labor in Paris, and the strike failed. The pattern was repeated in 1889. As the opening date of the international exposition drew closer, ordinary coachmen anticipated that the cab firms would increase the daily moyenne. Both sides began to prepare for a strike. When the exposition opened in May, the moyenne was set high, and a strike was called. This one failed, too, broken by scabs. Although the strikes are dealt with fully in the next chapter, it is important to note here that as the exposition of 1889 approached, the discourse flowing from the Chambre Syndicale des Cochers became more radical, a development that continued after the exposition closed.

Scattered reports in *Le Rappel* in 1888 were the first signs of this new attitude.[52] In the summer of 1888, the Chambre Syndicale des

---

51. Nord, *Paris Shopkeepers*, 315, 314–15, 312.
52. See *Le Rappel*, August 4, 15, 1888, p. 2.

Cochers was sympathetic to a strike by ditchdiggers and used the occasion as an opportunity to articulate some of its own demands, including an appeal for higher wages and the suppression of the mise à pied. To further these ends, the coachmen's union began holding meetings in the various Parisian quartiers and, what is most significant, warned that if justice was not forthcoming, the union would call for a general strike. Commenting on the mood of the times in 1888, the Chambre Syndicale des Cochers estimated that "a general movement of rebellion has been fomenting among us, generated also by the situation resulting from the strikes which took place at that time."[53] Coachmen began to increase the frequency of their meetings during 1888 and to see themselves as part of a larger movement of workers frustrated by the lack of relief from difficult times.[54]

The strike of 1889 reinforced a growing identification of coachmen with traditional Parisian workers, a process already under way in the Chambre Syndicale des Cochers. After the strike, the union continued its efforts to join with other workers organizing in Paris and throughout France. This development is rather significant since coachmen had previously considered themselves to be the bastard children of the working class. For their part, industrial workers and especially other transportation workers, such as omnibus or tram coachmen, either did not pay attention to cochers de fiacres or were patently hostile to them. It is a mark of their sense of working-class identity that in the late 1880s and early 1890s coachmen in the Chambre Syndicale des Cochers ceased referring to their inferior status among Parisian workers. They simply assumed they were members of the Paris working class, like all other industrial workers, and plunged into the organizational activities of the nascent labor movement. Their first contacts were with other transportation workers.

Parisian omnibus and tram coachmen had formed their own chambre syndicale in 1881, and over the next decade similar unions of municipal transportation workers were formed in other French cities. The first meeting to attempt to unite French urban transportation workers nationally took place in Paris in July, 1893.[55] At this

53. *Ibid.*, December 18, 1888, p. 4.
54. See *Le Rappel* for August, 1888, which was an especially busy month for the coachmen.
55. See *Le Réveil du cocher: Organe du syndicat*, July 24, 1893, pp. 2–3.

time, Poudrat of the Syndicat d'Omnibus de Paris, Carrière and Calmels of the Chambre Syndicale des Cochers de Paris, and Clément
of the Syndicat des Tramways de la Ville de Lyon energetically supported a proposition to form a *fédération des moyens de transport en
commun* (including cochers de fiacres). The public record is silent on
the outcome of this meeting, but no national federation of urban
transportation workers emerged in 1893.

The effort was revived in 1895, when Moreau of the Parisian
omnibus drivers' union invited delegates of provincial urban transportation workers to meet in Paris to establish a national fédération
des moyens de transport. Victor Darme, secretary of the union Employés de la Compagnie des Tramways de Lyon, refused to join the
Paris gathering or any federation that resulted from it. The Lyon
transportation workers did not wish to come under the "tutelage" of
the Paris organizations, which favored France's national revolutionary syndicalist labor confederation, the Confédération Générale du
Travail (CGT); the Lyon workers were already members of a second
national labor confederation, the Fédération Nationale des Syndicats
(FNS). Finally, the Lyon union objected to a general strike, which
the CGT favored, and to partial strikes as tactics against cab companies. The general strike, it believed, was too sophisticated a concept
for workers to grasp currently. As for partial strikes, the Lyon union
held that they only dissipated the workers' energies. It preferred "to
employ all its force and trade union power in order to impose, by
law, the work conditions which [could] assure transportation employees greater well-being and a measure of job security."[56]

The Paris and Lyon transportation workers obviously subscribed
to two different concepts of union activity. The FNS, to which
Darme's union belonged, had been formed in 1886 and until its dissolution in 1898 was largely under the influence of Guesdist Marx-
ists. They did not condone the notion of the general strike, which
implied a complete cessation of work throughout the country in all
public industries, or at least the essential ones, as well as in the public
service sector. Such a work stoppage might be violent, they feared,

---

56. For a review of this debate, see FNMT: Tramways, omnibus, bateaux-
omnibus, métropolitain, voitures de place, *Compte rendu du Congrès, tenue à la Bourse
du Travail de Lyon, les 16 et 17 septembre 1902* (Lyon, 1902), 7–20, esp. 35–36.

and could lead to a successful social revolution against capitalism and the liberal state but not under the control and direction of the Guesdist party. The Guesdists preferred to have the workers' movement subordinated to their socialist political party. The socialist party, they were convinced, could capture political power through elections and could effect social change through democratic legislation. The CGT, formed as a confederation of industrial federations in 1895, believed, partly as a reaction against the Guesdist use of unions for electoral purposes, Guesdist domination of the labor movement, and Guesdist reformism, that workers' organizations should be completely autonomous and free of political influence of any kind. The CGT placed its hope for the ultimate liberation of the working class in the general strike.[57]

After 1895, Paris and Lyon transportation workers traveled separate and rival paths. The Chambre Syndicale des Cochers de Paris aligned itself with the CGT and the Paris omnibus drivers; cochers de fiacre had been at the founding congress of the CGT in Limoges in 1895. As to the reasons for this orientation, the public record is silent. However, the experience of the Parisian coachmen during the international expositions was a decisive factor in pushing them toward the CGT. All French transportation workers underwent hardships as a result of the economic crisis of the 1880s. Parisian coachmen, though, suffered the additional burden of the expositions. In addition, from 1889 on, most owners, large or small, openly combined their resources to oppose the Chambre Syndicale des Cochers de Paris and any potential coachmen's strikes. This coalition of employers accounts for the growing radicalism among Parisian cabbies. Unification with the omnibus coachmen represented a natural alliance. Therefore, when a Fédération des Transports Parisiens was formed

57. The literature on revolutionary syndicalism is vast. The following are excellent starting points: Edouard Dolléans, *Histoire du mouvement ouvrier* (Paris, 1936–60); Jacques Julliard, *Fernand Pelloutier et les origines du syndicalisme d'action directe* (Paris, 1971); Louis Levine, *Syndicalism in France* (New York, 1914); Moss, *Origins of the French Labor Movement*; F. F. Ridley, *Revolutionary Syndicalism in France: The Direct Action Movement of Its Time* (Cambridge, Eng., 1970); Peter N. Stearns, *Revolutionary Syndicalism and the French Labor Movement* (New Brunswick, 1971); Jeremy Jennings, *Syndicalism in France: A Study of Ideas* (New York, 1990). See also Claude Willard, *Le Mouvement socialiste en France (1893–1905): Les Guesdistes* (Paris, 1965).

on July 1, 1901, hired coachmen joined it. By 1902, the federation included coachmen of omnibuses, fiacres, trams, and the operators of the Seine steamships, the *bateaux-mouches*. Attempting to become truly national, the federation tried to sign up workers from other departments but was unsuccessful. Its major rival was a federation of transportation workers formed in Lyon in 1902, the FNMT, which had a legitimate right to call itself "national." It represented unions from ten different French cities, whereas membership in the Paris-based federation was limited to the Seine Department. The Paris federation represented 8,434 workers, however, compared to the Lyon federation's 1,645 members. The fundamental reality of numbers prompted one member of the Lyon federation to remark, "We cannot pretend to constitute a national federation, since we are in a minority, owing to the absence of our comrades from Paris."[58]

Despite this division, several factors favored unity. In 1902, the CGT had merged with a rival labor association, the Fédération des Bourses du Travail, making it the largest and most viable French labor confederation to date. Its general policy was that all unions belonging to the same industry, even those organized along craft lines, should join together in one national federation to represent all the workers of that industry. The CGT officially encouraged all French urban transportation workers to unite into a common federation. At this time there was also an international federation of transportation workers. Founded in London by the International Federation of Ship, Dock, and River Workers in June, 1898, the International Federation of Transport Workers met in Paris in September, 1900. The countries represented at this meeting were Germany, England, Austria, Belgium, Denmark, Spain, France, Holland, Norway, and Sweden. The French delegates, not officially members of the international federation, were transportation workers from the Seine Department.[59]

58. AN, F7 13825, report of Paris, October 20, 1908, M/2143; Ministère du Commerce de l'industrie, des postes et des télégraphes, Office du Travail, *Les Associations professionnelles ouvrières* (Paris, 1904), IV, 597–600; FNMT: Tramways, *Compte rendu*, 21.

59. AN, F7 13825, report of Paris, October 20, 1908, M/2143; Ministère du Commerce, *Les Associations professionnelles ouvrières*, IV, 602–605; *Congrès international des unions des travailleurs de transport tenu les 19, 20, et 21 septembre 1900, Paris* (Paris, 1900), 11.

The major topic on the agenda was "various means to create a national organization in each country."[60] The French delegates proposed, and the international federation agreed, that transportation workers should be organized into several distinct federations: (1) docks and ports; (2) merchant marine; (3) railroad; and (4) urban transportation. These federations would then be linked in a national confederation of transportation workers. The French delegates declared that when such an organization had been achieved, they would officially join the international federation.

At this meeting, the Paris transportation workers also issued a general call for the unity of all French transportation workers under their aegis. They had a certain logic and natural strength on their side. The major French transportation firms, the CGT, and most national industrial federations all had their headquarters in Paris. Moreover, more transportation workers were concentrated in and around Paris than anywhere else in France. By 1904, the Lyon transportation workers had accepted this argument and joined their Parisian counterparts in a new national federation of urban transportation workers with the same name as the Lyon federation, FNMT, but in this instance a truly national organization.[61] This federation, in turn, joined the CGT.

A measure of how far cabbies had come in the world of professional trade unions is indicated by a proposal submitted to the unity congress of the FNMT by J. Mazaud, cosecretary of the Chambre Syndicale des Cochers. At the 1904 congress, the issue that provoked the longest debate was whether there should be a residency requirement for employment in the transportation industry of a particular locale.[62] Such a requirement would be binding only on federation members and not on the cab companies or the government. One delegate argued that a residency requirement contradicted socialist and internationalist ideals and was arbitrary. Another, speaking in favor of the principle, reasoned that unemployed workers, moving from town to town, could act as strike breakers. The great migration

---

60. For what follows, see *Congrès international des unions des travailleurs de transport*, 25–37, 40–42.

61. See its unity congress: FNMT, *Compte rendu du 1er Congrès, tenu à Paris, Bourse du Travail, les 2, 3, 4 mai 1904* (Paris, 1904).

62. *Ibid.*, 20–21.

of workers to the cities, the speaker continued, was causing a decline in working conditions and salaries. To alleviate these problems, he proposed a one-month residency requirement for union transportation workers. Mazaud agreed in principle with the proposal, suggesting a one-year rather than a one-month waiting period. He argued that such a regulation was necessary to protect the corporation and also the public: during the year in which the worker was fulfilling his residency requirement, he could, as an apprentice, acquire and perfect his driving skills, making him a much safer coachman. A residency requirement, he said, would also inhibit coachmen who hoped to come to Paris to make a "harvest of money" and then return immediately to the countryside. The unspoken fear was that such workers would simply not join the union. Mazaud's aim, however, was to create a highly disciplined labor force, which, he believed, would result in a more effective union movement. Calmels, his cosecretary, supported his arguments. The congress, too, agreed and adopted a one-year residency requirement for its members, an ironic step, if we consider the widespread incidence of seasonal labor in the cab trade.

A similar line of reasoning caused Mazaud to sponsor a national law concerning coaching and driving licenses. At the federation's 1911 congress, he argued that urban traffic was becoming "more intense" and consequently "more difficult," resulting in more traffic accidents, which were caused for the most part by inexperienced coach conductors. He proposed, therefore, that the Ministry of Public Works require anyone conducting any kind of street vehicle to possess a license, to be issued by a commission of transportation workers, employers, and employees of the pertinent locale. In addition, any transportation worker not operating a vehicle for six months or more for any reason other than illness or an accident would be required to take the operator's examination over again. This last requirement was obviously aimed at cabbies who came to large cities for a few months each year and then returned to their homes in the countryside to pursue other occupations, workers the cabbies' union found it difficult to organize. Mazaud also conceived the strict state licensing requirements for coachmen as another means of achieving a disciplined and more professional labor force. Since of all urban transportation workers the cochers de fiacre were the most difficult to organize, any measures of control passed by the state or the federation would make the task easier.

Mazaud and the cabbies' union were also strong supporters of a highly centralized federation of transportation workers, and they favored strong ties between their own federation and the CGT.[63]

Despite the development of a more consistent working-class identity among ordinary coachmen in the Chambre Syndicale des Cochers and no matter how firmly entrenched the union had become in the revolutionary syndicalist camp, it was still difficult to organize such widely scattered workers as coachmen. It was even more difficult to find a proper classification for the coachman who was also the owner of his cab. A classic industrial union could appeal to workers conveniently concentrated in and around large factories or mines by the very structure and archaeology of the capitalist establishment, though the earliest unions were frequently rival craft associations.[64] Until 1909, for example, metalworkers were divided along craft lines and were not members of one federation: copper workers' locals formed a national federation of copper workers in 1893, but machinists and iron molders had separate federations. Since 1883, however, there had existed in the metals industry an industrial federation, the Federation of Metalworkers, which strove to unite all metalworkers irrespective of specialization. The CGT encouraged these efforts, and in 1903, the copper workers and metalworkers united in the Federation of Metalworkers. The Federations of Iron Molders and of Machinists remained outside the new organization. In 1908, the CGT mandated that workers in the same industry belong to a common federation of that industry, even if they practiced different trades. This order served as a catalyst for the unification of the Federation of Metalworkers with the Federation of Iron Molders and with most machinists' unions. The timing was prompted by the CGT's fiat, but the organization of the different types of metalworkers into a centralized unit was facilitated by their proximity to each other.[65] This

63. FNMT, *Compte rendu du congrès extraordinaire, tenu à Paris, le 23, 24 et 25 novembre 1911* (Clichy, n.d.), 22–30, 35–36; FNMT, *Compte rendu du congrès fédéral, 1910, tenu à la Bourse du Travail de Toulouse du 29 septembre au 1er octobre inclus* (Paris, 1911), 22–23.

64. See Moss, *Origins of the French Labor Movement.*

65. For a discussion of unity among French metalworkers, see Nicholas Papa-

condition did not exist among coachmen, who conducted and parked their vehicles throughout the city, with depots in every arrondissement under the watchful eyes of their employers and the police. To organize this trade was difficult.

The Chambre Syndicale des Cochers therefore adopted a decentralized structure, unlike that of the typical industrial union, which was centralized and tightly grouped around its federation.[66] The Chambre Syndicale des Cochers, whose sovereign body was the annual general assembly of its membership, was divided into seven sections, which corresponded to seven geographic areas of cab-depot concentration in and around Paris: the Bastille, La Villette, Montmartre, Étoile, Batignolles, Grenelle, Montrouge and Levallois-Clichy. Each section of the union elected its own secretary and treasurer. Overall direction of the union was invested in its board of directors (*conseil syndical*), composed of twenty-one delegates, fourteen elected from the sections (two per section) and seven elected by the general assembly. In turn, the board of directors appointed an executive committee (*bureau*), composed of a secretary, an assistant secretary, a treasurer, an assistant treasurer, an archivist, and two members of the union's finance committee. The executive committee conducted the day-to-day business of the union. Two more offices completed its central bureaucracy, the Control Commission (*Commission de Contrôle*) and the General Committee (*Comité Générale*). The Control Commission of seven was chosen by the general assembly to review and verify the union's receipts and expenditures, to report monthly on financial matters to the board of the directors, and to attend meetings of the board as a nonvoting body. The General Committee consisted of each section secretary and treasurer, as well as five delegates from each section, the board of directors, and the Control Commission. Required by the union's statutes to meet at least once every three months, its prime function was to adjudicate any important issues of principle or differences within the union. The union assigned to the

---

yanis, *Alphonse Merrheim: The Emergence of Reformism in Revolutionary Syndicalism, 1871–1925* (Boston, 1985), 7–12, 48–51.

66. A printed copy of the bylaws of the Chambre Syndicale des Cochers is extant only for the period after 1884 and can be found in Bernaud and Laloy, *Guide pratique*, 209–14. What follows is based on this source.

seven sections the fundamental work of propagandizing and organizing within their respective locales, in which they had considerable autonomy. Thus, the highly diffuse nature of the coachman's work site was provided for by the union's decentralized structure. Within a large cab firm, however, no such organizational disadvantage existed.

The composition of the Chambre Syndicale des Cochers made it difficult for the union to challenge cab owners consistently. Although no membership rolls, or union archives for that matter, are extant, a key paragraph in the union's charter points to an important dilemma for the union with respect to the qualifications for membership. The first article of the constitution, establishing the requirements for joining, stated that the union was composed of all cochers de voitures de place or de remise in the Seine Department, including members of cooperative societies as well as independent cab operators. Coachmen-owners could join the union as long as they owned only one cab and conducted it themselves. This requirement reflected a duality within the socialist cab union. On one hand, it did not seem unreasonable for the union to admit single-cab owners. The coachman owning a cab worked as hard as any coachman working for a cab company and was not that far removed from the traditional worker in the quality of his workday. Too, many ordinary coachmen still aspired to ownership of their own cabs. On the other hand, that ownership was not a disqualifying factor weakened the ideological force of the union. Another provision of the charter of the Chambre Syndicale des Cochers specified that the aim of the union was to unite all coachmen so they could obtain "the common right, that is to say, to obtain, as all other workers, a minimum salary and a limit of the hours of work." For a revolutionary syndicalist union, this "common right" hardly constituted a revolutionary goal.

The institution that held out hope of ownership to the average coachman was the cooperative society, which could transform a single coachman or a group of single-cab owners into a small company.[67] The great appeal of cooperative societies was to workers

67. No contemporary study or list of coachmen's cooperatives exists. For a list of several of these in the 1880s, see APP, B/A 1442. For a general discussion of coachmen's cooperatives, see Barberet, Le Travail en France, IV, 313–19. For a list of the major cooperatives in the early twentieth century, see Bernaud and Laloy, Guide pratique, 52–53. For some useful information on these societies, see also Boudou, "Les Taxis parisiens," 255–66.

without large financial resources who nevertheless wished to become entrepreneurs. Thus, in 1881, Letellier, provisional secretary of the cooperative Union Libre des Cochers de la Seine, affirmed that "the goal of the society is to put at the disposition of the member coachmen, as quickly as possible, equipment that belongs to them at a price lower than that demanded by the companies." He concluded that coachmen-cooperators would be working only for themselves, a lure for the independent-minded coachman. Letellier knew well how to play to the socialist instincts of some coachmen by trying to recruit those "wishing to emancipate themselves and to become the sole possessors of the entire fruit of their labor."[68] A coachman-cooperator was simultaneously an owner and a worker.

An individual could become a member of a cooperative society in several ways. First, independent cab operators could pool their resources and form a cooperative.[69] Second, a group of ordinary coachmen could invest their savings to purchase coaches and horses collectively.[70] Finally, a single, ordinary coachman could join an already existing cooperative by purchasing shares in the society.[71]

Contemporary estimates of the amount of capital needed for membership in a coachmen's cooperative vary from 3,000 to 4,000 francs. One writer in 1883 suggested that if a coachman "could accumulate some serious savings," he would have the necessary capital in two years. A study of eight cooperative societies by one contemporary researcher helps in establishing the amount of capital that was required. Three of the eight, each with a membership of seven to eight people, had initial capital of less than 10,000 francs. Four cooperatives, with seven to sixteen members, had initial capital from 20,000 to 26,000 francs. One society had an initial capital investment of over 1,000,000 francs, making it virtually a large cab company. That four of the societies were established with relatively little initial capital indicates that an individual coachman with less than 2,000 francs could become an entrepreneur. The operation of such a society was expensive, grain alone ranging in cost from 400 to over 10,000

68. *Le Rappel*, June 4, 1881, p. 3, May 13, 1881, p. 3.

69. As an example, see *La Gazette des cochers*, September 27, 1883, an issue that discusses the formation of a cooperative named "L'Avenir."

70. For a few examples of this method, see *Le Fouet*, June 30, 1879, and *La Gazette des cochers*, December 6, 1883, February 8, 1884.

71. *La Gazette des cochers*, September 27, 1883.

francs annually.[72] The point is not that a society could fail if inadequately capitalized but rather that individual coachmen with little capital among them could realistically hope to start a cab cooperative with a chance for success.

We must also note that an ordinary cabbie might wish to buy his own coach and horse and operate as an independent coachman (*cocher libre*), which a number of them did. Of thirty-three bankruptcy proceedings of independent cab operators detailed in one study, one-quarter had previously been coachmen, demonstrating both the tenacity of their desire to own their own cabs and the fragility of the enterprise. The same study estimates that an individual could start a cab firm for about 10,000 francs, the same amount necessary to begin a cooperative society.[73] Although starting up a cab firm required a lower initial investment than was needed to start a firm within some other industry, the cooperative society still provided a more accessible means by which the average coachman could enjoy the fruits of ownership.

No archives contain the membership rolls of any of the cooperative societies. However, a brochure published by one of the large cab companies, Des Confortables, illuminates the types of people who formed cooperatives and their reasons for participating in such ventures. Membership in cooperatives, it reported, was made up of "those coachmen coming out of bourgeoisie homes [as coachmen], who have with them some savings and who wish to *establish themselves:* they buy one or two cabriolets." The brochure, obviously prejudiced because of the competition represented by cooperatives, also noted that "these cab entrepreneurs, and they are in the majority, live under the constant threat of ruination: for them, the rent of a stable and of a coach house is always too expensive; for them, the illness of a horse, a broken axle or shaft are grave accidents which condemn them to days *without yield,* while the expenses of parking, of feed, of police fees, and of their homes test them without respite." The brochure did not take into account the powerful pull that ownership exercised over many coachmen—a pull strongly affirmed by

72. Dulucq, in *La Gazette des cochers*, December 20, 1883, pp. 2–3; Docin, "Les Sociétés coopératives," *La Gazette des cochers*, December 6, 1883, p. 3; Boudou, "Les Taxis parisiens," 258, 246–47.

73. Boudou, "Les Taxis parisiens," 239, 243.

the constant presence of coachmen's cooperatives in the cab trade. One 1906 Parisian guidebook intended for coachmen listed eighteen well-established cooperatives that cabbies could join.[74] Even if it were possible to determine the percentage of ordinary coachmen entering the ranks of owners through coachmen's cooperatives, such data are less significant than the perception shared by coachmen that under the right circumstance they could become owners or part owners of a cab firm. Coachmen's journals throughout the late nineteenth century were replete with advertisements for such cooperatives, dangling the opportunity for ownership before the eyes of the ordinary coachmen, who realistically anticipated stepping up to their ranks.[75]

Describing what was wrong with the cooperative society as opposed to a purely working-class union, Dulucq, in his proworker phase, went to the heart of the matter when he wrote that a cooperative created a false image for workers. To become a member of a cooperative, a worker needed a minimum of 3,000 francs, according to him. "Therefore, these societies can only be comprised of such minority of men who possess this capital, that is to say men who already possess a certain well-being." Only the smallest portion of the coachmen could meet these standards, he concluded. Most workers, family men like himself, could never save enough capital to become members of a cooperative society. The appeal for recruits to such a society was thus an illusion and a cruel hoax. Worse still, he wrote, "these workers, to a small extent . . . retard the advent of social justice and well-being for all."[76]

Coachmen who owned their own cabs, whether they actually drove them or not, had had unions to represent their special interests since the early part of the nineteenth century. These unions encouraged cooperation between ordinary coachmen and owners until the 1880s. As the economic crisis grew and many ordinary cabbies became radicalized, the owners' associations reacted by coordinating their policies, by becoming more exclusive, by cooperating with the

74. Société en Commandite pour l'Exploitation des Confortables, *Voitures et cabriolets sous remise* (Paris, 1838), 1–2, in BN, 4°V.54, emphasis in original; Bernaud and Laloy, *Guide pratique*, 52–53.

75. See such journals as *Le Cocher: Organe de tous* (1864), *La Gazette des cochers*, *Le Fouet*, and *Le Rappel*.

76. Dulucq, in *La Gazette des cochers*, December 20, 1883, pp. 2–3.

large cab firms, and by attacking the members of the Chambre Syndicale des Cochers. On August 23, 1887, Charles Pernette founded the Union Syndicale des Cochers, a successor to the 1862 Union des Loueurs. Pernette, a former coachman, dedicated himself "to the task of harmonizing capital and labor, the employee and the employer, the cab entrepreneur and the coachman."[77] To this end, he established the École d'Apprentissage des Cochers de Paris.[78] The École Pernette, as it became known, was designed to turn out "capable" and "polished" coachmen and, one might add, compliant cabbies. In addition, in 1890 Pernette began to edit *La Voie publique,* an avidly prorepublican and proindependent cab-owner newspaper, the official newspaper of the Union Syndicale des Cochers. Indicative of the changing times, this newspaper focused its criticism not against the large cab firms but against the Chambre Syndicale des Cochers. It especially disapproved of the union's socialist and radical inclination. The Chambre Syndicale des Cochers, for its part, now viewed the independent cab operators and the large cab firms alike as oppressors, condemning both as owners of property that exploited labor.[79] In October, 1899, the independent cab operators formed a national organization, the Syndicat Général des Loueurs de Voitures de France. Its official organ was *Le Loueur de voitures,* which was published from 1901 to 1909.

Further complicating this picture was the fact that specialized coachmen, owners or not, also had their own associations. The Chambre Syndicale des Loueurs et Cochers de Grande Remise de Paris, founded in 1890, was a union composed of both ordinary coachmen and owners. Mixed membership in this case did not contradict the general tendency of coachmen in the late 1880s and the 1890s to split ranks on the basis of ownership. Coachmen of the grande remise, as well as private coachmen for individual families, always believed

77. *Réveil des cochers,* June, 1898, p. 1. This last page contains a laudatory biographical portrait of Pernette. See also Ministère du commerce, de l'industrie, *Annuaire des syndicats professionnels* (Paris, 1896), 398.

78. Ernst Nomis, "L'Éducation d'un cocher de fiacre," *Le Monde et les sports* (April, 1901), 556–59.

79. See APP, B/A 1365, note of Paris, June 27, 1893. This report describes a meeting of the Chambre Syndicale des Cochers at which Pernette and Bixio were linked and where one municipal councillor in attendance made this remark about Pernette: "[He] has promised to kick me in the rump; I am waiting for him; he can come with his confederates. But in the mean time I send them dung."

themselves superior to the coachmen of the common fiacre. They adopted the values and attitudes of their private masters or wealthier clients, cultural values taking precedence over class values. Thus, the coachmen of the grande remise had a separate union, the Syndicat des Cochers de Grande Remise du Départment de la Seine. Founded in 1888, this union had 520 members in 1896.[80] There was also the Cercle de l'Union des Cochers des Maisons Bourgeoises de Départment de la Seine, essentially a mutual aid society rather than a classic trade union.[81] Bourgeoisie employers would not knowingly have hired union labor.

The most powerful owners' union, perhaps the most powerful union in the cab trade, was the Chambre Syndicale des Entrepreneurs de Voitures de Place du Départment de la Seine. This association represented the larger cab firms whose owners were not members of the Union Syndicale des Cochers. In 1893, it had in its coffers 500,000 francs and had united two-thirds of the large cab firms of Paris. It was led for eleven years by Maurice Bixio, president of the CGV and a major contributor to its financial well-being. In 1893 alone, the CGV donated to the strike fund of the Chambre Syndicale des Entrepreneurs close to 500,000 francs, a sum almost equal to the union's entire treasury. During the series of strikes that affected the cab industry in 1892 and 1893, the CGV's policy was "to assist those who [were] seriously attacked." During the 1900 strike of Parisian coachmen, the CGV distributed to the independent cab operators 10 francs daily for each of their cabs on strike.[82] Antistrike funds were distributed either through the Chambre Syndicale des Entrepreneurs or through a secret strike fund the CGV had established.[83] Given its existence as a powerful employers' union, the CGV believed it

80. Chambre Syndicale des Loueurs et Cochers de Grande Remise de Paris et Professions Similaires, *Livret* (Paris, 1897); Ministère du commerce, de l'industrie, *Annuaire des syndicats professionnels*, 398–99.

81. See the several reports on this association in APP, B/A 348. This carton includes a copy of the union's statutes.

82. CGV, *Assemblée générale ordinaire du 28 avril 1893, rapport* (Paris, 1894), 35–36; ACGV, CGV, *Conseil*, reg. no. 5, January 29, 1892, p. 1193, and *Comité*, reg. no. 12, October 24, 1900, pp. 4869–70.

83. For information on the creation by the CGV of the secret antistrike fund, see ACGV, CGV, *Comité*, reg. no. 12, October 24, 1900, pp. 4869–70, as well as *Comité*, reg. no. 12, March 11, 1892, p. 1999, and reg. no. 6, April 1, 1892, pp. 2003–2004.

"must be able to come to the moral and material aid of those . . . colleagues who have been hit by such unjust and whimsical work stoppages." The money it spent supporting its principles was, in its opinion, "money very well placed for the defense of the interests which [were] entrusted to [it]." This kind of cooperation and concentration of resources among large cab companies extended into the era of the automobile. In January, 1909, the four leading Paris autocab companies, the Compagnie Française des Automobiles de Place, the CGV, the Compagnie des Auto-Fiacres, and the Société Météor, formed a consortium, one of whose major aims was the establishment of a strike fund against the ordinary cabbie.[84]

Compared with this power, the resources of the Chambre Syndicale des Cochers were paltry. Although no records exist to provide an accurate measure of the union's finances, we have some inkling of its material condition. In 1877, it had approximately 600 members and a treasury of 11,396 francs. According to a government publication, membership in the union had risen to 6,532 by 1896; the publication fails to include financial data.[85] The constitution of the union for this era indicates that each member had to pay a franc on being admitted to the union and 50 centimes in dues each month thereafter.[86] These figures add up to a treasury of 45,724 francs. This estimate is necessarily rough since many members may not have paid their dues on time and the government membership figures may be inaccurate. In addition, the union may have obtained funds from its national federation or from the CGT. Inflated or understated, the general level of its treasury was nonetheless only a fraction of the treasury of the owners.

Another area in which the owners and the coachmen's union were opposed was the cab meter. Owners were unwilling to entertain such an innovation until its worth was thoroughly proven; the union saw the meter as an important step toward its goal of fair wages. So important was it that in no other aspect was the radicalization of the

84. CGV, *Assemblée générale ordinaire du 28 avril 1893, rapport*, 35, 36; ACGV, CGV, *Conseil*, reg. no. 8, January 22, 1909, p. 2921, February 12, 1909, p. 2924, April 7, 1909, pp. 2932–33, June 25, 1909, p. 2943.

85. APP, B/A 1442, "Chambres syndicales ouvrières. Minute"; Ministère du commerce, de l'industrie, *Annuaire des syndicats professionnels*, 398–99.

86. See Bernaud and Laloy, *Guide pratique*, 210, 214.

Chambre Syndicale des Cochers more evident than in its position on the installation of these meters in Parisian cabs.

On January 30, 1868, the prefect of the Seine Department ordered cab companies to develop a device that would accurately measure the time elapsed and the distance traveled when a cab was hired by a client. From the 1890s on, the Chambre Syndicale des Cochers was one of the most ardent supporters of the idea of an accurate cab meter. Seeing itself as basically a workers' union, it believed that its members should receive a straight wage, like all industrial workers. Tips, which companies took into consideration when establishing coachmen's daily wages, were regarded by the union as too degrading and too precarious to be considered part of the coachman's wage structure. However, it was impractical for the union to demand a straight wage for coachmen in the absence of a method to calculate accurately the productivity of the cab. Without such a method, the cab owners charged, a straight wage would encourage coachmen to be lazy and perhaps not work at all. Not only would a meter guard against these possibilities, but it would also eliminate fraud, and this consideration, too, strengthened the union's argument for a fixed wage. In the 1890s, therefore, the Chambre Syndicale des Cochers took the position that all cab owners should install accurate electronic meters and that ordinary coachmen should receive a fixed wage of 7 francs for a maximum twelve-hour workday.

To add weight to its demand, the Chambre Syndicale des Cochers staged strikes against select cab companies several times in 1892 and 1893.[87] The Paris authorities had already mandated electronic meters for all cabs in 1891, and a recurrent theme of the strikes of 1892 and 1893 was the union's demand that cab companies comply with the law. In a letter to the employers' union, dated June 6, 1893, Carrière, secretary of the Chambre Syndicale des Cochers, made the union's position explicit: "We claim purely and simply that the regular use of the meter shall permit us to obtain a fixed salary to be determined in an equitable manner without dealing a blow to the benefits that the cab entrepreneurs are used to harvesting."[88] Carrière

87. See the police files and press clippings in APP, B/A 1365.
88. A typed copy of Carrière's letter is *ibid*. Bixio's formal printed response is attached to this letter in the archives.

anticipated the owners' argument that coachmen working for a fixed salary would have no incentive to perform a full day's work. He compared the cab owner to a master carpenter who employed 100 workers. The master carpenter, he noted, paid his men a salary of 7 francs daily. Among these workers he might find 20 who did not measure up to his standards. These he would simply replace. Cab owners could easily discover which coachmen were not productive. He concluded: "You know almost exactly the average yield per coach per day. That is the certain foundation that would permit you to appraise the more or less satisfactory work of each of your coachmen."

The union's demand was rooted in its belief that only a scientific device such as a meter could rationalize the hours and wages of the coachmen. Not only would it make life easier for the cabbies, but it was also compatible with the union's working-class ideology. The 1892 and 1893 strikes elicited from the Chambre Syndicale des Cochers its most decidedly socialist rhetoric to date. At one meeting in June, 1893, Carrière referred to himself as an "international revolutionary." At another meeting in the same year, a coachman called for a general strike and a revolution to end exploitation, the strike to begin at the Paris City Hall. Carrière, speaking in the name of the union, publicly called on the municipal authorities "to transform the cab trade controlled by insatiable capitalists into a public service controlled by the public."[89]

The position of the cab companies with respect to meters was more ambiguous than the stance of the union. Initially, the cab companies raised various technical objections to the many meters proposed by inventors during the 1880s and early 1890s. They insisted that a meter should simultaneously measure the distance a cab traveled and the time elapsed on the basis of a certain speed and that it should also register a reading based on a fictional speed when the cab was at rest. No inventor came up with a device that could perform all of these functions until the late 1890s. Other technical and legal problems constantly postponed the installation of meters: where they should be placed, for instance, and whether they could be made tamper-proof called for much debate. These were important issues

---

89. APP, B/A 1365, note of Paris, June 14, 1893, report of Paris, June 27, 1893, and petition, *A messieurs les conseillers municipaux de Paris* (Paris, n.d. [1893]).

since neither the cab companies, the cabbies, nor the public trusted one another. Another issue was ownership: would the manufacturer of the meters remain their owner and lease them to the cab companies or would the cab companies own them outright? The cab companies also questioned whether the municipal authorities had the right to mandate meters in the first place. The city had never doubted its power to do so, and though cab companies fought the principle, the city prevailed. Cab companies then suggested that the public authorities help bear the expense of installation, but they were defeated on this point, too. The cab companies did, however, extract from municipal authorities enough time to allow for the perfection of an accurate meter. One police ordinance had made the installation of meters mandatory in all cabs by April 1, 1891. That ordinance and several others were extended, so it was not until 1904 that all Parisian cabs began to be equipped with meters.

Only when all of the technical difficulties had been solved and an efficient meter developed did cab owners embrace the installation of cab meters. They had come by this time to see the meter as an effective means of control over the coachmen. The owners rejected outright any discussion of a fixed wage, suggesting instead that coachmen receive 33 percent of their cabs' daily receipts. This proposal was based on the owners' desire for control and on their perception of the coachman as a breed apart from the classic industrial worker. Mazuc, a former member of the Chambre Syndicale des Cochers and later an associate of the independent operators' union, repeated the owners' standard argument that if coachmen were guaranteed a minimum wage, they would become lazy and less productive. Coachmen, he wrote, should receive a salary commensurate with their output, for thereby they would become interested in the outcome of their own production and thus associates of the owner. *La Voie publique* stated editorially that coachmen should receive a third of the cab's daily receipts because "this system raises the dignity of the coachman and makes him into a veritable associate of the owner."[90]

Cab owners did not wish to regard coachmen as classic workers, citing as their reason the nature of the cabbies' work, for cabbies had

90. *La Voie publique: Organe de la corporation des cochers*, August 8, 1891, p. 2; Mazue [*sic*], August 15, 1891, p. 2; *La Voie publique*, August 8, 1891, p. 1.

a great deal of individual control over their own productivity. The refusal to define coachmen as traditional workers also had the advantage of avoiding potential class conflict within the cab industry. An in-house memorandum of the CGV summed up perfectly the cab firms' arguments. It began with the categorical view that "the coachman of the voiture de place is not a worker."[91] A worker, it noted, was someone who worked under the surveillance of a foreman and who produced a determined number of pieces within a fixed time. Such a worker had neither influence over the sale of the final product nor control over its quality. Such a worker received a fixed salary and was subject to unemployment. A coachman, however, "is master of when to begin and when to finish his work, whenever it seems right to him." Moreover, it stated, "he works as if he doesn't anticipate any surveillance," and "he is not threatened by unemployment," though both of these assertions were not true. The memorandum concluded that a coachman "has a preponderant, decisive and capital influence on the sale of the product of which he is in sole charge." There was certainly a great deal of truth to this last assertion. To overcome all these difficulties, therefore, the owners enthusiastically championed the cab meter and the concept of a salary for coachmen based on the cab's daily receipts.

Ordinary coachmen and the Chambre Syndicale des Cochers did not prevail in the 1892 or 1893 strikes. Nor did they succeed in any other of their major strikes in the nineteenth century. One of the main reasons for the coachmen's failure was that the corporation of Parisian coachmen was plagued by the internal inconsistencies examined in this chapter. It was divided within itself by different points of view: ordinary cabbies with a decidedly working-class mentality, those who still aspired to ownership, the coachmen-cooperators, driver-owners of a single cab, and coachmen who saw a proportional wage system as an opportunity to earn higher wages. Juxtaposed to the multiplicity of coachmen was the power of the single-minded large capitalist cab firms. These issues emerge more clearly when examined in light of the coachmen's strikes during the international expositions in Paris, the subject of the next chapter.

91. CGV, "Note et renseignements sur la question des voitures de place à Paris," in *Rapports divers* (typescript in ACGV). These opinions found their way into print in Bixio, *Note adressée à la Commission permanente*, 5–7.

# 6 — COACHMEN, INTERNATIONAL EXPOSITIONS, AND STRIKES

Parisian coachmen never missed an opportunity to strike while Paris was host to an international exposition.[1] They expected such strikes to succeed because during the expositions a work stoppage would severely reduce the higher revenues for the cab companies that an influx of visitors would bring. The police and other public authorities also dreaded cab strikes at such times because they put a strain on the public transportation system, they caused confusion, they erupted in unpleasant incidents between strikers and strikebreakers, and they tarnished the public image of France. For the otherwise scattered coachmen, who worked for different and varied cab companies out of depots and public cab stations spread throughout Paris, the exposition strikes became a single unifying force in a very diverse profession.

Since the universal expositions put an obvious strain on the normal transportation services of Paris, those responsible for transportation added special facilities to provide for increased ridership.[2] In 1878, for instance, the city added a special omnibus line from the Hotel de Ville to the exposition. In 1889, it added three extra omnibus lines for the exposition. The first went from the Palais Royal to the École Militaire; the second from the Gare Saint-Lazare to the

1. Perrot, *Les Ouvriers en grève*, I, 333.
2. The best sources for the subject of transportation and the expositions are the

Porte Rapp; and the last from the Place de la République to the Quai d'Orsay. At the time of the 1878 Exposition, 12,000 voitures de place and de remise circulated throughout Paris; in 1889, Paris was served by 13,350 cabs.[3]

The general perception of the public was that such transportation services should be sufficient to accommodate visitors to Paris during an international exposition, and they would be, except in the case of a strike. A tourist carrying a lot of baggage or traveling with a large party, the normal condition for visitors to the exposition, would be dependent on the Parisian cabs. Guidebooks to the expositions strongly advised tourists with little baggage to take either public mass transportation or an omnibus provided by the railway companies—advice intended to spare the newcomer to Paris misadventure at the hands of an unscrupulous cocher de voiture de place. For those with considerable baggage or with a large party, however, the guidebooks recommended the voiture de place as the best means of transportation. For Parisians and visitors, with or without baggage, the private cab, despite suggestions by guidebooks to use mass transportation, was "the preferred means of transportation."[4] A strike of Parisian coachmen would force such clientele to use the public mass transportation system and severely strain these resources. However, a strike during the exposition would also focus attention on the problems of the coachmen and bring more pressure to bear on the owners to come to terms with their employees.

---

many guidebooks that appeared on the occasion of an exposition. For this study, the following have been especially useful: A. Bitard, *Guide pratique dans Paris pendant l'exposition* (Paris, 1878); F. de Donville, *Guide complet de l'étranger dans Paris suivi d'un guide à l'exposition universelle* (Paris, 1878); Gautier and Desprez, *Les Curiosités de l'exposition de 1878*; Charles Moonen, *Cook's Guide to Paris and Its Exposition, 1878. With a Plan of Paris* (London, n.d. [1878]); Exposition de 1889, *Guide bleu du Figaro et du Petit Journal* (Paris, 1889); *Guide dans l'exposition. Paris et ses environs* (Paris, 1889); Georges Grison, "Les Moyens de transport," *L'Exposition de Paris de 1889*, May 18, 1889, p. 95; Emile Lequien, *Les Merveilles de l'exposition en 1889. Guide du visiteur à l'exposition universelle dans Paris et ses environs* (Paris, 1889); Paris Universal Exhibition, 1889, *Guide to the Exposition* (London, 1889).

3. De Donville, *Guide complet*, 65; Préfecture de la Seine, *Annuaire statistique* (1891), 640; Gautier and Desprez, *Les Curiosités de l'exposition de 1878*, 227, and Préfecture de la Seine, *Annuaire statistique* (1889), 647.

4. Grison, "Les Moyens de transport," 95; de Donville, *Guide complet*, 2; *Guide dans l'exposition*, 8; Bitard, *Guide pratique*, 2–3.

That coachmen struck during every one of the universal expositions in Paris in the nineteenth century confirms this idea, but it also creates an impression of uniformity among the coachmen that is quite false. For the historian, the strikes are accurate and dramatic indicators of the conditions within and aspirations of the entire trade. They register not only broad tendencies but subtle splits and differences among the major factions within the corporation and even within a single union. An examination of each strike separately (the key ones of 1878, 1889, and 1900, in light of their extent, plus the strikes of 1855, 1867, 1884, 1892, and 1893) permits a topological grouping into two broad categories. The salient feature of coachmen's strikes prior to 1878 was that ordinary coachmen and the small cab entrepreneurs (the single-cab owners, cooperators, and small firms) stood together in some fashion against the large cab companies. The early strikes thus reflected a corporate mentality.[5] By 1889 the corporation of Parisian coachmen had split apart, as evidenced not only by the language unique to the different unions representing the various segments of the corporation but also by the 1889 strike itself. The small cab entrepreneurs changed allegiance, standing this time with the large cab firms against the ordinary coachmen. If we take the strikes of 1878 and 1889 as two successive points on a scale in the development of class consciousness among coachmen, between these points we must factor in the increasing cooperation and concentration of capital in the industry and the economic crisis of the 1880s, for concentration and crisis are the keys to understanding the differences between 1878 and 1889.

The Paris Exposition of 1878 was a decisive stimulus in the formation of the first industrywide coachmen's union, the Chambre Syndicale des Cochers de Paris. Throughout the nineteenth century, coachmen believed that their wages were too low and the method of payment unfair. They also believed that because they worked long hours outdoors in all weather conditions, they had to expend more money on food and especially drink than the average Parisian

---

5. For a discussion of corporate language and French workers, see Sewell, *Work and Revolution in France*. For an in-depth examination of the creation of a regional working class from the middle of the nineteenth to the beginning of the twentieth century, see Lequin, *Les Ouvriers de la région lyonnaise*. To better situate the coachmen of Paris at this time in relation to other Parisian workers, see Berlanstein, *Working People of Paris*.

worker. These problems were exacerbated during the expositions because the cab companies set a higher moyenne than usual, on the assumption that more people would be riding cabs. Although working à la moyenne was supposed to be voluntary, the cab companies, especially during expositions, expected all their coachmen to meet a daily target rate. Consequently, coachmen not only could not increase their wages during an exposition but had to work harder to meet the increased target rates. This situation, existing throughout the cab trade and across all depots, incited the coachmen to organize and to strike.

Coachmen had already experienced the negative effects of a universal exposition on their wages in 1867, and they anticipated the 1878 exposition warily. During the 1867 exposition, François-Joseph Ducoux, director of the CGV, raised the moyenne expected of each cab from thirteen to twenty-five francs. His coachmen struck briefly to have it lowered, but with no Paris-wide organization to back them, their protest failed. In 1872, a few coachmen tried to form a union but without success. In terms of organization, they were beset by two fundamental disadvantages compared to other workers. Coachmen could only assemble in groups for three relatively short periods during their long workday: when they reported to a company depot to receive their cabs, when they lined up at public cab stations to await clients, and when they returned their cabs to the depot. These opportunities to congregate were carefully circumscribed by cab owners or by the police, and during the workday coachmen were scattered throughout Paris, with little chance of meeting or of talking with each other. Although many coachmen lived in neighborhoods close to their depots, organizing them was difficult, especially since coachmen worked for many different and varied employers. Nonetheless, in January 1877, an industrywide chambre syndicale of coachmen was born. It was the forthcoming exposition, however, that unified so disparate and scattered a work force and that galvanized many coachmen to join.[6]

Between January, 1877, and May, 1878, Michel Moritz, secretary of the Chambre Syndicale des Cochers, defined the issues at stake

6. APP, B/A 178, report of Paris, August 23, 1878; Perrot, *Les Ouvriers en grève*, I, 333; Barberet, *Le Travail en France*, IV, 242–46.

and prepared the way for a possible strike. In January, 1877, he issued a circular to the entire corporation of Parisian coachmen.[7] First, he demanded that coachmen be able to park anywhere in Paris as long as they did not tie up traffic or interfere with private interests. Second, he wanted the police to abolish the obligatory fares they had stipulated for each kind of cab ride and to open the trade to *la liberté du travail*, that is, coachmen and their clients between them should set the fare for a cab ride. Third, he demanded that cab firms pay their coachmen à la planche, using monthly income as the basis for getting the daily target rate. The union also requested that the government establish the right to a civil trial for any coachman accused of violating the police driving ordinances.

Nearly a year later, on December 16, 1877, Moritz published a letter in Joseph Barberet's "Bulletin du travail," in which he complained of the cab companies' terrible treatment of their horses.[8] The companies, he claimed, skimped on food, horse grooms were too busy to care for the horses properly, and the animals themselves were "above all badly boarded." In addition, he wrote, the police forced coachmen to travel miles to find an empty cab station, exhausting the horses.

Fretting publicly about the CGV's treatment of its horses was a clever tactic. For too long coachmen had been the ones accused of cruelty to horses. They were among the special targets of middle-class moralists and reformers who wished to tame what was considered the rude and rough manners of the lower classes and to socialize these people with middle-class values.[9] The Society for the Protection of Animals noted the obvious, that the horse was the most visible animal in Paris, adding that it was "too frequently a martyr." In 1843, two years before the official formation of this society, its early

7. Barberet, *Le Travail en France*, IV, 246–47. See also *ibid.*, IV, 249–74, for an excellent survey of the 1878 strike, including copies of the major petitions and statements presented by each side.

8. *Ibid.*, IV, 249.

9. For a discussion of this issue, see Robert J. Bezucha, "The Moralization of Society: The Enemies of Popular Culture in the Nineteenth Century," in *The Wolf and the Lamb: Popular Culture in France, from the Old Regime to the Twentieth Century*, ed. Jacques Beauroy, Marc Bertrand, and Edward T. Gargan (Saratoga, Calif., 1976), 175–87.

partisans pressured the prefect of Paris police, Gabriel Delessert, to forbid coachmen "to hit their horses with the handle of their whip or to mistreat them in any manner whatsoever." One observer, in an article defending the owners, wrote in 1867 that the Paris cab cavalry was basically well fed and in excellent health and that the "coarse and cruel coachmen" had no reason to whip their horses.[10]

During the strike of 1878, the coachmen turned these class-based attacks around. Hoping to elicit the sympathy of the Parisian populace, they portrayed themselves as the champions and friends of the suffering horse. Their accusations of malnourished horses called attention to the essential fact that the physical state of the horse was central to the coachman's livelihood. A healthy and well-fed horse would pull his coach as quickly as possible in the course of the workday. The quicker the ride, the more clients and hence the more tips a coachman could obtain. It was to ensure the assignment of a healthy horse that drivers felt obliged to tip horse grooms each day. Parisians frequently did see coachmen whipping their horses to make them move faster, and the Society for the Protection of Animals often cited them for such behavior. Coachmen wanted the Parisian public to understand, however, how important a healthy horse was to a cabbie's wages and to shift the blame for unhealthy horses and the coachman's own occasional cruel treatment of the animals to the cab companies.

The union repeated its claims of January, 1877, in March and in May, 1878, in the form of petitions sent to the National Assembly, to the Paris Municipal Council, and to the Paris prefect of police.[11] When the exposition opened on May 20, 1878, slightly later than anticipated, there had still been no response.

Rather than easing the rules as the coachmen had wished, on July 16 the prefecture of police issued a new ordinance requiring each cab to display a sign indicating whether it was occupied or empty. The ordinance was scheduled to go into effect on August 5. The

10. Société Protectrice des Animaux, *Exposé de l'oeuvre* (Alençon, 1891), 4; Gustave Dumaine, "La Société protectrice des animaux, ses origines, son histoire," *La Nouvelle Revue*, CXL (December 1, 1935), 195; Henry Blatin, *Nos Cruautés envers les animaux, au détriment de l'hygiène, de la fortune publique et de la morale* (Paris, 1867), 33–34.

11. See APP, B/A 178, report of Paris, March 30, 1878, no. 2, and *Les Droits de l'homme*, May 15, 1878.

entire cab trade, ordinary coachmen and owners alike, was outraged by what it regarded as another bureaucratic curtailment of freedom of trade. Militant coachmen, spurred by the agitation the new ordinance evoked, decided that this was the moment to strike. The fundamental reason for the strike, however, was that the largest cab firm of Paris, the CGV, had begun to raise its daily moyenne as people flocked to the capital for the exposition. One police agent reported that the CGV's moyenne sometimes went as high as thirty-four francs, representing seventeen hours of work. This police agent became quite sympathetic to the coachmen's point of view, noting that the elevated moyenne "constituted a charge too heavy for the coachmen." He interviewed several coachmen and believed their charges that "the General Cab Company [did] not maintain its cavalry suitably." In fact, he reported, "the good coachmen" daily spent one franc, fifty centimes of their own money to supplement their horses' diets. This same agent confirmed that though working à la moyenne was voluntary and only a fraction of the CGV's coachmen subscribed to the system, the company nonetheless expected all of its coachmen to meet the daily average. Reporting this information in late July, he noted that rumors of a possible coachmen's strike had begun to circulate in Paris.[12]

Talk of a strike brought to the surface the first serious schism in the Chambre Syndicale des Cochers. The division was over tactics: whether the union should or should not urge a strike to protest the new ordinance. On July 20, the Executive Committee voted nine to eight against a strike. On August 5, the first day of the strike, the union itself remained neutral, but committee members were already polarized and active.[13] Once the first vote had been taken, those who had voted for the strike earnestly began to prepare for it, and those who had voted against took measures to block it. How each faction of the Executive Committee proceeded is interesting for what it reveals about the tactics of the coachmen's strike and about the basic causes of the split.

Among the proponents of the strike were Joseph Godefroy,

12. APP, B/A 178, reports of Paris, August 23, 1878, July 17, 1878, no. 27, and July 28, 1878, pièce 34.

13. *Ibid.*, reports of Paris, August 1, 1878, no. 44, and August 7, 1878, no. 228; "La Grève des cochers," *Le Pays: Journal de l'empire,* August 6, 1878; "La Grève des cochers," *Le Petit Parisien,* August 5, 1878.

Michel Moritz, his brother Jean Moritz, and a man named Osmont, a former municipal councillor and a supporter of the coachmen. Immediately after the July 20 vote, the eight who favored the strike began visiting depots and public cab stations, declaring that the union had voted for a strike on August 5. Godefroy encouraged the coachmen of his own firm, Vernaz et Fils, to protest and was fired "for having incited the coachmen to . . . strike."[14] This dismissal did not deter Godefroy; on August 3, police agents spotted him visiting cab stations on the boulevards Montparnasse and des Invalides and on the avenue du Maine.[15] Activists printed petitions and posted them on kiosks or in wine merchants' shops, where they also organized local ward meetings of the union.[16] These local meetings took place in neighborhood meeting halls, as well as in the back rooms of wine merchants' shops, and were usually held in the evening, when many coachmen were off duty. Godefroy and Dulucq, another union leader, organized a series of such meetings in July.[17]

Union opponents of the strike were quick to respond. The most important member of this group was Leclerc, associate secretary of the Chambre Syndicale des Cochers.[18] He first reacted to talk of a strike by publishing a letter in a major Parisian newspaper as early as May 11, declaring his position: "Experience has too often proved that we have nothing to gain by initiating these strike procedures. Moreover we shall not choose a moment like the time of an Exposition to bring about cruel disagreements with the public about a service which functions as the basis of our daily existence." The strike as a vehicle for promoting demands, he wrote, was an unsatisfactory tactic. Rather, he thought, "the means that the chambre syndicale

14. APP, B/A 178, reports of Paris, August 1, 1878, nos. 44 and 43.

15. *Ibid.*, report of Paris, August 3, 1878, no. 64. See also *ibid.*, report of Paris, May 10, 1878, no. 21. This last report notes that another coachman, Charles Guérin, who had been fired from the Maison Rieussec, 68, rue de l'Université, "has gone to propagandize near the coachmen of the Compagnie Parisienne des équipages de grande remise, rue de l'Université." This pattern of activists visiting depots was very typical of the organizing methods of the union.

16. *Ibid.*, reports of August 1, 1878, no. 43, and August 6, 1878.

17. See APP, B/A 178, which contains examples of the fliers sent out to announce such meetings.

18. Leclerc voted against the strike at the July 20 meeting; see APP, B/A 178, report of Paris, August 7, 1878, no. 228.

has taken, a system of petitions, is the best." Here was a personal preference for reformist tactics, a position shared by many cabbies in the corporation of coachmen who wished to continue working during the exposition. The police reported that Leclerc and Tremolière, the treasurer of the union and another opponent of the strike, had in their care the two keys of the union's treasury. Leclerc had arranged with Tremolière that in the event of a strike they would seize the treasury, remove it to a "safe place," and thus sequester the union's funds from those who favored a strike.[19] Several years after the strike, Leclerc became a wine merchant and a member of the Society for the Protection of Animals, not especially a favorite organization with coachmen.[20]

While the leaders of the union were thus divided, the rank-and-file coachmen of the CGV took matters into their own hands. On August 4, 1878, over six hundred coachmen of the CGV failed to present themselves for work. On August 5, the balance of the firm's coachmen did not report for work, making the strike against the CGV total. These men comprised a major portion of the cochers de fiacre in Paris. That most of them decided to go out on August 5, which was a Monday, rather than on the previous day reflected the custom of the workers, especially those with a rural background, to mark Holy Monday with a religious festival or to strike on that day during labor conflicts—a custom they seem to have transferred to this occasion. The idea of a religious festival might explain why, early in the strike, coachmen paraded festively by their depots and ended their day with a visit "to the wine merchants' shops."[21]

Once the strike broke out, the union closed ranks behind the coachmen of the CGV. Division continued, however, on the principles involved. On August 6, Michel Moritz issued, through the

19. "Les Cochers," *La Lanterne*, May 11, 1878, p. 2; APP, B/A 178, reports of Paris, August 2, 1878, no. 14, August 7, 1878, no. 228, August 2, 1878, no. 49.

20. *La Gazette des cochers*, September 13, 1883, pp. 1–2. It might be noted, too, that Leclerc's name is somewhat slippery, a not unusual phenomenon with coachmen's names. Barberet gives it as Leclère (*Le Travail en France*, IV, 249–50), whereas newspapers such as *La Gazette*, with information on or by this coachman, give his name as Leclerc.

21. APP, B/A 178, reports of Paris, August 4, 1878, pièce 67, and August 5, 1878, no. 81; Perrot, *Les Ouvriers en grève*, I, 109; APP, B/A 178, reports of Paris, August 5, 1878, no. 81, and April 4, 1878, no. 72.

press, seven demands in the name of the entire corporation of Parisian coachmen.[22] He began with the union's strongest point: "The coachmen have struck because they are tired of serving as instruments of torture over the poor horses who die of hunger and are badly boarded, badly groomed and work too hard." Moritz also demanded le travail à la planche, a share in the control of pension funds, the payment of interest by cab companies on the coachmen's major security deposit, reform of discriminatory police rules that denied coachmen le droit commun, the right to eat on the public roads, and la liberté du travail.

At the same time, a rival faction within the union submitted another set of demands to the Parisian press, including a maximum workday of fourteen hours and a fixed daily wage of five francs. It also demanded abolition of the moyenne au jour; coachmen, it stated, should turn over to the cab company whatever they earned each day. There was, however, some small confusion about what the workers were asking for. Police agents had learned from conversations among coachmen in the street that many strikers were demanding the abolition of the moyenne, a maximum workday of fourteen hours, but a fixed salary of six francs. The insurgents spoke for these coachmen but formally presented the lower claim for five francs. They demanded additionally that the coachmen be relieved of liability for broken shafts on their cabs and, finally, that the CGV stop forcing its coachmen to join the company Société de Secours Mutuels. It is impossible to determine the numerical strength of those who supported these demands, either in the union or at large.[23]

The major point of contention between the two main rival factions in the union was not the amount of wages but the wage system. The ideological positions of the factions, however, though beginning to be thought out, had not yet surfaced. Those demanding a fixed salary for a determined number of working hours regarded coachmen as traditional workers with no stake in the cab's production and thus no involvement in the owners' success. To make a stake in the cabs' fares part of coachmen's wages was, they believed, to exploit

22. See *Le Rappel*, August 7, 1878, p. 1.
23. *Ibid.*, August 9, 1878, p. 1; APP, B/A 178, report of Paris, August 5, 1878, no. 81.

the cabbies' labor. Not until the 1890s did those favoring a wage system based on a share of the cab's total receipts formally separate from those championing a fixed wage, each faction within the cab trade forming its own union. During the 1878 strike, the division was not severe or its significance evident.

Paris remained relatively calm during the strike, though there were scattered violent incidents between strikers and nonstrikers or strikebreakers.[24] One striker, Alexandre Barré, thirty-nine years old and a native of the Marne, was outside the CGV's depot at 20, boulevard de la Chapelle, where the CGV was hiring new coachmen as strikebreakers. As several were leaving the depot, Barré shouted, "Down with the cowards, slackers, as if you didn't have work elsewhere without coming to prevent these people from their strike; if it were up to me I would fix you." He was immediately arrested by the police guarding the depot. In another incident a nonstriker was returning his cab at 2 A.M. when he was assaulted by several people at the corner of the boulevard des Invalides and the avenue de Tourville. One assailant held the horse's bridle while the others dragged the coachman by the feet from his seat high atop the cab. He fell and hit his head on the hard pavement. The strikers kicked and punched him and took his work sheet and his wallet, which contained twenty-five francs. This coachman, caught on a lonely road early in the morning, was a quite vulnerable target for the strikers' anger. Attacking strikebreakers on public roads rather than near guarded cab stations or depots thus became a favorite tactic of the strikers. Another strategy employed by striking coachmen was to involve their wives and children. The police reported that the wives, children in hand, would visit depots and express agitation and excitement, thereby stirring up emotions, venting their anger, and perhaps eliciting some sympathy. Most reports covering this strike, however, indicate that violent incidents were not typical.[25]

In the absence of public survey polls, it is difficult to determine the reaction of the Parisian populace to the strike. Newspapers reported the mood of Parisians but through the filter of their own po-

---

24. For all that follows, see APP, B/A 178.

25. *Ibid.*, note of Paris, August 11, 1878, no. 427, and report of Paris, August 8, 1878, no. 292.

litical prejudices. Conservative newspapers attacked the strikers for creating chaos in the streets, whereas the liberal press painted a kinder picture. *L'Union* editorialized that "the traffic disturbance caused by the strike, especially at the moment of the Exposition, justifies the intervention of the Prefecture of Police." It went on to describe the confusion at train stations, where travelers, bags in hand, searched in vain for a cab to take them to the center of Paris. It was impossible, it continued, to find a cab to the Champs de Mars or the Trocadéro, central locations of the exposition. *Le Moniteur* was more moderate; it did not editorialize but merely described the scene near railroad stations: "Whatever it is, the face of Paris is rather curious this morning. At the cab stations there arrive a crowd of clients who wait in vain; and then they end up hearing the news. Very embarrassed at first, each exercises his resources to find a means of locomotion: some run to omnibuses and others to delivery vans, for it is only the lucky chaps who succeed in grabbing the rare free coaches that circulate on the public road." *La Lanterne* blamed the strike on the CGV but believed that the work stoppage could harm the exposition. It called for an equitable settlement of the conflict. This journal also described an attitude it found among Parisians: "The most curious thing is that Paris seems to have gotten used to traveling on foot; the pedestrians invade the streets, and in the evening they have an air of disdain for the rare coaches which remain at the disposition of the public."[26]

The police seem to have had the most accurate picture of daily life during the strike. Police agents, who traditionally patrolled the Paris streets and public cab stations, were also assigned during the strike to each depot of the CGV.[27] For the most part, they reported, Parisians blamed the CGV and not the coachmen for the strike, faulting the large firm for undernourishing its horses. The public even criticized the Society for the Protection of Animals for constantly taking to task the coachmen, as opposed to the CGV, for maltreating

26. "La Grève des cochers," *L'Union*, August 7, 1878; "La Grève des cochers," *Le Moniteur*, August 7, 1878; *La Lanterne*, August 2, 1878, p. 3, and August 9, 1878, p. 2.

27. For what follows, see APP, B/A 178, reports of Paris, August 6, 1878, no. 174, August 7, 1878, no. 227, August 9, 1878, no. 308, and August 10, 1878, no. 386.

the horses. They demanded that the society inspect the company's stables. Parisians also found the CGV too inflexible and "too absolute" in its negotiations with the strikers, a charge that was true. As for the public's opinion of the strikers, one police report stated that "by their attitude, by their moderation, thanks to the intelligence with which they have presented their claims, the strikers have obtained the sympathy of the entire Parisian population."[28] This opinion must be taken seriously; police agents were not noted for their partiality toward strikers.

Three more observations by the police round out this sampling of the public's attitude toward the striking coachmen. First, beginning on August 7, the CGV began to hire new cabbies as strikebreakers, a tactic that eventually broke the strike. At the same time, this measure reinforced the public's hostility toward the CGV, since the new cabbies were inexperienced and frequently caused accidents on the road. Second, the treatment of the carriage horses became a point of controversy among the CGV, the cabbies, and the public. Typical of the public's sentiment was the way people reacted in an incident involving one of the CGV's new cabbies. As he conducted his coach along the Place du Châtelet, he was whipping his horse. Parisians quickly surrounded the cab, and only the intervention of the police saved the cabbie from the anger of a hostile crowd. The people who witnessed this scene blamed the harsh treatment of the horse on the CGV for hiring such a cabbie.[29]

Third, it is important to note, apropos of public opinion, that the police and many newspapers reported a rumor circulating in Paris that Bonapartists had played a role in the strike.[30] Bonapartists, some argued, urged the coachmen to strike to embarrass the government. Others believed that Bonapartists in the management of the CGV may have inspired the strike. There was even talk that Bonapartists among the police welcomed it. No matter what element of truth these speculations may have, though, they can be dismissed as explanations of the cause of the strike. It is illogical to accuse the CGV of

28. *Ibid.*, report of August 10, 1878, no. 308.

29. See *ibid.*, report of August 10, 1878, no. 386.

30. As an example, see *ibid.*, report of Paris, August 6, 1878, as well as other reports in this carton. See also *La Revue politique et littéraire*, August 17, 1878, pp. 165–66.

promoting a strike during the exposition, for the company stood to lose a great deal from a strike during this busiest cab season in a decade. Nor did the police instigate the strike. Everything we know about the history of the coachmen's corporation points to the adverse conditions under which cabbies labored, to their difficulty in organizing, and to the advantageous conjuncture of the exposition as the fundamental and immediate causes of this strike.

Throughout the strike, the coachmen focused their hopes as well as their hostilities on Maurice Bixio, president of the CGV. His decisions determined the policy of the cab company. Bixio was born in 1836 to a prominent republican family.[31] His father, Alexandre, represented Doubs in the Constituent Assembly and in the Legislative Assembly of 1848. In the latter body, he sided with moderate republicans against the monarchical right. With France under Napoleon III's regime, he left politics for the world of industry and agriculture. An associate of the Pereire brothers, he sat on the boards of the Crédit Foncier de France, the Crédit Foncier d'Italie, Gaz de Paris, and other companies. Earlier he had been a cofounder of the *Revue des deux mondes* and had directed several agricultural reviews, among them the *Journal d'agriculture pratique*, the *Almanach du jardinier*, and *L'Almanach du cultivateur*. When he died in 1865, his son Maurice, who had taken a degree at the École des Mines, took over the direction of the Librairie Agricole, which Alexandre had also founded. Three years later, Maurice Bixio left the Librairie and joined the CGV's board of directors. He became president of the CGV in 1873, a post in which he became famous. Bixio was also a member of the Municipal Council of Paris from 1874 to 1881, representing the sixth arrondissement, and he served on the Voirie de Paris, the commission dealing with the city's roads. The strike made him and others in

31. There exists no biography of this fascinating captain of industry. (I am currently preparing such a study.) Biographical references have been gathered from the following: *Dictionnaire de biographie française* (Paris, 1954), VI, 538 (also contains information about his father Alexandre); Conseil Municipal de Paris, *Listes des membres du Conseil Municipal de Paris de 1871 à 1890* (Paris, 1890); Albert Petrot, *Les Conseillers municipaux de Paris et les conseillers généraux de la Seine* (Paris, 1876); *Bulletin mensuel de l'association amicale des elèves de l'école nationale supérieure des mines* (February, 1906), v–vii. Debra Perry very generously shared her notes on Alexandre Bixio.

his administration unpopular figures with his cabbies and the Parisian public.

Bixio's reactions to the strike were swift and clever. On August 6, he issued the order of the day, to be posted on the walls of all the CGV's depots, appealing "to the good sense and to the patriotism of the coachmen" and inviting "them to resume their work immediately."[32] He pointed out how very embarrassing the strike was for France, coming, as it did, at the moment of the exposition. He blamed the strike on "foreign persons." Several days later, he issued a detailed rebuttal to the strikers' charge that he underfed his horses and housed them badly.[33] Admitting that the accusation had "deeply affected public opinion," he noted in his own defense that his stables represented an enormous capital investment of five million francs and that surely he would protect it properly. The issue of the horse had struck such a deep chord, though, that neither the public nor the press accepted Bixio's studied and thorough response. *Le Rappel*, partial to the strikers, summed up the general Parisian feeling on this subject: "We wish to believe with him [that he fed his horses adequately], but there is an argument more powerful than all rationalizations, and that is the very look of the horses. It is impossible to maintain that they have an air of being healthy and solid. If the food is sufficient then the work is excessive."[34] Bixio had only himself to blame for the public's perception; he once wrote, in his treatise *De l'alimentation des chevaux*, that "considering the horse as an *engine*, it must be subject to ordinary rules of mechanics, that is to say it is necessary to find a means to make him produce *the greatest sum of work possible*, with the *least expense possible.*" Long after this strike was over, Bixio, still sensitive to charges that his firm mistreated its horses, tried to shift the responsibility to the coachmen, pointing out that they paid for extra food for their horses so they could work them harder. He observed that in a typical afternoon a horse worked an average of forty-five kilometers and that the CGV provided enough food for that distance. To earn more, the coachmen worked their

32. APP, B/A 178, report of Paris, August 6, 1878, no. 137. A copy of Bixio's poster is also in this carton.
33. See *Le Rappel*, August 12, 1878, pp. 3–4.
34. *Ibid.*, pp. 1–2. See also APP, B/A 178, report of Paris, August 23, 1878.

horses fifty or fifty-five kilometers and thus were at fault for the animals' ill health.[35]

During the strike, Bixio tried to soften his public image, but he was also resolved to break the strike by hiring new cabbies. On August 6, just one day into the work stoppage, Bixio ordered his depot chiefs to issue temporary cards to any new coachman wishing to work for the CGV. In addition, he told the company to require only a token security deposit from these new cabbies rather than the usual payment of two hundred francs, to assure their rapid integration into the company. When the new cabbies got to work (the CGV accepted five hundred new workers on one day alone), the company closed its eyes to their inadequacies and to the complaints of the public. On August 7, Bixio publicly advertised for new coachmen, publishing the address of each depot where new recruits could report for work.[36]

Bixio's policy succeeded, for general unemployment was then high in Paris. New cabbies, former coachmen, and even horse grooms rushed to fill the vacant posts. As early as the morning of August 8, just three days after the strike had begun, 742 cabs of the CGV were out on the streets of Paris. That figure grew to 1,395 by late afternoon of the same day, to 2,369 by August 9, and to over 3,000 by August 10.[37]

Not only did Bixio establish a strike-breaking policy to assure the rapid conclusion of the strike, but he also took this opportunity to rid the CGV permanently of both politically dangerous and incompetent coachmen. He met with his depot chiefs on August 10, asking them to send to the central administration the dossiers of three types of cabbies: (1) those who regularly did not perform well, (2) those who abused their horses, and (3) those who had expressed decided hostility toward the CGV during the strike. The last category, rather vague in formulation, was probably aimed at strike leaders and their principal supporters. Bixio's policy was effectuated,

35. Maurice Bixio, *De l'alimentation des chevaux dans les grandes écuries industrielles: Cinq ans d'expériences sur une cavalerie de 10,000 chevaux. Rapport adressée au conseil d'administration de la Compagnie Générale des Voitures à Paris* (Paris, 1878), 6–7, emphasis in original; Bixio, *Note adressée à la Commission permanente*, 4–5.

36. APP, B/A 178, reports of Paris, August 6, 1878, and August 9, 1878, no. 305.

37. *Ibid.*, reports of Paris, August 23, 1878, August 8, 1878, nos. 239 and 281, August 9, 1878, no. 245, and August 10, 1878, no. 385.

for when some cabbies began to drift back to work while the strike was still officially in progress, the CGV refused to hire back those it considered dangerous or inadequate, a practice consistent with the company's wish to send a message to the strikebreakers that their new jobs were secure.[38]

The prefecture of police facilitated Bixio's policy of hiring new cabbies. On August 8, the prefect of police attended a meeting of the Paris Municipal Council to explain the policy of the police toward the strike.[39] He reported that the prefecture of police was determined to remain neutral in the conflict. Desiring to protect the "freedom of work," he insisted, the police would keep order in the depots; his agents had also apprehended potential agitators. In particular, he wished to mitigate any inconvenience to the Parisian population and to the foreigners visiting the exposition, he informed the council. For this reason, the prefecture of police was granting, on very easy terms, provisional driving papers to those coachmen capable of handling a horse and cab. The tone and substance of this testimony indicate that the police, contrary to their official position, were hardly neutral during the strike.

On the evening of August 8, 1878, the Chambre Syndicale des Cochers organized a general meeting of the corporation of Parisian coachmen, held at the Cirque Fernando on the boulevard Rochechouart in the eighteenth arrondissement. Approximately four thousand coachmen gathered in and around the circus building, which could accommodate only slightly more than two thousand people.[40] Moderates controlled the meeting. Moritz took charge and outlined an agenda on which debate continued from 9:00 to 11:30 P.M. When the meeting was over, the cabbies had forged five demands. The first, written with an eye toward the Parisian public, was that the CGV improve the feeding and housing of its horses. Second, the cabbies asked that membership in the CGV's mutual aid society be voluntary and that the coachmen themselves be placed in charge. Third,

38. *Ibid.*, reports of Paris, August 11, 1878, nos. 427, 435, and 434.

39. Conseil Municipal de Paris, *Procès-Verbaux*, no. 42, August 8, 1878, pp. 735–37.

40. Reports differ on the number in attendance at this meeting. A median point between three thousand and five thousand has been arrived at from the APP, B/A 178, reports of Paris, August 9, 1878, no. 3000, and August 8, 1878, no. 242.

and this was the major claim, was that cabbies be paid à la planche, with the target fare determined by a panel composed of both cabbies and management. The fourth demand, representing the position of a more militant and politically radical segment of the union, was for a maximum workday of fourteen hours. Finally, the strikers requested two days' rest per month. This claim was not for two days of paid vacation but rather for the right to take two days off per month without being fired.

The meeting passed these demands unanimously, partly because of the police intervention the union's directors had requested. The incident that had precipitated the intervention was indicative of a sharp difference of opinion within the union—a difference that became more pronounced as the century drew to a close. Before the meeting at the Cirque Fernando, the union's leaders, determined to impress the police with their moderation, petitioned them for permission to hold a general meeting "with the aim of conciliation and in effect to shorten as much as possible this strike which is so injurious to the interests of all Paris." The police readily agreed to the meeting and sent "a squad of policemen . . . to maintain order."[41] When debate at the meeting focused on the issue of wages, several partisans of a fixed wage began to disrupt the assembly. Looking to reach consensus quickly, the union's leaders, rather than entertain the position of these coachmen, labeled them troublemakers and asked the police to expel them, which the police did.

Once the union had a consensus, it could move to negotiations, which were central to its tactics. It was financially too weak to remain on strike for a long period of time. Furthermore, other Parisian workers, who did not yet consider cabbies authentic members of the working class, did not actively support the strike. A long strike might also turn the people of Paris against the cabbies. The meeting at the Cirque Fernando, therefore, chose a commission of twenty to talk with the cab owners; seventeen would negotiate with the CGV and three with the independents. All twenty were presumably partisans of travail à la planche. The key negotiations were with the CGV, since it, not the small entrepreneurs, was the focus of the strike. The

41. "La Grève des cochers," *Le Rappel*, August 8, 1878, p. 3, and August 10, 1878, p. 2.

seventeen designated for talks with the CGV gathered the next morning at union headquarters and chose from among themselves a delegation of five to present the union's demands in person at the company's offices. A coachman named Mazuc was president of this delegation. He and his co-delegates met with Bixio at 5 P.M. on August 9. Bixio refused to capitulate to or even compromise on any union demand.[42] The coachmen then requested permission to convene another general meeting of cabbies in the Cirque Fernando to consider the CGV's negative stance.

When the union met again on August 11, an important shift in its position emerged. Mazuc, who chaired the assembly, suggested that in view of the CGV's absolute refusal to consider travail à la planche, the meeting should consider a new set of proposals. After some debate, a new platform was approved, at its core five demands: (1) that the CGV abolish "all the moyennes," (2) that all cabbies work à la feuille, (3) that the workday be limited to fourteen hours, (4) that a basic wage of five francs be established, and (5) that membership in the company's mutual aid society be voluntary. This was the agenda of the minority faction of the union, which had apparently taken the initiative after the setback dealt the first negotiating team. Supporters of travail à la planche disagreed, becoming quite agitated, and the meeting ended in a great deal of commotion and confusion. The press account of the gathering reported that Mazuc restored order by declaring the vote on the new program final and debate terminated.[43] It also noted that Mazuc, who had previously favored travail à la planche, now allied himself with the supporters of travail à la feuille.

There is more behind this shift in position than is contained in the public record. In light of both the union's earlier and its subsequent history, there is no doubt that partisans of travail à la feuille represented a bona fide tradition in the union—a tradition that eventually became dominant in the 1880s. In 1878, however, a shift from moderate to radical is questionable. There is no evidence that those who captured the August 11 meeting were not legitimate strikers or

42. APP, B/A 178, report of Paris, August 9, 1878, pièce 299; "La Grève des cochers," *Le Rappel*, August 11, 1878, pp. 1–2.

43. "La Grève des cochers," *Le Rappel*, August 13, 1878, p. 2.

union members, though a dissident minority, but how they seized control of the meeting is another matter. No information exists on precisely when during the meeting the vote was taken or on whether it reflected a majority opinion. Given the rejection of the union's initial position by Bixio, the vote might have been an accurate gauge of the members' response at that moment. Mazuc's key position as chair of this assembly is certain and provocative. If we read between the lines of the news reports, it does seem that he permitted the radical program to surface and then cut off debate once the vote was recorded. Mazuc's stance is highly suspect, however. The position of the dissidents was consistent, but Mazuc's turnabout was abrupt and dramatic. In addition, he left the public stage after this strike, to reappear only in the 1890s, this time in the owner's camp and as an outspoken foe of the Chambre Syndicale des Cochers. Coachmen suspected after the 1878 strike that someone on their negotiating team, unnamed but clearly Mazuc, had been sabotaging their efforts because he was in the employ of Bixio.[44]

On August 12, a new delegation met once more with Bixio and other officials of the CGV, but Bixio still refused to compromise. By this time his policy of hiring new cabbies had almost succeeded in destroying the strike. He did grant the strikers a few minor concessions, though, to mollify public opinion, which generally favored the strikers.[45] The CGV agreed to suspend application of the moyenne for one month after work was resumed and would thereafter apply this wage system only to those cabbies whose minimum daily earnings were noticeably low.[46] The company also agreed not to charge coachmen for breakdowns of their cabs caused by horses falling on the public road, and it granted coachmen the right to two days' rest per month without pay. It also agreed not to fire any cabbie for participation in the strike. However, Bixio denied a request for a fourteen-hour workday, refused to grant a base pay of five francs,

44. See APP, B/A 178. Mazuc became an occasional contributor to *La Voie publique*, a newspaper representing the employers' interests in the cab trade.

45. This was the view of the police and of most of the Parisian press. See APP, B/A 178, report of Paris, August 23, 1878.

46. For a report on the settlement of the strike, see *ibid.*, as well as the following: *Le Rappel*, August 14, 1878, p. 1; APP, B/A 178, report of Paris, August 13, 1878, pièce 584.

and would not alter the requirement that coachmen must participate in the CGV's mutual aid society. The union leaders knew that Bixio would go no further and that the strike had already been broken by the CGV's new recruits. On the night of August 13, therefore, the union announced that the strike was terminated.[47] Work resumed on August 14.

Bixio's victory was far more decisive than the above terms indicate. In practice, he circumvented his public position on the wage system. Coachmen were initially given the chance to work à la feuille or à la moyenne, but at the end of the month, those working à la feuille who did not meet the CGV's posted target rate were issued a preliminary warning that they were not working efficiently. If they failed to meet the target rate for a second consecutive month, they were fired. Despite his apparent concessions, Bixio had de facto reimposed payment à la moyenne on all his cabbies.[48] Moreover, he blatantly broke his promise not to fire any strikers. On August 14, the day the strikers were to resume work, the CGV issued an order regularizing the employment of the so-called temporary cabbies it had hired during the strike.[49] This order invited all provisionally employed coachmen who wished to remain with the CGV to so advise their respective depot chiefs. The CGV would assist any acceptable coachman in obtaining his coaching papers from the police. As the CGV's directors explained to the company's shareholders, they thus established a pool of excess cabbies from which to draw so as to replace as many strikers as possible.[50] The company wanted to fire as many incompetent cabbies as it could and began almost immediately to fire strike leaders and coachmen it regarded as *mauvais sujets* (bad characters) or drunkards.[51] By its own count, the CGV was eventually able to hire 2,000 new cabbies, more than half its total work

47. See *Le Rappel*, August 15, 1878, p. 1.

48. APP, B/A 178, reports of Paris, August 31, 1878, pièce 584, and August 21, 1878, pièce 570.

49. For a copy of this order, see *ibid.*, August 15, 1878, pièce 567.

50. CGV, *Assemblée générale du 28 avril 1879. Rapport sur l'exercice 1878* (Paris, 1879), 6–7.

51. APP, B/A 178, report of Paris, August 23, 1878, pièce 582. See also *ibid.*, report of Paris, August 14, 1878, pièce 563, and a letter from a fired coachman in *Le Rappel*, August 17, 1878, p. 3.

force of about 3,500 (on the books, as opposed to on the streets on any one day) before the strike.[52]

Some of the reasons for the failure of this coachmen's strike are apparent. The union was split between two opposing points of view and represented only a fraction of all Parisian coachmen.[53] A job shortage and the cooperation of the police supported Bixio's intransigence and his resolve to break the strike; an agent provocateur sabotaged key union negotiations. The small entrepreneurs also contributed to the strike's failure, which is ironic, since they hoped it would succeed. The relationship between the small entrepreneurs and the ordinary coachmen was not only fundamental to the strike but also helped define the state of political consciousness within the corporation at that time.

The small cab entrepreneurs, the majority of whom owned no more than ten cabs, favored a strike against the CGV, for they would be its major beneficiaries.[54] Since the CGV operated approximately half the cabs circulating in Paris, a strike of its cabbies would force the Parisian populace and visitors to the exposition to use public omnibuses and trams, voitures sous remise, and the cabs of the small firms. If the coachmen of the smaller cab firms were poorly paid, they might strike, too, but the small firms tended to be more solicitous of their employees than the large cab companies were. After the conflict Joseph Godefroy reflected on the difference in treatment: "Many small entrepreneurs acted with more or less good conscience. The coachmen of these entrepreneurs have not followed those of the Company [CGV], because they have not had serious enough griev-

---

52. CGV, *Assemblée générale du 28 avril 1879*, 6–7.

53. In 1878, 3,539 new coachmen registered to drive in Paris, as compared to 2,419 the previous year. Moreover, in 1878 there were 48,310 coachmen registered to drive, though probably less than half were really active. See Préfecture de la Seine, *Annuaire statistique* (Paris, 1882), 639.

54. There are no accurate data on the number of independents and their holdings for this period. Statistics are available for later periods, however, and there is no reason to believe that the structure of this part of the cab trade changed radically over the last part of the nineteenth century. Anne Boudou has studied a small sample of independents for the period 1898–1914 and estimates that 54 percent had less than ten cabs; see Boudou, "Les Taxis parisiens," 242–43. On the subject of their favoring the strike, see APP, B/A 178, reports of Paris, March 30, 1878, no. 2, and August 23, 1878.

ances to leave the voitures sous remise." Conducting the voiture sous remise was also a more pleasant and prestigious assignment; the vehicle was generally cleaner than an ordinary cab and the working conditions better. The small firms hired out ordinary cabs as well, but the bulk of their trade was in the larger cab. The police noted that these firms generally recognized that their coachmen were entitled to a better salary during the exposition and for the most part had granted wage increases.[55]

No doubt such an attitude was due in part to their small scale. In these companies coachmen and owners knew each other personally. However, in being good to their cabbies, the small companies were not merely being magnanimous or expressing fraternal and corporate values. On the contrary, they had devised clever strategies that simultaneously satisfied most of their coachmen, augmented their profits, and enabled them to take advantage of the 1878 strike. The key to their success was not just that they augmented their coachmen's salaries but that they did so in a manner that manipulated most of their cabbies into remaining basically satisfied. A typical example was the firm of Brion et Cie, which employed 150 coachmen.[56] On April 29, 1878, 49 of Brion's coachmen petitioned the owner for higher wages; they asked for 250 francs per month for coachmen of regular cabs and a franc overtime for each hour of work after midnight. They demanded an answer to their demands by May 1. He responded immediately, taking several measures simultaneously. Having learned that a coachman named Gosjean engineered the petition, Brion fired him at once. He also took advantage of the moment, firing seven other signatories because they were poor coachmen. At the same time, he raised the wages of the remainder of his cabbies, though not to the level they had requested. The wage increase, concurrent with the firings, convinced the remaining coachmen to continue working.

Other small cab operators responded with similar tactics. The coachmen of Chez M. Paul, at 67, rue Croix-Nivert in the fifteenth arrondissement, complained that their moyenne was too high. Paul

55. Godefroy, in *Le Fouet*, June 30, 1878, pp. 2–3; APP, B/A 178, reports of Paris, May 4, 1878, no. 4, and August 23, 1878.

56. For the incident described, see APP, B/A 178, reports of Paris, April 29, 1878, May 3, 1878, and May 4, 1878, no. 1.

closed his depot for two days, fired and replaced his worst cabbies, and reopened without incident. When the cabbies of Lanquet, père et fils, at 49, rue de la Chausée d'Antin in the ninth arrondissement, asked for higher wages, the owners rejected their demands but agreed to give a bonus of 100 francs for August (the month of the exposition) to good and loyal coachmen. They fired the three who had organized the request for higher wages. Some small cab operators used subtler tactics. M. Bordier of 16, rue de la Tours-des-Dames, also in the ninth arrondissement, employed 30 coachmen. As the time for the exposition approached, he promised his cabbies exemption from the payment of accident insurance and a bonus of 10 francs per month during the period of the exposition. He did not have to fire anyone. Some small cab operators negotiated with their contract clients to pay higher fees and then passed the increment along to their coachmen. Other small owners bought social peace. On May 1, the eve of the exposition, M. Chretien, loueur, located at 22, rue Bayard in the eighth arrondissement, began paying his coachmen 10 francs per day. Generally speaking, throughout the cab trade the coachmen of the voitures sous remise were relatively satisfied, since their pay normally ranged from 250 to 500 francs a month.[57]

A final reason for the continued operation of small cab firms during the strike was that the Chambre Syndicale des Cochers did not mount any strike action against them. The major enemy in the union's eyes was the giant capitalist firm, in this instance the CGV. The small cab firms were in complete agreement. Moreover, their trade association, the Chambre Syndicale des Loueurs de Voitures de Place de Paris, publicly supported the coachmen against the CGV with petitions to the police and to the Municipal Council but not by a sympathy strike.[58] This action, or lack of it, was crucial to the outcome since the small cab firms provided Parisians with an alternative source of transportation. Other transportation workers, including those in public mass transport, did not actively support the strikers

57. Ibid., reports of Paris, May 18, 1878, no. 26, May 4, 1878, no. 1, May 6, 1878, no. 7, May 4, 1878, no. 4.
58. See Le Rappel, August 14, 1878, p. 4; APP, D/B 505, petition, A messieurs les conseillers municipaux (Paris, September 10, 1878); APP, B/A 178, reports of Paris, August 4, 1878, no. 15, August 5, 1878, no. 16, and August 6, 1878, no. 148.

either, helping to doom the action to failure. Had there not been these alternative modes of transportation, greater pressure would have been exerted on Bixio and the CGV to give in to the demands of the striking cabbies.

The strike of Parisian coachmen during the 1889 exposition differed from the 1878 one in several ways. Most important, the Chambre Syndicale des Cochers comported itself more like a classic workers union. Its sharply defined working-class outlook was evident in its initial demands and in the nature of those to whom it made them.

The 1889 Universal Exposition officially opened on May 5. The coachmen's strike broke out on June 12, but the union had begun to prepare for it long before. In January, 1889, the Chambre Syndicale des Cochers had met and formulated two basic claims for presentation to the cab firms. It demanded recognition of the principle that ordinary coachmen should receive a fixed salary for a determined number of hours of work. Specifically, the union asked for a straight wage of 7 francs for a twelve-hour workday.[59] There was no rhetoric this time about sharing in a percentage of the cab's receipts as in the last strike. The union was now firm in its belief that a coachman was like any other Parisian worker and should be treated as such by his employers.[60]

Equally important, the Chambre Syndicale des Cochers presented its demands to small as well as large cab companies. Gone was any talk about common values and mutuality of interests within the corporation of Parisian coachmen. Once the union had formulated its position, it named a commission of eleven members to contact all cab companies and loueurs "and force them to declare whether they have decided, yes or no, to do right by the just demands of the union." The negotiating team paid separate visits to Bixio, to H. de Lamonta, president of the CGV's largest competitor, the Urbaine, and to the trade association of the small entrepreneurs. In its preparations for the strike, the Chambre Syndicale des Cochers was fully aware that, in contrast to the last strike, "*the companies and the entre-*

59. "Les Cochers de fiacres," *La Lanterne*, February 11, 1889.

60. The newspaper *La Lanterne* warned that a strike would break out if these claims were not met by cab firms; see *ibid.*

*preneurs* [were] going to demand [as a moyenne] the fabulous sums of 25 to 30 francs a day."[61] The small entrepreneurs banded together with the large companies; Bixio, de Lamonta, and Camille, president of the Chambre Syndicale des Loueurs, all took a united stance and negotiated in common.[62] The press reported that "the coachmen have voted the strictest agreement among the members of the union *against certain entrepreneurs* that they accuse of wanting to cause a strike."[63]

An exception to this clear perception of class interests was the cooperative society. The data on its role in this strike, though minuscule, permit some conclusions to be drawn.[64] One journal noted that the eleven-member commission of the Chambre Syndicale des Cochers did not present its demands to cooperative societies. There are no figures on the number of cooperative coachmen, but if these cabbies continued to operate, they could only weaken the force of the strike. The same journal provided a partial explanation for the commission's failure to contact the cooperatives. Members of cooperatives, it wrote, were "owners of horses and equipment, they are responsible vis-à-vis themselves for the use of their day." Another newspaper, *Le Petit National*, explained matters a little differently: members of cooperative societies are "at the same time owners and employees."[65] As basically owners, then, the cooperative coachmen did not strike in June, nor did the Chambre Syndicale des Cochers ask them to do so. The union could not readily place the cooperative cabbies in the same category with those who hired other coachmen. They were like any other hard-working coachmen, since they drove cabs themselves, but as owners they would only harm their own interests if they struck. Thus, the Chambre Syndicale des Cochers left them alone. For their part, the cooperative cabbies welcomed the

61. "Le Travail," *Le Rappel*, February 7, 1889, p. 3, February 15, 1889, p. 4; "Les Cochers," *ibid.*, May 6, 1889, p. 3, emphasis added.

62. See *Le XIXe Siècle*, June 15, 1889.

63. "Réunion générale des cochers," *Le Rappel*, April 7, 1889, p. 2, emphasis added.

64. See *Loir*, February 9, 1889; F. Serizier, "Une Grève à l'horizon," *Le Petit National*, February 10, 1889; and APP, B/A 179, report of Paris, June 14, 1889, pièce 537.

65. *Loir*, February 9, 1889; Serizier, "Une Grève à l'horizon."

June strike because they stood to gain so much extra business from the exposition.

During the days preceding the June 12 strike, the language coming out of the Chambre Syndicale des Cochers was more forceful than in the last strike. The exposition was to be a celebration of the French Revolution of 1789, and the union played on this theme in an open letter to the president of the Republic, Sadi Carnot.[66] Stating that while France was celebrating the anniversary of the French Revolution, the cochers des voitures de place were "still deprived of the common law and treated as outsiders from the moral and material point of view," the union petitioned President Carnot to use the celebrations as the occasion to eliminate all traces of tyranny, to suppress the dreaded mise à pied, and to guarantee "that the coachman has his livelihood assured while working." Other public declarations were more strident. In February, the union declared that "it is necessary to leave this frightful misery that tortures us, demolish this citadel [of exploitation], recall what our ancestors did in '89, and we shall celebrate with dignity this anniversary with our deliverance." Carrière, secretary of the union, indicated that he did not eschew the "spirit of conciliation," but he warned of "serious consequences" if reforms were not forthcoming.[67]

Not only did the union use stronger language than it had before, but it also had more contact with other Parisian workers. When Cyprien Ribanier, secretary of the Paris Bourse du Travail, learned that the Chambre Syndicale des Cochers wanted to organize a major meeting in March, 1889, he informed the union that the *grande salle de réunion* in the Bourse headquarters was available to it. Although this meeting eventually took place in the Salle Wagram, the Chambre Syndicale des Cochers did hold many of its smaller deliberations in the Bourse du Travail's building. Other Parisian workers' groups actively sided with the coachmen's union. A week before the strike began, the FNS encouraged the coachmen "to persevere with the greatest energy for their just claims"; it would "aid and assist them in the triumph of their cause." Unfortunately for the coachmen, a key group of Parisian workers did not cooperate with them, which

66. See "Les Cochers," *Le Rappel*, May 6, 1889, p. 3.
67. *Ibid.*, February 23, 1889, p. 3, and March 15, 1889, p. 4.

weakened the force of the 1889 strike. The omnibus coachmen's union refused to support the coachmen's strike, thus ensuring that Parisians again had a major alternative means of transportation during an exposition.[68] Cooperation among all public transportation workers in Paris came about only later, with the organization of a general transportation federation.

The Paris Universal Exposition of 1889 officially opened on May 5, the anniversary of the first meeting of the Estates General in 1789. Before it was over, the exposition would attract over twenty-four million visitors to Paris.[69] Coachmen were once more preparing to tie up Paris traffic to obtain their goals. On March 16, the Chambre Syndicale des Cochers had held a meeting in the Salle Wagram to add another demand to its initial claims: it wanted the coachmen to have a seat on the Commission d'Examen, the body within the cab industry that oversaw coachmen's examinations and generally acted as a watchdog over the cab trade. According to the union, the cabbie on the Commission d'Examen should also "become part of the Commission of the mise à pied, while waiting for the suppression of the latter." It asked that "the corporation of coachmen be permitted to profit from the jurisdiction of arbitration councils in the same measure as other workers' corporations" and, too, that the Municipal Council formally serve as an arbitration council between cabbies and owners.[70] At this stage in its preparations for a strike, the union said nothing about the level of the moyenne, for the exposition had not opened yet, and few companies had begun raising their daily target fares.

As in the last strike, rank-and-file cabbies did not wait for a signal from the Chambre Syndicale des Cochers to strike. In early March, coachmen working for the Compagnie Urbaine and the Compagnie Métropolitaine, another large cab firm, spontaneously walked off their jobs, though only briefly. The men of the Urbaine knew that the cabbies of the CGV were expected to bring in daily fares of fif-

68. APP, B/A 179, report of Paris, February 20, 1889, pièce 344; L'Intransigeant, June 13, 1889; APP, B/A 179, report of Paris, June 23, 1889, pièce 700.

69. Gazette des cochers et des gens de maison: Journal professionnel des serviteurs des deux sexes, April 13, 1890, p. 2.

70. "Le Travail," Le Rappel, March 19, 1889, p. 3. See also ibid., March 17, 1889, p. 3, for a copy of the poster announcing the March 16 meeting.

teen to sixteen francs in March. Consequently, when the Urbaine announced a moyenne of sixteen francs, seventy-five centimes on March 6, some one hundred coachmen from one of the company's depots refused to take their cabs out.[71] The strike ended the following day when the company lowered the moyenne by a franc.[72] Similar events were responsible for a one-day walkout by the cabbies of the Métropolitaine on March 7.[73]

These early outbreaks are significant for two reasons. First, while the Chambre Syndicale des Cochers was busy defining issues along one avenue, rank-and-file cabbies imposed their own different, but pressing, needs on union leaders. The immediate concern of the coachmen was the level of the moyenne. Second, these spontaneous walkouts portended an open break between the union's leaders and the insurgents within the corporation over control of the strike during the exposition. Both themes were present in the crucial events of June 12, 13, and 14.

On June 12, 1889, the Chambre Syndicale des Cochers invited all Parisian coachmen to a public meeting that evening in the Salle Wagram. According to the police, six thousand people attended the meeting.[74] The union's leaders hoped the gathering would arrive at a common resolution they could present to the owners, demands they would be prepared to back up with a strike. By the end of the evening, though, events had gotten away from them. At first, the assembly provided what the leaders wanted: it unanimously passed a resolution incorporating the union's current position. It demanded from public authorities and employers the suppression of the mise à pied, the presence of a union coachman on the Commission d'Examen and on the Commission de Discipline (the body that tried coachmen for violations of public ordinances), and a twelve-hour workday at seven francs.[75] The assembly also agreed to petition the

71. *Paris*, March 8, 1889.

72. APP, B/A 179, report of Paris, March 7, 1889, pièce 354. See also *ibid.*, report of Paris, March 6, 1889, pièce 345, and *L'Intransigeant*, March 12, 1889.

73. See "Le Travail," *Le Rappel*, March 9, 1889, p. 3, and March 10, 1889, p. 3. See also *L'Intransigeant*, March 10, 1889, and APP, B/A 179, reports of Paris, March 7, 1889, pièce 356, and March 8, 1889, pièce 358.

74. APP, B/A 179, report of Paris, June 13, 1889, pièce 499.

75. This meeting was covered in much of the Parisian press as well as by the

Paris Municipal Council to refuse a parking permit to any company that did not accept the above claims. Finally, the coachmen warned that they would refuse to work for more than twelve hours a day or for less than seven francs, a statement intended as a threat to strike. The Chambre Syndicale des Cochers, however, preferred to negotiate and to strike only if the public authorities and the cab companies rejected its demands. This position was challenged by the rank-and-file at the meeting, who vociferously demanded a strike the following day; they were quieted only when union officials capitulated somewhat and agreed to a peaceful demonstration on June 13.[76]

During the next day, the divergence in aims and tactics between the union leaders and the strikers became very evident.[77] At 10 A.M. on June 13, a delegation consisting of a deputy (Basly) and three municipal councillors (Daumas, Longuet, and Chauvier) visited Minister of the Interior Ernest Constans to present the case for the coachmen, including the claims passed the evening before. Constans, expressing his sympathy with the plight of the cabbies, agreed to meet with a delegation of coachmen later that afternoon, but he denied the request for a large public demonstration, fearing it would disrupt the exposition. That same morning, despite a union policy of negotiation first, cabbies were already refusing to report for work. By early afternoon, the spontaneous walkout against the large cab companies was nearly total. Union secretary Carrière admitted that "the strike broke out accidentally against the will of the union."[78]

The union delegation met again with Constans in the late afternoon of June 13. Adopting a conciliatory stance, the minister steered the discussion toward the issue of the moyenne, indicating that cab

---

police. See, for example, *La Petite République*, June 14, 1889, for a copy of the resolution presented to the meeting; *Le Gaulois*, June 13, 1889, for the outcome; and "La Réunion des cochers," *Le Rappel*, June 14, 1889, p. 2, and APP, B/A 179, report of Paris, June 13, 1889, pièce 499, for a summary of the meeting.

76. APP, B/A 179, report of Paris, June 13, 1889, pièce 499, and *Le Petit Journal*, June 14, 1889.

77. The events that follow are covered very thoroughly in the following: "Les Cochers," *Le Rappel*, June 15, 1889, pp. 1–2; *Paris*, June 14, 1889; *Le Matin*, June 14, 1889; and APP, B/A 179, report of Paris, June 13, 1889, pièce 464. Sources are cited individually here only if they present special information; otherwise, the account given is a synthesis of them all.

78. See "Le Travail," *Le Rappel*, June 22, 1889, p. 3.

owners might lower it somewhat. The cabbie representatives wanted a guaranteed wage.[79] Neither the owners nor the minister, who was perfectly aware that most strikers were more concerned with the moyenne than with a fixed wage, was prepared to consider this last request, however. The meeting concluded with an agreement to continue the talks on the following day.

On June 14, the leaders of the Chambre Syndicale des Cochers met with the owners, represented by Bixio, de Lamonta, and Camille.[80] The union delegation, now taking into account rank-and-file sentiment, asked for fixed wages and limited hours but also for a maximum moyenne of twenty francs per day during the period of the exposition. The union leaders had asked the cabbies to suspend their strike while negotiations were in progress, but the strikers continued their protest, demanding one specific reform.[81] They would agree to end the strike if the owners fixed the moyenne at twenty francs while the exposition continued; the coachmen refused to discuss fixed wages and fixed hours. Knowing the coachmen's disposition, the owners rejected union claims for fixed wages and a shorter workday but said nothing about the moyenne. An impasse was reached, broken only when the Paris Municipal Council, wanting a successful exposition and social peace, decreed on June 17 that any cab firm fixing a moyenne above twenty francs as of July 1 would lose its rights to public parking.

In principle, the strikers had obtained the relief they wanted, though not what the Chambre Syndicale des Cochers had hoped for. Worse, the owners frequently ignored the Municipal Council's order. In a real sense, the strike was a double failure: it did not realistically reduce the moyenne nor did it win a fixed wage and fixed hours.

Like the strike of 1878, this one had failed, too. The difference lay in the clear perception by the leadership of the Chambre Syndicale des Cochers in 1889 that its interests were fundamentally at odds

79. *Le Matin*, June 14, 1889, provides an excellent summary of this afternoon meeting.

80. The events of this day are covered in the Parisian press, most notably in "La Grève des cochers," *Le XIXe Siècle*, June 15, 1889, in "Les Cochers," *Le Rappel*, June 16, 1889, p. 2, and by the police, most notably in APP, B/A 179, reports of Paris, June 15, 1889, pièces 607 and 608.

81. *Le Matin*, June 14, 1889.

with those of the men with enough capital to own cabs and to hire drivers to conduct them. Small and large cab companies alike were foes. Only the cooperative coachmen who operated their own cabs escaped this antagonism.

If the Chambre Syndicale des Cochers had become relatively class conscious and proworker by 1889, why did its leadership appear moderate? The paradox is resolved when we see that the union's moderate stance was only tactical. Its leaders were behaving in a classic trade-union fashion. They used the threat of a strike in their negotiations, but they feared and resented any strike action not under their direction or control. The union's claims, however, were not at all moderate; they were presented from a working-class perspective. Its leaders believed that coachmen were like any other Parisian workers, albeit in the service sector of the economy, and ought to receive a fixed salary for a determined number of hours of work. The strikers themselves, ironically, did not fully share this vision. They were extremely forceful but only because a high moyenne would, at the least, reduce their wages and would prevent them from reaping the benefits of the exposition's large crowds. They were quite willing to work long hours to earn extra money for themselves. The strikers thus played into the hands of the owners by accepting the owners' wage system.

The union leaders and many of its members (there is no way to determine how many strikers belonged to the union and supported its claims) had a fairly clear vision of themselves as members of the working class. Only the owner-operator of the single cab remained a stumbling block to the union's total antipathy toward capitalists. The small cab firms, who had dropped efforts to collaborate and any pretense that they wished to cooperate with unionized cabbies, would do whatever was necessary to defend their private property. Between the union members and the cab firms stood the unorganized coachmen who were, for whatever reason, averse to joining a workers' union. The strike of 1889 crystallized class division in the cab trade, but it also exposed a lingering ambivalence. All those who drove cabs were not classic workers. Coachmen's cooperatives and the aspiration of many unorganized cabbies to own their own cabs or to share in the cab's receipts, especially during an event such as an exposition, proved fatal to the development of a clear political and class consciousness in the cab trade.

# 7 — COACHMEN AND THE AUTOMOBILE

In Europe and America the decade of the 1880s witnessed, on the part of many enterprising engineers and inventors, an intense preoccupation with efforts to devise an effective mechanical means of replacing animal power for vehicles of all types.[1] There were many successes before the century was over, and by the 1890s, a transformation of the entire cab industry had begun. It was apparent to most people by 1907 that the days of the horse-drawn vehicle were numbered; existing cab companies would soon be converting all their stock to mechanical methods of power. New cab companies bypassed the horse completely. The coachman's days were numbered as well. Although the name *cocher* would survive into the automobile era (the CGT cab driver's union still retains "cocher" alongside "chauffeur" in its name), the trade itself would virtually disappear. What happened to the coachmen and how they coped with the automobile era are the subjects of this last chapter.

Many international efforts fueled the automobile revolution. In Germany, Karl Benz finished building a gasoline-driven tricycle in January, 1886; the Peugeot hardware firm built its first steam tricycles in 1889. Several gasoline and steam engines were on display at

---

1. See James M. Laux, *In First Gear: the French Automobile Industry to 1914* (Montreal, 1976), and Patrick Fridenson, *Histoire des usines Renault* (Paris, 1972).

the Paris Universal Exposition of 1889. Émile Levassor finished his first motorcar in September, 1890. In 1892, the firm of Panhard and Levassor published what is believed to have been the first catalog offering motorcars. They sold 16 automobiles in that year and 37 in 1893. Peugeot produced 29 automobiles in 1892 and 24 in 1893, but automobiles were still a sideline for these manufacturers. Peugeot, for example, constructed 8,000 bicycles in 1892. Moreover, it was not evident in the early 1890s whether the gasoline or the steam engine would power the motor cab of the future. It was not until the middle of the 1890s, when gasoline-powered cars decisively surpassed steam models in some well-publicized automobile races, that the gasoline engine began significantly to outpace the steam engine.

Even when technical problems concerning the engine's efficiency began to be solved and more motorcars began being built, these vehicles were used not for transportation but primarily for sport or as playthings for the rich. Motorcar racing was especially popular at the turn of the century. According to James Laux, these uses of the automobile eclipsed any utilitarian function until about 1905.[2]

Cab entrepreneurs quickly recognized the advantage of the motorized vehicles. In 1896, the first *fiacre automobile*, or motor cab, began to circulate on the streets of Paris.[3] This vehicle was the idea of a horse-drawn-cab driver, one Monsieur Biguet, who worked with a cab manufacturer and the Association of Cab-Makers to produce a motor cab. It was in the style of a landaulet. Its length was three meters, compared to the five meters that made up the length of a horse-drawn cab with its horse. The motor cab's interior was designed primarily for two people, but it could accommodate a third person on a retractable seat in front of the main seat. Without the third passenger, the interior of the landaulet was large and comfortable enough for clients to stretch out their legs. The motor, whose power was equivalent to the power of five horses, was fueled by gasoline. The cab's speed varied from a minimum of ten to twelve kilometers per hour to a maximum of twenty-two to twenty-four. The total weight of the cab was nine hundred kilograms, or just under two thousand pounds.

2. Laux, *In First Gear*, 21.
3. For what follows on this vehicle, see "Le Premier Fiacre Automobile à Paris," *La Nature: Revue des sciences*, December 5, 1896, pp. 1–2.

Paris soon saw a second motor cab on its streets, and a Société de Fiacres Automobiles to produce auto-taxis was forming in Bordeaux. By the end of 1896, the Société Anonyme Française de Fiacres Automobiles was planning to produce a substantial number of motor cabs for use in the capital. In light of these activities, one reporter came to this conclusion: "[We] are taking part in an evolution whose importance cannot be predicted. Paris shall always remain the classic paradise, but it shall cease being a horse's hell: we can only applaud this humanitarian progress and wish all success to the first motor cab."[4]

The largest cab company in Paris, the CGV, recognized the value of motorized cabs. Maurice Bixio, president of the firm from 1873 to 1905, announced to his shareholders in 1897 that he wished to replace animal power with *la traction méchanique*. The CGV had been studying the question for over a year, and Bixio reported that automobilism "is currently the most important question of the day in our industry; it is the major subject of our work, our studies and our assiduous research."[5] He predicted that the introduction of the motorcar would be as significant as the coming of the railway in an earlier epoch.

Although Bixio was committed to adopting the automobile as a cab, he was not certain whether its engine should be powered by electricity or by gasoline. Electrically powered streetcars were being introduced in the 1880s in Germany and in the United States. Even though they were heavy and costly, they created a strong interest in electric propulsion between 1897 and 1900, particularly for cabs. Electric cabs were quiet, easy to operate, and relatively safe compared to those driven by gasoline or steam. Bixio's initial preference in 1897 was for electricity. Two years later, on April 2, 1899, the CGV put the first 6 electrically powered fiacres automobiles onto the streets of Paris as a test of their feasibility. The experiment failed. In 1899, a French electrically powered cab weighed five thousand pounds, too great a weight for the pneumatic tires of the day. Without better tires, the batteries storing the electricity would suffer too many shocks to last for an extended period of time. Electric cabs, moreover, needed frequent recharging, and this process proved to be

4. *Ibid.*, 2.
5. CGV, *Assemblée générale . . . du 26 avril 1897* (Paris, 1897), 25–30.

expensive and inefficient. So the CGV changed to a gasoline engine, a modification started under Bixio's administration and completed by Edouard Jéramec, Bixio's successor.[6]

In July, 1907, the CGV put into circulation the first new gasoline-powered automobile with its own colors. By the end of 1909, it had 500 gasoline-driven motor cabs circulating in Paris. Close to 4,000 auto-taxis belonging to other companies were also on the streets of Paris in 1909. Although concerned with the competition, Jéramec was impressed with the "enormous and rapid development [of] this exploitation."[7] By 1911, the CGV had 1,200 auto-taxis doing business in Paris and 400 more under construction, but it still had 3,500 *voitures hippomobiles*, or horse-drawn vehicles. In contrast, a company founded in 1902, the Compagnie Française des Automobiles de Place, also known as G7, already had 2,500 *automobiles de place* in circulation.[8] The automobile revolution was well under way in the cab industry.

The overall statistics for cabs in Paris provided by the *Annuaire statistique* indicate a dramatic shift in the relationship between the numbers of horse-drawn cabs and of motor cabs beginning in 1907. Table 28 demonstrates the changes from 1900 to 1914. I include in this table totals for only the second-class voitures de place, the basic Parisian cab, but combine, as does the *Annuaire statistique*, totals for all types of motor cabs. The steep decline in the number of horse-drawn and motor cabs in 1914, the first year of World War I, was to due to the army's requisition of horses and motor vehicles for its use.[9] During the war years, though, the cab industry was able gradu-

6. *Ibid.*, 28–29; CGV, *Assemblée générale . . . du 30 avril 1898* (Paris, 1898), 3–5; Laux, *In First Gear*, 90–94; CGV, *Assemblée générale . . . du 29 avril 1907* (Paris, 1907), 20.

7. CGV, *Assemblée générale . . . du 28 avril 1908* (Paris, 1908), 23; CGV, *Assemblée générale . . . du 29 avril 1910* (Paris, 1910), 22; Mareschal, *Les Voitures de place*, 32 n. 11. Préfecture de la Seine, *Annuaire statistique* for 1906, p. 375, and for 1909, p. 382, give slightly higher totals for auto-taxis in Paris, 974 and 5,037, respectively, than the CGV provides. In any case, the percentage increase of auto-taxis from 1906 to 1909 is very large: 500 percent using the CGV's figures and 416 percent using the data of the *Annuaire statistique*.

8. Boudou, "Les Taxis parisiens," 293; Laneyrie, *Le Taxi dans la ville*, 28.

9. Because of the war, the CGV's cavalry was reduced from 7,671 to 3,114 horses. See CGV, *Assemblée générale annuelle du 29 avril 1915. Rapport . . . l'exercice 1914* (Paris, 1914), 6–7.

TABLE 28
Horse-drawn Cabs and Motor Cabs in Paris, 1900–1914

| Year | Total number of second-class voitures de place | | | Total number of automobiles (first and second class and de grande remise) | | |
|---|---|---|---|---|---|---|
| | Cabs | Absolute change | Percentage change | Cabs | Absolute change | Percentage change |
| 1900 | 11,097 | | | 115 | | |
| 1901 | 10,455 | −642 | −5.8 | 127 | +12 | +10.43 |
| 1902 | 10,424 | −31 | −0.3 | 189 | +62 | +48.81 |
| 1903 | 10,333 | −91 | −0.9 | 277 | +88 | +46.50 |
| 1904 | 10,123 | −210 | −2.1 | 369 | +92 | +33.21 |
| 1905 | 9,995 | −128 | −1.3 | 546 | +177 | +47.97 |
| 1906 | 9,911 | −84 | −0.8 | 974 | +433 | +79.30 |
| 1907 | 9,608 | −303 | −3.2 | 2,359 | +1,385 | +142.20 |
| 1908 | 8,784 | −824 | −9.4 | 3,916 | +1,557 | +66.00 |
| 1909 | 8,006 | −778 | −9.7 | 5,037 | +1,121 | +28.63 |
| 1910 | 7,426 | −580 | −7.8 | 7,374 | +2,337 | +46.40 |
| 1911 | 6,162 | −1,264 | −20.5 | 8,266 | +892 | +12.10 |
| 1912 | 5,252 | −910 | −17.3 | 9,315 | +1,049 | +12.69 |
| 1913 | 4,302 | −950 | −22.1 | 10,002 | +687 | +7.38 |
| 1914 | 3,152 | −1,150 | −36.5 | 6,333 | −3,669 | −36.68 |

ırce: Préfecture de la Seine, "Voitures publiques," in *Annuaire statistique* (Paris, 1900–14).

ally to increase its material stock. In 1915 there were 6,712 motor cabs on Parisian streets, but only 2,939 were horse-drawn. In the next three years, the same trends continued, with auto-taxis on the rise and horse-drawn carriages declining: in 1916, there were 7,579 motor cabs and 2,640 horse-drawn cabs; in 1917, 7,808 motor cabs and 2,273 horse-drawn cabs; and in 1918, 8,163 motor cabs and 1,249 horse-drawn cabs. By 1919, out of 14,651 public cabs circulating in Paris only 1,144 were drawn by horses.[10]

Data are not available on the vital question of how many coachmen wanted and were able to make the transition to motor cabs. The *Annuaire statistique* merely records the number of horse-drawn and motor cabs for each year. Nor is there information in the ACGV to indicate what proportion of the company's coachmen became motor-cab conductors. The demise of the coachman's trade must therefore be grasped somewhat impressionistically.

10. Préfecture de la Seine, *Annuaire statistique* (1915–18), 521; *ibid.* (1919), 340.

With the advent of the automobile and the phasing out of horse-drawn coaches, an enterprise like the CGV naturally turned its attention to training motor-cab conductors. The CGV established its own *école d'apprentissage* to train automobile drivers and in 1898 already had 220 coachmen enrolled.[11] In 1900, it reported to its shareholders that it established the école d'apprentissage because it had decided "that the personnel of conductors shall be taken exclusively from among [its] coachmen." The CGV maintained this policy for almost a decade, believing that its coachmen had a superior knowledge of Paris and that when they mastered the operations of the motor cab they would "secure satisfactory professional qualities."[12] The company was also convinced that its coachmen had an active interest in becoming motor-cab conductors.[13]

From the outset, however, the CGV encountered difficulties in training automobile conductors. In 1899, when the company was experimenting with electrically powered cabs, it issued an internal memorandum on the status of its automobile operation.[14] A major part of the report was devoted to the progress its coachmen were making in learning how to conduct the new automobile. From one sample of 43 "coachmen," the name the firm still called its conductors, the CGV concluded that twenty-five practice trips were the minimum necesary to constitute a novice driver. At least one hundred trips were needed for the coachman to develop into a competent driver. The report also noted that the largest number of cabbies, 29, averaged from five to twenty breakdowns per one hundred trips—breakdowns blamed on the conductor's lack of experience in maintaining the automobile, especially its batteries.

How many of the CGV's coachmen who attempted to learn the art of conducting an automobile actually passed into the ranks of the

11. See CGV, *Assemblée générale . . . du 29 avril 1899* (Paris, 1899), 30–31.

12. CGV, *Assemblée générale . . . du 28 avril 1900* (Paris, 1900), 28–32; CGV, *Assemblée générale . . . du 29 avril 1909* (Paris, 1909), 26; and CGV, *Assemblée générale . . . du 28 avril 1908* (Paris, 1908), 25.

13. ACGV, CGV, *Conseil*, reg. no. 8, May 25, 1906, p. 2807, and July 20, 1906, p. 2817; *Comité*, reg. no. 15, May 25, 1906, p. 6052. For the terms for admission to the école d'apprentissage, see ACGV, CGV, *Conseil*, reg. no. 8, January 10, 1908, p. 2877.

14. "Rapport sur l'exploitation des voitures automobiles pendant l'année 1899," *Annexes aux Procès-Verbaux du conseil* (Ms in ACGV), 145–47.

TABLE 29
CGV Coachmen in the Automobile Training Program, 1899

| Number of trips per cab | Number of cabbies entering auto service | Number of cabbies remaining by December 31, 1900 | Total number of trips | Total number of breakdowns | Ratio of breakdowns to total number of trips (expressed as a percentage) |
|---|---|---|---|---|---|
| 200–238 | 5 | 4 | 1,136 | 130 | 11.4 |
| 150–199 | 10 | 7 | 1,781 | 285 | 16.0 |
| 100–149 | 8 | 5 | 1,084 | 135 | 12.4 |
| 50–99 | 10 | 1 | 586 | 193 | 22.3 |
| 25–49 | 10 | 3 | 362 | 103 | 28.4 |
| 10–24 | 20 | 6 | 325 | 54 | 17.0 |
| 0–9 | 53 | 5 | 158 | 41 | 26.0 |

Source: CGV, "Rapport sur l'exploitation des voitures automobiles pendant l'année 1899," *Annexes au procès-verbaux du conseil* (MS in ACGV), 147.

conductors? The CGV memorandum disclosed that 116 coachmen were in its automobile training program during 1899. The memorandum included a chart, reproduced here as Table 29, detailing the number of trips per automobile each coachman made, the number of coachmen who successfully completed the automobile apprenticeship program, the number of coachmen who remained in the automobile program, the aggregate number of trips these coachmen took, and the relationship of the number of trips to the number of breakdowns.

The CGV concluded "many coachmen become disgusted very quickly with automobile cabs, since 48 coachmen have handed in their resignations before making ten trips." We also learn from the report that only 31 of the 116 coachmen who entered the automobile training program successfully completed the course. That is, only 27 percent of the CGV's early sample of motor-cab-conductor candidates were able to make the transition to the automobile. There are no similar data for other years before 1914, but many of the CGV's coachmen had as much difficulty making the change to the gasoline-driven motor cab as to the electrically powered cab. Since the skills required to master the gasoline-driven cab were somewhat more complex than those required for the electrically powered vehicle (the shifting of gears as opposed to battery maintenance, for instance), we may safely assume that an even greater proportion of coachmen were unable to learn the intricacies of a gasoline-powered automobile than were unable to operate the electric motor cabs. The 1899 memorandum concludes by reporting that it took an average of 11.4 days per coachman to produce a competent automobile conductor. It took a considerably longer time, however, as Table 29 demonstrates, "before the coachman [came] to an understanding of the part he [could] play in maintaining his automobile" and before he realized that "he [had] an interest in caring for his batteries."[15]

The next time the CGV reported on motor-cab conductors was in 1908, by which time the firm was committed to the gasoline-driven car. The president of the company reported to his Administrative Council that the policy of hiring conductors exclusively from the ranks of the CGV's coachmen was no longer sufficient and that the Executive Committee had decided to recruit conductors from outside the firm, a policy shift made while the CGV was still publicly committed to converting its own coachmen into motor-cab conductors. The original policy was clearly not working. Regrettably, the CGV never reported the reasons for the policy's failure. Did the company not obtain enough candidates from among its own coachmen, or did many of those it did recruit fail to learn the new and more complex driving skills? In a 1914 meeting, the CGV's Administrative Council hinted at what the problem might be in a one-sentence statement: "The Council is advised of the greater and greater difficulties in the recruitment of conductors because of the increasing severity of the Examination Commission."[16] The Commission d'Examen, as the state's licensing and examination body for coachmen of horse-drawn carriages, would clearly be responsible for testing the expertise of motor coachmen. Apparently, many coachmen were not mastering the skills necessary to conduct a motor cab, a finding consistent with the company's similar experience in trying to teach them how to drive the electric cab. Unfortunately, there are no data on what proportion of those coachmen who did try the automobile succeeded in learning its operations.

15. *Ibid.*, 147.
16. ACGV, CGV, *Conseil*, reg. no. 8, August 28, 1908, pp. 2903–904, reg. no. 16, November 24, 1908, p. 6428, and reg. no. 8, May 22, 1914, p. 3128.

In this context, the evaluation sheets that were filled out by the depot chiefs on the CGV's employees are useful, for they rate the performance of those coachmen who did make the transition to the automobile. Moreover, it is generally the same drivers being evaluated here as motor-cab conductors that were judged as coachmen. Thus, the sheets give us a kind of progress report on the coachmen we saw back in Chapter 4 as they now take to Paris streets in motor cabs. The only differences in the evaluation sheets for motor-cab drivers are that category 1 measures the cabbie's automobile driving proficiency instead of his horsemanship and category 4 judges the care of the automobile instead of the coach. The same scoring codes are used to arrive at numerical values: 4, very bad; 5, bad; 6, mediocre; 7, passable; 8, good; 9, very good; 1, no; 2, yes; and 3, sometimes. Table 30 reproduces the results of all the available evaluation sheets as they apply to motor-cab drivers, with the results expressed as a mean for each category at the end.

The scores indicate a significantly better rating for driving proficiency than these drivers received for horsemanship. Only 30 percent of the cabbies were good to very good horsemen, whereas 49 percent of the evaluations rated motor-cab drivers as good to very good. Not a single evaluation sheet out of 2,552 stated that cabbies were "very bad" drivers. Of the rest, 98 percent of the evaluations rated motor-cab drivers as passable to very good drivers, compared to only 75 percent for those who drove horse-drawn carriages. This difference is to be expected, given the more complex skills, and therefore greater training, involved in driving an automobile. To become a motor-cab coachman an individual had to pass through a training program and licensing examination more rigorous than the one for simple coachman. The technical skills cabbies mastered to become effective automobile conductors involved the care of the vehicle as well, as is clear from the table. In category 4, the care of the automobile, 92 percent of the evaluation sheets reported that motor-cab drivers had a passable to very good performance rating, compared with 78 percent for horse-drawn-cab drivers.

In the categories applicable to character evaluation, categories 3, 6, and 7, automobile cabbies have a much better record than their earlier counterparts. For instance, there is a dramatic improvement in attitude toward their superiors, 94 percent rating good to very good compared to 77 percent in the earlier era. In category 7, the

TABLE 30
Summary of Evaluation Sheets for Motor Cab Cabbies, *ca.* 1900–1914

| Category 1 Driving Proficiency | | | Category 2 Receipts | | |
|---|---|---|---|---|---|
| Judgment | Frequency | Percentage | Judgment | Frequency | Percentage |
| Missing ones | 7 | | Missing ones | 2,322 | |
| Bad | 5 | 0.2 | Bad | 18 | 7.6 |
| Mediocre | 35 | 1.4 | Mediocre | 2 | 0.8 |
| Passable | 1,269 | 49.7 | Passable | 45 | 19.0 |
| Good | 1,224 | 48.0 | Good | 163 | 68.8 |
| Very good | 19 | 0.7 | Very good | 9 | 3.8 |

| Category 3 Attitude Toward Public | | | Category 4 Care of Automobile | | |
|---|---|---|---|---|---|
| Judgment | Frequency | Percentage | Judgment | Frequency | Percentage |
| Missing ones | 470 | | Missing ones | 244 | |
| Very bad | 1 | 0.0 | Very bad | 119 | 5.1 |
| Bad | 3 | 0.1 | Bad | 208 | 9.0 |
| Mediocre | 1 | 0.0 | Mediocre | 13 | 0.6 |
| Passable | 379 | 18.1 | Passable | 1,386 | 59.9 |
| Good | 1,705 | 81.6 | Good | 575 | 24.8 |
| | | | Very good | 14 | 0.6 |

| Category 5 Care of Personal Property | | | Category 6 Attitude Toward Superiors | | |
|---|---|---|---|---|---|
| Judgment | Frequency | Percentage | Judgment | Frequency | Percentage |
| Missing ones | 241 | | Missing ones | 241 | |
| Very bad | 1 | 0.0 | Bad | 13 | 0.6 |
| Bad | 41 | 1.8 | Mediocre | 4 | 0.2 |
| Mediocre | 18 | 0.8 | Passable | 120 | 5.2 |
| Passable | 1,080 | 46.6 | Good | 2,166 | 93.4 |
| Good | 1,151 | 49.7 | Very good | 15 | 0.6 |
| Very good | 27 | 1.2 | | | |

| Category 7 Character | | | Category 8 Excessive Drinking | | |
|---|---|---|---|---|---|
| Judgment | Frequency | Percentage | Judgment | Frequency | Percentage |
| Missing ones | 18 | | Missing ones | 8 | |
| Very bad | 6 | 0.2 | No | 2,542 | 99.6 |
| Bad | 400 | 15.7 | Yes | 5 | 0.2 |
| Mediocre | 21 | 0.8 | Sometimes | 4 | 0.2 |
| Passable | 234 | 9.2 | | | |
| Good | 1,866 | 73.4 | | | |
| Very good | 14 | 0.6 | | | |

TABLE 30 (continued)
Results of Table Expressed as a Mean

| Category | N | Mean | Standard deviation |
|---|---|---|---|
| Driving proficiency | 2,522 | 7.476 | 0.551 |
| Receipts | 237 | 7.603 | 0.889 |
| Attitude toward public | 2,089 | 7.811 | 0.410 |
| Care of automobile | 2,315 | 6.920 | 1.046 |
| Care of personal property | 2,318 | 7.475 | 0.632 |
| Attitude toward superiors | 2,318 | 7.934 | 0.333 |
| Character | 2,541 | 7.415 | 1.115 |
| Excessive drinking | 2,551 | 1.005 | 0.090 |

Source: ACGV, personnel files of coachmen.

general character category, 74 percent of the evaluations reported that auto-taxi cabbies had a good to very good character, compared to 63 percent for the cabbies who drove horse-drawn coaches. There is a rating drop only for the category on attitude toward the public, 82 percent good compared to 92 percent in the era of the horse-drawn cab. However, if we total the ratings of passable to very good for the horse-drawn-cab era and the motor-cab era, the results are precisely 98.5 percent and 99.7 percent, respectively. The overall performance in this category is thus very similar from one epoch to the other, and if we compare the mean scores for each era in this category, the cabbies' performance gets slightly better. An obvious conclusion is that there was an overall general improvement in the character ratings of the cabbies from the age of the horse to the age of the motorcar.

How can this improvement be accounted for within exactly the same population sample? A number of factors work together to give an adequate explanation. Driving an automobile was a pleasanter experience than dealing with a horse. Automobiles, if in working order, were not temperamental. The speed of a motor cab, unlike that of a coach, could be as constant as the driver desired. The cabbie could reach his destination more quickly and more confidently with an automobile than with a horse-drawn coach. Thus, a motor cab was less taxing to handle. Financially, it was more rewarding. The evaluations on receipts bear this out. Depot chiefs believed that motor cab receipts were good to very good 73 percent of the time compared to 60 percent during the horse-drawn-cab age. Cabbies were more content with the automobile, a fact reflected in their attitudes, character reports, and earnings.

This new spirit may also have accounted for the slight increase in the scores on care of personal property. Auto-taxi cabbies received a good to very good rating 98 percent of the time, compared to 92 percent for horse-drawn-carriage coachmen. With respect to alcohol consumption, it was the depot chiefs' opinion, as in their judgment of the earlier coachmen, that automobile cab drivers did not drink excessively.

The kind of reaction coachmen had to the transformation of their trade depended on whether they were owner-drivers or working-class cabbies. Whatever the specific response of each group, though, its fundamental nature was peaceful. The pages of *La Voie publique*, an independent cab owners' publication, heralded the coming of the automobile. As early as 1895, one of its correspondents wrote that progress was being made in the automotive field. He hailed this new form of transportation as beneficial because "the horse can be easily frightened, vicious, sick, hungry, thirsty or very tired; it can strike out or make a very sudden movement capable of causing an accident." The automobile, he concluded, was predictable, elegant, tireless, and quick. It "shall have no difficulty in replacing the current cabs." Another article asserted that automobiles would reduce costs in the cab industry. There would no longer be thousands of horses to be fed or enormous stables needed to house them.[17]

The cab entrepreneurs believed the automobile was desirable also because of its probable effect on ordinary coachmen. One writer for *La Voie publique* noted that the coming of the automobile would oblige many cabbies to become "mechanics," by which he meant that the new conductor would have to be better trained and more skilled than a coachman. Many would be called to the profession of conducting a motor cab, "but few would be elected," he wrote, for "one cannot drive an automobile the way one currently conducts the vulgar coach." Driving an automobile was relatively complex, he noted, and only the most intelligent coachmen could become skillful

---

17. Degrange, "Les Fiacres automobiles," *La Voie publique*, November 17, 1895, p. 1; "Les Fiacres automobiles," *La Voie publique*, December 22, 1895, p. 1.

drivers. Many of them would be eliminated from the trade by the automobile, and for him this was a happy development. Drunks and similar types, he concluded, would disappear from the ranks of the cabbies. The same theme, that the automobile would attract only serious workers and eliminate the dangerous class within the cabbies' trade, was echoed by a coachman, probably an owner, in a letter to *La Voie publique*. These views reflected the general attitude of this publication, and the many who subscribed to it, with respect to the advent of the automobile in the cab industry.[18]

The journal *Le Réveil du cocher*, a pro-union, pro-working-class, cabbie publication, had a rather different perspective. It, too, embraced the automobile revolution but suggested a policy with respect to the new vehicle that would favor the simple coachman. One of its correspondents wrote in 1897 that one did not have to be a prophet to realize that the time was fast approaching when at least half the vehicles in circulation would be motor-driven. The author accepted this development but wanted to ensure that cabbies would benefit from it. Cab companies, he suggested, should guarantee coachmen a minimum salary and fixed hours, claims easily granted given the potential for profit the automobile promised. He concluded that coachmen were becoming chauffeurs, that they were adopting the automobile, but that they also wanted to benefit from the changes in the cab industry.[19]

By 1906, *Le Réveil du cocher* had become *Le Réveil du cocher et chauffeur*. The transformation of the cab trade, it reported, was inevitable and incontestable. Such a change represented progress, and coachmen should be able to share in the benefits of the automobile revolution. The journal urged coachmen and motor-cab drivers to organize into one united labor union to match the united stance of the cab entrepreneurs.[20] The working-class trade union that did form in the cab industry never protested the coming of the automobile; it

18. A. Gervois, "Le Cocher mécanicien," *La Voie publique*, May 15, 1898, p. 1; Hubert, cocher, dépot Letort, "Le Cocher d'automobile," *La Voie publique*, July 31, 1898, p. 1.

19. C. Aygalenq, "De l'automobilisme," *Le Réveil du cocher*, February 18, 1897, p. 2.

20. M. Grandeau, "Vers le progrès," *Le Réveil du cocher et chauffeur*, July, 1907, p. 2.

merely wanted to secure for the cabbie a decent fixed minimum wage and a reasonable workday.[21]

The absence of any protest against these new technological advances from the different spokesmen for the cabbies is noteworthy. On the contrary, they actually welcomed the changes, in contrast to the forceful protests of the corporation during the great strikes at the time of the Paris expositions when their wages were threatened. Each faction in the corporation of Parisian coachmen now saw potential advantages. Does this mean that no coachman regretted the loss of a way of life that revolved around the horse? Hardly. The silence on this point in the record merely indicates that the old coachmen's day had come and gone. Transformation was accepted as inevitable. Paris would still have cabbies, so the coachmen's trade would continue, but the manner of the vehicle's operation would be radically transformed. All other aspects of the trade, its independence, the having to drive by the rules of the road, the surveillance by police, the hostility of the public, the scrambling for tips, and the like, remained central features for the new coachmen, the conductors or chauffeurs, as they were called. The trade itself did not disappear; it was merely transformed. Coachmen either retired, learned how to drive automobiles, or left the profession. The classic horse-drawn-coach driver left the historical stage very quietly. His successor in this uniquely organized industry slipped fairly easily and quietly into the vacancy, where he operated within similar parameters and was just as concerned with his social mobility or material status.

The year 1907 formed a watershed in the transformation of the coachman's trade, yet in that year the press was far more interested in an obviously and immediately newsworthy development. In November, 1906, three women began apprenticeships to become cochers, or, as the press referred to them, *cochères* or *femmes cochers*. In February, 1907, the first two women cochers took to the streets of Paris, an event covered on the front pages of the Parisian press.[22] This

21. For some early unionism, see *Le Réveil du cocher et chauffeur*, April, 1907, pp. 2–3.

22. For what follows, see Fernand Hauser, "Les Femmes-Cochers," *Le Journal*, November 15, 1906; "Les Femmes-Cochers," *Le Rappel*, February 4, 1907; "Elles entrent dans la carrière," *Le Matin*, February 21, 1907; and "Les Femmes-Cochers: Leur Première Sortie," *Le Rappel*, February 22, 1907. For a collection of picture postcards featuring these early cochères, see APP, Iconography, Carton 20. Women

event is worth lingering over, for it summarizes perfectly the kinds of interests and concerns that prevailed in the nineteenth century with regard to coaching. A woman cab driver was a curiosity, and Parisians wanted to follow her progress from training school to her first workday on the streets of Paris. The press obliged. *Le Journal* reported that in November, 1906, several women had applied and were accepted into apprenticeship programs leading to a coachman's diploma. Their month-long course of study was the same as for the men and included theoretical and applied sections. To obtain a diploma one was required to demonstrate a thorough knowledge of handling a horse, horse medicine, techniques of harnessing a horse, familiarity with the new electronic meter, a knowledge of the driving code, and a grasp of the geography of Paris and its suburbs. With a diploma from their schools, the women could apply to the Prefecture of Police to take its examination.

That is what a male candidate would do. Was there anything in the driving code to block the entrance of women into the coaching profession? The division of traffic police informed the reporter for *Le Journal* that the law merely specified that to conduct a cab a person had to be eighteen years of age and in possession of a coachman's diploma. The ordinance said nothing about women, and it was the opinion of the police that women with the proper credentials could conduct cabs in Paris. The ultimate consideration was whether cab firms would hire female coachmen.

Two of the women who had entered the coachmen's training program, Clémentine Dufaut and a Madame Charnier, passed their courses, were granted driving licenses by the police, and were hired by the same cab company. On February 20, 1907, these two women made history when they took out their first cabs. Their first passengers were members of the press, and wherever they went that day, they were followed by a cortege of reporters and photographers.

---

did not conduct public cabs in the nineteenth century, though one popular writer wrote that occasionally "the *cocher* of a *coucou* was a woman" (see Nicolas Brazier, "Les Cochers de Paris," *Paris, ou le livre des cents-et-un*, XI, 187–88). A *coucou* was a two-wheeled post-chaise designated for trips to the outskirts of Paris. The woman cocher this writer observed was the wife of a cocher de coucou; she conducted one coach her husband owned while he conducted the other. For information on coachmen and the coucou, see Achille Jubinal, "Le Conducteur de coucou," *Paris, ou le livre des cent-et-un*, XIV, 285–319.

People crowded the streets of Paris to catch a glimpse of the first women cab drivers. In the central marketplace of the capital, the Les Halles district, merchants cried out, "There they are! there they are!," when the women drove by. At lunchtime, both of them were surrounded by reporters asking about their adventures during the morning. Madame Charnier responded that all had gone well and that she was not tired. Madame Dufaut was very happy with her morning, and both she and her colleague posed for photographers as they cared for their horses and cabs. One press account concluded that the public was sympathetic and amused by the sight of two women cabbies but also noted that some male cabbies had "betrayed their bad humor" when confronted with females in their trade.[23]

In 1907, there were thus two important developments in the cab trade. The first, the hiring of women cab drivers, was a major story in the press. The second and more revolutionary, the large increase in the number of automobiles in the cab trade, which represented the turning point in a transformation of the cabbie's occupation that had been in the making for a decade, was not noted by the press. The advent of the automobile, however, certainly had about it an irony reflective of the interest Parisian society took in cabbies. Most Parisians, even most other workers, never took cabbies too seriously. Anecdotes, folklore, and amusing stories passed for knowledge of cabbies. It was thus no wonder that the first women cabbies created such a commotion. Most contemporaries did not grasp the irony in that development: the trade of horse-drawn-cab driver was doomed to extinction in the very year Madame Dufaut and Madame Charnier made history by becoming that kind of driver.

23. "Les Femmes-Cochers," *Le Rappel*, February 22, 1907, p. 1.

# CONCLUSION

The point of departure for this book was Michelle Perrot's observation, noted in her magisterial thesis *Les Ouvriers en grève*, that Paris coachmen always seized the opportunity to strike when the capital was host to an international exposition.[1] This remark suggested several obvious questions. How could such a widely scattered work force combine and organize to produce city-wide work stoppages? What were the strikers' major claims and against whom were they directed, the municipal authorities, cab firms, or both? How did a strike in the cab industry affect other branches of public transportation in Paris? What was the reaction of the public and of government authorities to a transportation strike during the middle of a prestigious international event in the capital? Because of the magnitude and importance of these strikes, contemporary newspapers and police reports provide an exhaustive account of the issues and events and go a long way toward answering the above questions. The files of the leading Paris cab company of the late nineteenth century, the CGV, also report on these labor conflicts, though not so fully as the police archives.[2]

1. Perrot, *Les Ouvriers en grève*, I, 333.
2. See the ACGV for the minutes of the Comité de Direction and of the Conseil d'Administration.

The coachmen's strikes manifest more than particular issues and outcomes, however. Writing about all workers' strikes in the nineteenth century, Perrot makes this astute observation: "Silent sufferings, desires buried beneath the exhausting monotony of everyday life, rise up here and find expression. Full of sound and gestures, a strike is an outpouring of words, a psycho-drama in which repressed drives are liberated."[3] Coachmen's strikes did indeed embody a wide range of rich and nuanced discourse, some articulated by strike leaders, some emerging from the rank-and-file, all as it crystallized, bringing into focus claims long in the making. Moreover, these strikes were neither accidental nor exceptional events. Their occurrence throughout the entire nineteenth century, not just during every Paris international exposition but at other times as well, makes it possible to establish a series that lends itself to systematic analysis. Beyond singular details and issues, such analysis reveals certain attitudes and significant shifts in attitude, competing factions within the corporation of Parisian coachmen, and even factional disputes and subtle differences within a single block of coachmen.

Strikes were not the sole expression of the coachmen's deepest feelings and aspirations. An exceptional number of publications were devoted exclusively to their trade—publications that span the same time period as do the strikes. Most of them seem to have been written or edited by coachmen, former coachmen, or coachmen's representatives. Coachmen were also represented throughout the nineteenth century by their own associations and unions. A large body of ideas and opinions emerges from these publications and associations over a long period of time, divulging the same pattern of attitudes, aspirations, and factions as those revealed in a study of the strikes.

The investigation of coachmen's strikes, publications, and associations over the long term led me to an identification of the dominant trends and issues dealt with in Chapters 5 and 6 of this study. It is apparent that at midcentury a corporate identity prevailed in the corporation of Parisian coachmen, without, however, completely masking an awareness on the part of cab owners and ordinary coach-

3. Michelle Perrot, *Workers on Strike: France, 1871–1890*, trans. Chris Turner with Erica Carter and Claire Laudet (New Haven, 1987), 4. This translation of an abridged version of Perrot's thesis, cited above, is currently in print and easily accessible.

men that cab ownership was potentially divisive. As the century wore on, a working-class consciousness began gradually to germinate within a faction of the corporation, resulting in the formation of traditional working-class unionism by the late 1880s. This consciousness did not extend to all ordinary coachmen, however, for many of them aspired to join the ranks of the petit bourgeoisie as owners or part-owners of a cab or some other modest enterprise. Ordinary coachmen who shared working-class attitudes also sympathized with the owner-coachman of the single cab, a worker who had to toil long and difficult hours to earn his living.

I have attempted in this book to account for the formation of these class attitudes among coachmen, at the same time avoiding an analysis based on a simple reductionism or assumptions that there is ideology "out there" reflecting some "reality below" or some monocausal determinism. My starting point was a research strategy that did not set out to demonstrate the importance of any group of variables or the priority of any one historical agent over another. Since coachmen were not a well-known historical subject, I wished to situate them within their Paris setting. Using as much hard data as I could obtain from any source that had reference to les cochers, I constructed their social portrait, ever mindful that much of the information on coachmen reflected the bias of the reporting person or agency. The charge of bias is certainly true for the nonstatistical literature. The bourgeois cab clientele, frustrated by slow rides or seemingly insolent coachmen, cannot be trusted to have represented these workers accurately. Nor are coachmen, trying to stretch a ride or violating a police ordinance to increase their earnings, the most reliable of sources for evaluating the transportation system of Paris or the needs of the public. Too, statistical sources have their own traps, for they mirror the bias of the statistician; the choice of one subject over another for evaluation is itself the product of a preconceived value system.[4] My aim has been to get behind the popular image of a coachman by disengaging statistical data, to the extent

4. For a discussion of objectivity in statistical surveys, see Joan W. Scott, "Statistical Representations of Work: The Politics of the Chamber of Commerce's *Statistique de l'industrie à Paris*," in Steven Laurence Kaplan and Cynthia J. Koepp, eds., *Work in France: Representations, Meaning, Organization, and Practice* (Ithaca, 1986), 335–63, reprinted in Joan W. Scott, *Gender and the Politics of History* (New York, 1988).

possible, from the uses originally intended for them and to provide an optimum account of reality for this occupational category.[5]

All the statistical surveys employed here have been approached in this fashion. Fortunately for my purposes, as the growth of Paris continued to be of great concern to urban planners throughout the nineteenth century, statistical studies multiplied. I have examined all of them and have supplemented the many official and semiofficial inquiries with the private records of the CGV, the statistical investigations of scholars interested in coachmen, and the marriage certificates of coachmen, that is, with anything that contained statistical information on coachmen or could be subjected to statistical analysis. Data from these sources were compared with each other or with data from different sources, where appropriate. The outcome was the accumulation of a large body of statistical knowledge of varying degrees of accuracy. Statistical data, as Perrot has noted, makes "it impossible . . . to write in a random fashion," because "numbers impose a discipline" over conclusions and judgments.[6] On the basis of all these data on coachmen's socioprofessional and geographic backgrounds, their marital status, their wages, the occupations of their friends, and the like, I concluded that the occupation of coachman was an ideal vehicle for seasonal workers to supplement their incomes, a means for rural inhabitants with low-level skills to make the transition into urban life, and a stepping stone toward modest social advancement for rural and urban workers.

Once in the capital, coachmen developed collective attitudes, the subject of a major portion of this book. Various and varied elements combined to forge collective identities and alliances among coachmen: common neighborhoods, the influence of friends, the opinions of and contact with other occupational groups, the treatment clients accorded them, the influence of socialist and revolutionary syndicalist ideas, and the ideals of political freedom stemming from the French Revolution. Singular events and economic structures, among them strikes and a short-term, but severe, economic crisis, also acted on the collective mentality of these workers. None of these factors,

---

5. See Perrot, *Workers on Strike*, 310, where she refers to an "optimum account" of reality in a different context than that used here.
6. Perrot, *Workers on Strike*, 310.

however, shaped a consistent attitude or relatively uniform value system throughout the corporation of Parisian coachmen. None can explain the particular shifts of alliances or the competing doctrinal positions that characterized this trade. And none can accommodate, as an analytical category, the factors that caused an individual to become a coachman in the first place.

Judging from the structure of coachmen's daily lives and routines and from the motives that had caused them to become coachmen, I concluded that the unique features of the cab industry and the daily work-site experiences of coachmen were the critical factors in shaping their collective values. The economic structure of the cab industry was not an abstraction for the individual coachman; it was the setting within which he worked and within which he might improve his life, including his chances for cab ownership or for accumulating enough capital to begin some other modest enterprise. Cab company and police regulations beset coachmen at every turn, constituting their most immediate and pressing concerns. To understand this trade it is important to know that over the last half of the nineteenth century the larger cab firms that emerged coexisted with the small- and medium-sized firms, with the single-cab owner-driver, and with the coachmen's cooperative society. The degree of work-site autonomy, independence, and fiscal responsibility enjoyed by coachmen, unique to them among all French workers, persisted alongside the increased intensification of surveillance. These mixed elements, experienced daily and viscerally, constituted the critical setting for the development of a working-class consciousness among some Parisian coachmen while others clung to aspirations for social mobility.

# Bibliography

In those instances in which a work may be difficult to locate from its title and / or author alone, the depository in which it may be found has been indicated.

## Manuscripts

### Archives Nationales, Paris

BB$^{24}$ 348–60, Cochers en grève, February 2, 1848. [Dossier S. 3-9925].

BB$^{30}$ 299, Conducteurs-cochers, March 6, 1848.

C 2233, Assemblée Constituante. Correspondance. Comité du Travail [includes conducteurs des "Tricycles," 1848].

C 2257, Assemblée Constituante. Correspondance. Comité du Travail [includes transports parisiens, 1848].

C 2284, Assemblée Constituante. Correspondance. Comité du Travail [includes cochers, 1848].

F7 13825, Syndicats des Transports. Congrès (1900–28). Fédération des Transports (1900–1908).

F7 13826–27, Fédération des Transports (1909–19).

F7 13831–32, Travailleurs de la Voiture (1910–34).

F7 13926, Grèves des tramways, du métro, des chauffeurs de taxi et transports-camionneurs (1908–24).

F7 13931–32, Travailleurs de la Voiture: cochers, laveurs de voitures, mécaniciens, chauffeurs, carrossiers, garagistes, ouvriers en automobiles (1910–34).

F12 2210, Inventions relatives aux voitures (1811–28).

F12 3483, Exposition Universelle de 1878. Manutention et service des transports.

F12 5749–50, Grèves en France et à l'Étranger (1879).

F12 6064, Estimation des immeubles de la Compagnie Impériale des Voitures à Paris (avec plans) (1864).

F12 6758, "L'Alliance," société pour l'exploitation des voitures de place à Paris, ordonnance du 4 octobre 1846.

F12 6762–63, Compagnie Impériale des Voitures à Paris, société anonyme en commandite E. Caillard (1855, 1866).

F12 6804, Compagnie des Voitures, décret du 13 avril 1894.

F12 6816, Société anonyme pour le service des voitures de place (1817); voitures publiques de Paris à Versailles (1828).

F12 6817–18, Compagnie Générale des Voitures de Paris (1856).

F14 1965, Projets de lois, rapports et circulaires sur la police des routes et des voitures publiques (1814–43).

F18 1735, Maurice Bixio.

F22 364, Repos hebdomadaire (1906). Cochers.

Archives Rothschild: Compagnie Impériale [des Voitures à Paris].

Fonds 65 AQ:

Q370$^{1-4}$, Compagnie Générale des Voitures à Paris.


## *Archives de Paris*

4 AZ 1174, Lettre . . . sur la circulation des voitures, 5 mars 1848.

6 AZ 565, Voitures (Publiques et de place), n.d. [1826–28].

6 AZ 365, Voitures à 6 roues (1840–50).

DM$^4$9, Roulage, stationnement des voitures (1819–59).

DM$^4$11, Roulage, stationnement (1818–59); Omnibus de Contilly (1876).

DQ$^7$10.364, 16 juin 1866, Alexandre Bixio.

V$^2$F$^4$39, Stationnement des voitures d'approvisionnement et voitures publiques.

VI$^1$, Nettoiement des voies publiques de Paris; police locale; voirie [including grève de cochers, Ducoux].

VI², Préfecture de Police: l'éclairage (1808–52).
VN⁵, no. 56, Voitures de place. Tarifications et compteurs (1889–1902).
Registre des mariages (1860).

## Archives de la Préfecture de la Police

B/A 117–20, Exposition universelle de Paris (1878, 1889).
B/A 165, Chambre syndicale des employés de la Compagnie Générale des Omnibus et métiers similaires (1884–97).
B/A 178–79, Grèves des cochers de fiacre (1878–91).
B/A 348, L'Union des cochers de Maisons Bourgeoises du Département de la Seine.
B/A 444, Compagnie Impériale (1855–69).
B/A 462, "La Générale" (Cie. Anonyme de Voitures de Grande Remise, 1882–84).
B/A 1353–54, Grève des autos-taxis (1912).
B/A 1364, Grève des cochers de la Cie. Urbaine (1892).
B/A 1365–67, Grève des cochers de fiacre, de voitures de place de la CGV, et des laveurs (1892–1900).
B/A 1370, Grèves des cochers de fiacre (1900–1904).
B/A 1406, Grèves dans le Département de la Seine (1876–1920).
B/A 1412, Grèves des chauffeurs et cochers (1896–1910).
B/A 1426, Chambre Syndicale de l'Industrie et des Transports (1902–14).
B/A 1434, Chambre Syndicale de L'Omnibus (Cie. gle, 1891–1914).
B/A 1439–40, Chambres syndicales, Législation.
B/A 1442, Chambres syndicales (1872–84).
B/A 1443, Cercle de l'Union syndicale ouvrière.
B/A 1572–74, Cie. gle des Omnibus de Paris (1871–1919).
D/A 2, Personnel des stations; voitures et cabriolets.
D/A 22, Circulation et transports.
D/A 27–28, 67–68, Stationnement des voitures de place et les voitures de transport en commun.
D/A 180, 182, Circulation et transports. Visite générale des voitures de place, 1833–84.
D/A 251–53, Circulation et transports.
D/A 258–65, Circulation et transports, 1808–77.
D/B 226, Fourrière.
D/B 498–507, Circulation et transports dans Paris et le Département de la Seine.
Iconography, Carton 20.

## Archives de la Compagnie Générale des Voitures à Paris

Procès-Verbaux des séances du Comité de Direction. 19 vols. 1866–1924.
Procès-Verbaux des séances du Conseil d'administration. 9 vols. 1866–1928.
Plans des propriétés. N.p. [Paris], n.d. [1910].
Annexes aux procès-verbaux du conseil.
Rapports divers.
Personnel files of coachmen.

## PRINTED SOURCES

## Bibliothéque Historique de la Ville de Paris Newspaper-Clipping Collections

Actualité—Série 119, Travail. Généralités et grèves. (Material in this series is currently being integrated into the regular collection of the BHVP.)
Actualité—Série 125, Transports.

## Newspapers Consulted Regularly

Le Brancardier: Organe des cochers. 1886–87.
Le Cocher: Journal des annonces, de la littérature, de l'industrie, des sciences et des arts. 1846.
Le Cocher: Organe des intérêts de tous les cochers et des industries concernant la cavalerie, la sellerie, et la carrosserie françaises. 1890.
Le Cocher: Organe des intérêts professionnels des cochers de la Seine. 1884.
Le Cocher: Organe de tous les cochers et charretiers de France. 1864–65.
Le Cocher français. 1869–70.
Le Fiacre: Journal des cochers. 1846.
Feuille des cochers de place de Paris. 1879.
Le Fouet: Journal des cochers. 1879.
La Gazette des cochers. 1883–84.
Gazette des cochers et des gens de maison: Journal professionnel des serviteurs des deux sexes. 1887–91.

*La Lanterne des cochers de Paris.* 1880.

*Le Loueur de voitures.* 1901–1909.

*Le Moniteur des cochers: Journal indépendant des intérêts du cocher de Paris.* 1887.

*Le Moniteur des cochers: Organe spécial de la locomotion.* 1876.

*Le Moniteur des cochers et gens de la maison.* 1884.

*Paris-Voitures: Société internationale des distributeurs automatiques pour voitures publiques.* 1890–91.

*Le Pilori des cochers: Organe indépendant.* 1895.

*Le Prolétaire: Journal républicain des ouvriers démocrates socialistes* [later *Organe officiel de la fédération des travailleurs socialistes de France*]. 1878–91.

*Le Rappel.* 1869–1912.

*Réveil des cochers: Organe des cochers indépendants.* 1897–98.

*Le Réveil du cocher: Organe du syndicat* [later *Le Réveil du cocher et chauffeur*]. 1892–1908.

*Revue des transports parisiens et de la banlieue: Tramway, omnibus, chemins de fer, métropolitain, funiculaires, automobilisme, bateaux, voitures.* 1897–1900.

*Les Transports: Organe de la fédération nationale des transports.* 1905–25.

*La Tribune des cochers: Organe des intérêts corporatifs de l'industrie de la voiture.* 1902.

*L'Union des cochers: Journal des loueurs, conducteurs, palefreniers, piqueurs.* 1865.

*La Voie publique: Organe de la corporation des cochers.* 1891–1902.

### Newspapers Consulted Intermittently or from Clippings File

*Le XIXe Siècle.* 1889.

*Le Charivari.* 1883.

*Les Droits de l'homme.* 1878.

*Le Gaulois.* 1889.

*L'Intransigeant.* 1889.

*La Lanterne.* 1878.

*Loir.* 1889.

*Le Matin.* 1889, 1907.

*Le Moniteur.* 1878.

*L'Opinion nationale.* 1855.

*Paris.* 1889.

*Le Pays. Journal de l'empire.* 1855.

*Le Petit Journal.* 1889.

*Le Petit National.* 1889.

*Le Petit Parisien.* 1878.
*La Petite République.* 1889.
*La Révolution démocratique et sociale.* 1849.
*La Revue politique et littéraire.* 1878.
*L'Union.* 1878.


## Government Publications and Official Collections

Administration générale de l'assistance publique à Paris. *Renseignements statistiques sur la population indigente de Paris.* Paris, 1862.

Annales de la Chambre des Députés (nouvelle série). *Commission d'enquête parlementaire sur la situation des ouvriers de l'industrie et de l'agriculture en France et sur la crise industrielle à Paris* (documents parlementaires, Session ordinaire de 1884). Paris, 1885. In BN, Fol Le⁸⁹.36 (bis.).

*Annales du Sènat et de la Chambre des Députés. Session ordinaire de 1878.* 9 vols. Paris, 1878. In BN, 4°Le⁸⁹.36.

Caisse d'épargne. Assemblée générale des directeurs et administrateurs. *Rapports et comptes rendus.* Paris, 1855.

Chambre de Commerce de Paris. *Enquête sur les conditions de travail en France pendant l'année 1872. Département de la Seine.* Paris, 1875.

———. *Statistique de l'industrie à Paris résultant de l'enquête faite par la Chambre de Commerce de Paris pour les années 1847–1848.* Paris, 1851.

———. *Statistique de l'industrie à Paris: Résultat de l'enquête faite par la Chambre de Commerce pour l'année 1860.* Paris, 1864.

Conseil Municipal de Paris. *Listes des membres du Conseil Municipal de Paris de 1871 à 1890.* Paris, 1890.

———. *Procès-Verbaux (année 1878).* Paris, 1879.

———. *Rapports et documents (année 1878).* Paris, 1878.

———. *Rapport . . . sur les revendications des cochers de fiacre et sur les modifications à introduire dans la Chambre de discipline et dans la Commission d'examen.* Paris, 1899.

———. *Services de transport en commun à Paris et dans le département de la Seine et service des voitures de place et de remise. . . .* 2 vols. Paris, 1889–92.

*Corps législatif, Session 1855, no. 180. Projet de loi relatif à l'établissement d'une taxe municipale sur les voitures et les chevaux circulant dans Paris.* Paris, 1855. In BHVP, 4311.

France, Conseil d'État. *Projets de décrets et rapports, 1806–1809.* Paris, 1811.

Ministère de la Justice. *Compte général de l'administration de la justice criminelle en France pendant l'année. . . .* Paris, 1856, 1862, 1865, 1867.

Ministère du Commerce, de l'industrie [later Ministère du Travail]. *Annuaire des syndicats professionnels.* Paris, 1896.

Ministère du Commerce, de l'industrie, des postes et des télégraphes. Office du Travail. *Les Associations professionnelles ouvrières.* 4 vols. Paris, 1904.

————. *Résultats statistiques du recensement des industries et professions, 1896.* Paris, 1896.

————. *Salaires et durée du travail dans l'industrie français.* 4 vols. Paris, 1893–97.

————. *Statistique des grèves et des recours à la conciliation et à l'arbitrage* (1893–1914). 21 vols. Paris, 1894–1915.

Ministère du Travail et de la Prévoyance Sociale. Statistique générale de la France. *Statistique des familles en 1906.* Paris, 1912.

————. *Statistiques des familles et des habitations en 1911.* Paris, 1915.

Peuchet, M. *Ordonnances et réglements de police, depuis le 13e siècle jusqu'à l'année 1818.* 8 vols. Paris, 1818.

Préfecture de la Seine. Service de la statistique municipale. *Annuaire statistique de la ville de Paris.* 37 vols. Paris, 1880–1919.

————. *Recherches statistiques sur la ville de Paris et le département de la Seine.* 6 vols. Paris, 1821–60.

————. *Résultats statistiques du dénombrement de 1881 pour la ville de Paris.* Paris, 1884.

————. *Résultats statistiques du dénombrement de 1886 pour la ville de Paris et le département de la Seine.* Paris, 1887.

————. *Résultats statistiques du dénombrement de 1891 pour la ville de Paris.* Paris, 1896.

————. *Résultats statistiques du dénombrement de 1896 pour la ville de Paris.* Paris, 1899.

Préfecture de Police. *Collection officielle des ordonnances de police, 1800–1874.* 7 vols. Paris, 1844–74.

————. *Collection officielle des ordonnances de police, 1800–1880.* 4 vols. Paris, 1880.

————. *Compte d'administration des dépenses de la Préfecture de Police, pour l'exercice de l'année* [from 1817 to 1855]. 6 vols. Paris, 1817–55.

————. *Ordonnance concernant les voitures de place.* Paris, 15 janvier 1841. In BN, 8°Z Le Senne 11525 (3).

————. *Ordonnance concernant le tarif des voitures de place.* Paris, 25 mai 1842. In BN, 8°Z Le Senne 11525 (4).

Statistique de la France. *Prix et salaires à diverses époques.* Strasbourg, 1864.

————. *Résultats du dénombrement de la population en 1856.* 2eme série. Vol. IX. Strasbourg, 1856.

————. *Résultats généraux du dénombrement de 1866.* 2e série. Vol. XVII of 21 vols. Strasbourg, 1869.

Statistique générale de la France. *Résultats statistiques du recensement général de la population effectué le 24 mars 1901.* 5 vols. Paris, 1904–1907.

————. *Résultats statistiques du recensement général de la population effectué le 4 mars 1906.* Paris, 1909.

————. *Résultats statistiques du recensement général de la population effectué le 5 mars 1911.* 2 vols. Paris, 1911.

————. *Salaires et coût de l'existence à diverses époques, jusqu'en 1910.* Paris, 1911.

## Special Collection, Bibliothèque Nationale, Service des Recueils

4°V.54. Documents related to the following transportation companies and associations: Des Accélérées; Des Algériennes; Les Anciennes; Aron et Cie.; Batignolles-Monceaux; H.-M. Cardeilhac et Cie.; CGO; Cie. Parisienne des Équipages de Grande Remise; Compagnie Centrale du Factage Parisien; Compagnie Parisienne de Petites Voitures et Messageries; Dames Blanches; Des Dames Réunies; Des Dandys; Durant et Cie. (Des Confortables); EGC; Des Élégantes; Enterprise Générale du Transport des Prisonniers . . .; Enterprise Leloir-Ducler et Peigné jeune; Enterprise Sézanne; Éoliennes; De L'Étoile; Des Favorites; Gazelles-Réunies; Victor Lachèvre et Cie.; Des Lutéciennes; Les Mondaines; Petites Messageries Générales; Les Phaétons; Ravel et Farrouilh; Des Sylphides; Des Tricycles; Des Triolets; L'Urbaine; Union des Loueurs de Voitures de Paris; Des Vigilantes; Voitures Dites Francaises.

8°V.54. Documents related to the following transportation companies or associations: Des Boulonnaises; D.-M. Cardeilhac et Cie.; CGO; Cie. des Cabriolets . . .; CIV; Compagnie des Véloces Francaises à Paris; Compagnie des Voitures de Maîtres Sous Remise; Compagnie Générale des Équipages de Grande Remise; Compagnie Générale des Transports Parisiens; Compagnie Générale des Voitures de Luxe; EGC; Des Favorites; Les Gauloises; Des Jumelles; Messageries Générales de la France; Syndicat des Cochers de Grande Remise; L'Union des Loueurs de Voitures de Paris; Union des Loueurs de Voitures sous Remise; L'Urbaine; Des Voitures Nouvelles de Paris.

4°W 20919–20920, 20922–20925. Compagnie Générale des Transports Parisiens par le Matériel des Omnibus.

## Congresses

*Congrès international des unions des travailleurs de transport, tenu les 19, 20, et 21 septembre 1900, Paris.* Paris, 1900. In AN, F7 13825.

Fèdèration Nationale des Moyens des Transports en commun. "IVe Congrès national. Toulouse. Les 29, 30 septembre et 1er octobre 1910," in *Les Transports*, no. 17 (August, 1910), 1. [This is only an agenda for the congress.]

Fédération Nationale des Moyens de Transports. *Compte rendu du 1er Congrès, tenu à Paris, Bourse du Travail, les 2, 3, 4 mai 1904.* Paris, 1904. In BN, 8°V.14181.

———. "Compte rendu du 3e congrès national des moyens de transports, tenu à Saint-Etienne du 1er au 4 octobre 1908," in *Les Transports*, no. 2 (March, 1909), 4. [This is the only compte rendu of this congress, since the federation did not have enough funds to hire a stenographer to cover the meeting.]

———. *Compte rendu du congrès fédéral, 1910, tenu à la Bourse du Travail de Toulouse du 29 septembre au 1er octobre inclus.* Paris, 1911. In AN, F7 13825. The subsequent congresses, those of 1911, 1912, 1914, 1920, and 1921, under the heading "Fédération nationale des moyens de transports," are in BN, 8°V.14181.

Fédération Nationale des Moyens de Transports: Tramways, omnibus, bateaux-omnibus, métropolitain, voitures de place. *Compte rendu du Congrès, tenue à la Bourse du Travail de Lyon, les 16 et 17 septembre 1902.* Lyon, 1902. In BN, 8°V.13705.

*Séances du Congrès Ouvrier Socialiste de France. troisième session, tenue à Marseille du 20 au 31 octobre 1879.* Marseille, 1879.

## Financial Reports

COMPAGNIE GÉNÉRALE DES VOITURES DE PARIS

*Assemblée générale [Paris] [comptes rendus].* 1868–1919. In BN, 4°WZ.3383.

COMPAGNIE IMPÉRIALE DES VOITURES DE PARIS

There is no one depository that contains a complete run of the financial reports of the CIV.

*Assembée générale. Comptes rendus.* 1863, 1864, 1866. In BN, 4°WZ.3386.

The report for April 15, 1857, may be found in CIV, "Assemblée générale des actionnaires du 15 avril 1857," *Journal des chemins de fer* (April 18, 1857), 355–59. Two other financial reports for 1857 are: CIV, *Rapport présenté à l'assemblée générale des actionnaires de la Compagnie Impériale des Voitures de Paris, le 25 mai 1857,* handwritten report in AN, F12 6763, and CIV, *Rapport présenté le 30 juillet . . .* , Paris, [1857], in APP, D/B 505.

Reports with the titles *Assemblée générale des actionnaires, Assemblée générale ordinaire et extraordinaire . . .* , or *Assemblée générale annuelle* may be found in F12 6762 and APP, B/A 444 (1858); CGV Archives (1859); APP, D/B 505 and B/A 444 (1860); AN, F12 6762 (1861); AN, F12 6762 (1862); APP, D/B 505 (1863); AN, F12 6762 (1864); AN, F12 6762 (1865). For 1859, see also CIV, *Examen du rapport de l'expert et réponse à ses critiques. Première administration. février 1859*. Paris, 1859. In BN, V.13,648.

COMPAGNIE PARISIENNE DE VOITURES L'URBAINE

*Assemblée générale* [*Paris*] [*compte rendus*]. 1888–1907. In BN, 4°WZ.3397.

## Brochures, Pamphlets, Books, and Maps

*Acte d'union des entrepreneurs de voitures de place à Paris.* N.p., n.d. In BHVP, 132 534.

Agulhon, Maurice. *The Republican Experiment, 1848–1852.* Translated by Janet Lloyd. Cambridge, Eng., 1983.

———, ed. *La Ville de l'âge industriel: Le Cycle haussmannien.* Paris, 1983. Vol. IV of *Histoire de la France urbaine,* ed. Georges Duby.

*Almanach de l'étranger à Paris: Guide-pratique pour 1867.* Paris, 1867.

*Almanach des rues de Paris: Le Tarif des voitures de place; l'itinéraire des omnibus et leurs stations. . . .* Paris, 1852.

d'Almeras, Henri. *La Vie parisienne sous la Restauration.* Paris, 1910.

Amicis, Edmondo de. *Studies of Paris.* Translated by W. W. Cady. New York, 1882.

*L'Ami des chevaux, petit manuel vétérinaire, à l'usage des gens du monde.* Paris, 1841.

Aminzade, Ronald. *Class, Politics, and Early Industrial Capitalism: A Study of Mid-Nineteenth-Century Toulouse, France.* Albany, 1981.

André, Jean. *Manuel du cocher.* Paris, 1864.

*A propos du concours hippique: Les Voitures et les ordonnances de police.* Paris, n.d. [*ca.* 1889]. In BN, 8°Z Le Senne 6743.

Audiganne, Armand. *Les Populations ouvrières et les industries de France dans le mouvement social du XIXe siècle.* Paris, 1854.

d'Auriac, Eugène. *Histoire anecdotique de l'industrie française: Canaux et ri-*

vières. *Coches et carrosses. Postes. Messagers et messageries. Fiacres et voitures de louage. Carrosses à cinq sous. Omnibus.* Paris, 1861.

d'Avenel, Georges. *L'Evolution des moyens de transports: Voyageurs, lettres, marchandises.* Paris, 1919.

Babeau, Albert. *Paris en 1789.* Paris, 1891.

Baralle, A.-C. de. *Livret des voitures publiques: Guide des voyageurs dans Paris.* 8th ed. Paris, 1850.

———. *Nouveau Livret des voitures publiques.* Paris, 1857.

Barberet, Joseph. *Le Travail en France: Monographies professionnelles.* Vol. IV of 7 vols. Paris, 1887.

Barker, T. C. and Michael Robbins. *A History of London Transport: Passenger Travel and the Development of the Metropolis.* Rev. ed. 2 vols. London, 1975.

Bastié, Jean. *La Croissance de la banlieue parisienne.* Paris, 1964.

Beauroy, Jacques, Marc Bertrand, and Edward T. Gargan, eds. *The Wolf and the Lamb: Popular Culture in France, from the Old Regime to the Twentieth Century.* Saratoga, Calif., 1976.

Belloc, Alexis. *La Manière de voyager: Autrefois et de nos jours.* Paris, 1903.

Berlanstein, Lenard R. *The Working People of Paris, 1871–1914.* Baltimore, 1984.

Bernaud, E., and L. Laloy. *Guide pratique du cocher de fiacre à Paris.* Paris, 1906.

Bertier de Sauvigny, Guillaume de. *La Restauration, 1815–1830.* Nouvelle Histoire de Paris. Paris, 1977.

Bezucha, Robert J. *The Lyon Uprising of 1834.* Cambridge, Mass., 1974.

Bienayamé, Gustave. *Le Coût de la vie à Paris à diverses époques.* Pt. 1, *Moyens de transports publics.* Pt 2, *Profits, étrennes et pourboires.* Paris, 1902.

Bigey, Michel, and André Schmider. *Les Transports urbains.* Paris, 1971.

Bitard, A. *Guide pratique dans Paris pendant l'exposition.* Paris, 1878.

Bixio, Maurice. *De l'alimentation des chevaux dans les grandes écuries industrielles: Cinq ans d'expériences sur une cavalerie de 10,000 chevaux. Rapport adressé au conseil d'administration de la Compagnie Générale des Voitures à Paris.* Paris, 1878.

———. *Mémoire présenté au nom de la Chambre Syndicale des Entrepreneurs de Voitures de Place du Département de la Seine.* Paris, 1896.

———. *Note adressée à la Commission permanente du Conseil supérieur du Travail par la Chambre Syndicale des Entrepreneurs de Voitures de Place du Département de la Seine, sur la question de la possibilité de limiter les heures de travail des Cochers de Place.* Paris, 1903.

Blatin, Henry. *Nos cruautés envers les animaux, au détriment de l'hygiène, de la fortune publique et de la morale.* Paris, 1867.

Blot, A. *Du transport des visiteurs à l'Exposition de 1900 et de l'application à ce transport en chemin de fer dynamo-électrique à voie mobile.* . . . Paris, 1895.

Bottin. *Almanach du commerce de Paris.* Paris, 1830, 1840, 1845.

———. *Annuaire du commerce Didot-Bottin.* 36 vols. Paris, 1875–1911.

Bouchardon, Pierre. *Crimes d'autrefois.* Paris, 1926.

Bouchary, Jean. *Les Compagnies financières à Paris à la fin du XVIIIe siècle.* 3 vols. Paris, 1940–42.

Braudel, Fernand, and Ernest Labrousse, eds. *Histoire économie et sociale de la France.* 4 vols. in 8. Paris, 1970–82.

Brécy, Robert. *Le Mouvement syndical en France, 1871–1921: Essai bibliographique.* Paris, 1963.

Brousse, Paul, and Albert Bassède. *Les Transports.* 2 vols. Paris, 1907–12.

Cabaud, Michel. *Paris et les Parisiens sous le Second Empire.* Paris, 1982.

Cameron, Rondo. *France and the Economic Development of Europe, 1800–1914.* 2nd ed. Chicago, 1965.

Caron, François. *An Economic History of Modern France.* Translated by Barbara Bray. New York, 1979.

Castillon, A. *Déceptions de la Compagnie Impériale des Voitures de Paris: La Ville, le public et les actionnaires.* Paris, 1860.

Causse, Bernard. *Les Fiacres de Paris aux XVIIe et XVIIIe siècles.* Paris, 1972.

CGO. *Condition des employés et ouvriers. Institutions créées par la Compagnie.* Paris, 1867.

———. *Réglement et instructions à l'usage des conducteurs et cochers.* Paris, n.d. [ca. 1860].

———. *Salaires et condition des conducteurs et des cochers des omnibus de Paris.* Paris, 1865.

CGV. *Apprentissage des cochers: Itinéraires à suivre à pied.* Paris, n.d. [ca. 1868].

———. *Ateliers de la Villette: 2eme Concours pour la construction d'un type de voitures à quatre places et à un cheval: Séances du jury.* Paris, 1874.

———. *Explications du nouveau tarif des voitures de place.* . . . Paris, 1857.

———. *Locations des voitures: Tarifs et renseignements pour les services.* Paris, 1878.

———. *Plans des propriétés.* N.p. [Paris], n.d. [1910].

———. *Réglement des cochers.* Paris, 1868.

———. *Règlement des conducteurs de voitures automobiles.* Paris, 1908.

———. *Réglement sur le service des dépôts.* Paris, 1868.

———. *Statuts.* Paris, 1866.

Chambre Syndicale des Entrepreneurs de Voitures de Place. *A messieurs les conseillers municipaux de la ville de Paris.* Paris, 1878.

———. *A monsieur le Préfet de la Seine, à messieurs les conseillers municipaux de Paris.* N.p., n.d. [late 1860s].

Chambre syndicale des loueurs et cochers de grande remise de Paris et professions similaires. *Livret*. Paris, 1897, 1899.

Chaumeil, Louis. *Les Omnibus et les tramways à Paris: Historique—rapports des concessionnaires et des pouvoirs publics*. Paris, 1913.

Chevalier, Emile. *Les salaires au XIXe siècle*. Paris, 1887.

Chevalier, Louis. *La Formation de la population parisienne au XIXe siècle*. Paris, 1950.

————. *Laboring Classes and Dangerous Classes in Paris During the First Half of the Nineteenth Century*. Translated by Frank Jellinek. New York, 1973.

*Circulaire des cochers de Paris pour la rédaction d'une pétition* . . . . N.p.,n.d. [1706]. In BN, LB⁵³ 1706.

CIV. *Explication du nouveau tarif des voitures de place*. Paris, 1857.

————. *Livret des voitures publiques: Guide des voyageurs dans Paris*. Paris, 1857.

————. *Nouveau Tarif et ordonnances concernant les voitures de place*. Paris, 1857.

————. *Règlement du service des cochers*. Paris, n.d. [1856].

————. *Statuts*. Paris, n.d. [1855].

————. *Table of the Cab and Hackney Coach Fares of Paris*. Paris, 1866.

————. *Traité*. Paris, 1862.

Claretie, Jules. *Souvenirs du Diner Bixio*. Paris, 1923.

*Le Cocher vélophobe*. Paris, 1896.

Cochin, Augustin. *Paris, sa population, son industrie*. Paris, 1864.

Coleman, William. *Death is a Social Disease: Public Health and Political Economy in Early Industrial France*. Madison, 1982.

*Compteur pour les voitures et règlement*. Paris, 1827. In BN, 8°V.54.

*Conjoncture économique, structures sociales*. Paris, 1974.

Conservatoire National des Arts et Métiers. Centre de documentation d'histoire des techniques. *Analyse historique de l'évolution des transports en commun dans la région parisienne de 1855 à 1939*. Paris, 1977.

————. *Évolution de la géographie industrielle de Paris et sa proche banlieue au XIXe siècle*. 3 vols. Paris, 1976.

Coppée, François. *Souvenirs d'un parisien*. Paris, 1910.

Corbin, Alain. *Archaïsme et modernité en Limousin au XIXe siècle (1845–1880)*. 2 vols. Paris, 1975.

————. *Les Filles de noce: Misère sexuelle et prostitution (19e et 20e siècles)*. Paris, 1978.

Court, Émile. *Nouveau manuel du cocher*. Paris, 1886.

Crafty. *Paris à cheval*. Paris, 1883.

D***, le colonel. *Manuel du cocher, guide pour conduire à 1,2,3 et 4 chevaux, entretien des voitures et harnais. Installation des écuries*. Paris, 1900.

Daminville. *Réponse des cabriolets à la requête des fiacres*. London, 1768.

Day, Georges. *Les Transports dans l'histoire de Paris.* Paris, 1947.

Deflandre, A. *Répertoire du commerce de Paris et almanach des commerçans* [*sic*], *banquiers, négotiants* [*sic*], *manufactariens* [*sic*], *fabricants et artistes de la capitale.* Paris, 1828.

Déglise, E. *Tickets-Voiture: Feuille et contrôleur (ou timbre). Horaires. Nouveau système de location et d'exploitation.* Paris, 1870.

De Langle, Henry-Melchior. *Le Petit Monde des cafés et débits parisiens au XIXe siècle: L'Évolution de la sociabilité citadine.* Paris, 1990.

De Lizaranzu. *Nouveau Tarif et ordonnances concernant les voitures de place.* Paris, 1857.

*Dictionnaire de biographie française.* Vols. VI, XI. Paris, 1954, 1967.

Dolléans, Édouard. *Histoire du mouvement ouvrier.* 3 vols. Paris, 1936–60.

Donville, F. de. *Guide complet de l'étranger dans Paris suivi d'un guide à l'exposition universelle.* Paris, 1878.

Du Camp, Maxime. *Paris, ses organes, ses fonctions et sa vie, dans la seconde moitié du XIXe siècle.* 6 vols. Paris, 1869–75.

Duchêne, Georges. *L'Empire industriel: Histoire critique des concessions financières et industrielles du Second Empire.* Paris, 1869.

———. *La Spéculation devant les tribunaux.* Paris, 1867.

Ducoux, [François-Joseph]. *Notice sur la Compagnie Impériale des Voitures de Paris depuis son origine jusqu'à ce jour.* Paris, 1859.

Dulac, Henri. *Almanach des 2500 adresses des principaux habitants de Paris, pour l'année 1830.* Paris, 1830.

Dumerson, Gabriel, and Nicolas Brazier. *Les Cochers, tableau grivois, mêlé de vaudeville, en un acte.* Paris, 1825.

Durand. *Tarif des voitures de place.* Paris, 1857.

Duveau, Georges. *La Vie ouvrière en France sous le Second Empire.* Paris, 1946.

L'Écho des voitures publiques. *Livret des voitures publiques: Guide des voyageurs dans Paris.* Paris, 1847.

Éditions du Chêne. [Fargue, Léon-Paul]. *Dans les rues de Paris au temps des fiacres.* Paris, 1950.

Éditions du Figaro. *Les Types de Paris.* Paris, 1889.

Éditions Garnier. *Almanach du voyageur et du commerçant, tant à l'intérieur qu'à l'extérieur de Paris et des départements, pour l'an 1806.* Paris, n.d.[1806]. In BHVP, 10 930B.

Élouin, A. Trébuchet, and E. Labat. *Nouveau dictionnaire de police. . . .* 2 vols. Paris, 1835.

*Essai sur l'almanach général.* Paris, 1769.

Evenson, Norma. *Paris: A Century of Change, 1878–1978.* New Haven, 1979.

Exposition de 1889. *Guide bleu du Figaro et du Petit Journal avec 5 plans et 31 dessins.* Paris, 1889.

Exposition Universelle de 1878. *Guide-Itinéraire du visiteur.* Paris, 1878.

Exposition Universelle de 1889. *Huit jours à Paris pour cent francs: Guide et méthode.* Lyon, 1889.

Exposition Universelle de 1900. *Exposition centennale des classes 30 et 31 réunies. Notice sur l'exposition centennale des moyens de transport.* Preface by Maurice Bixio. Paris, 1901.

*Le fiacre, ou comme quoi il est prouvé qu'il y a des maris qui sont nés coiffés.* Paris, n.d.

Firmin-Didot. *Annuaire général du commerce et de l'industrie.* Paris, 1854–58.

Flaubert, Gustave. *Madame Bovary.* Translated by Eleanor Marx-Aveling. London, 1928.

Fournel, Victor. *Ce qu'on voit dans les rues de Paris.* Paris, 1858.

Fournier, Albert. *Métiers curieux de Paris.* Paris, 1953.

Foville, Alfred de. *La Transformation des moyens de transports et ses conséquences économiques et sociales.* Paris, 1880.

Franklin, Alfred. *Les Corporations ouvrières de Paris du XIIe au XVIIIe siècle: Histoire, statuts, armoiries, d'après des documents originaux ou inédits.* Paris, 1885.

———. *Dictionnaire historique des arts, métiers et professions.* Paris, 1906.

Fridenson, Patrick. *Histoire des usines Renault.* Vol. 1, *1898–1939.* Paris, 1972.

Gaillard, Jeanne. *Paris, la ville, 1852–1870.* Paris, 1977.

Gaillard, Marc. *Histoire des transports parisiens: De Blaise Pascal à nos jours.* Roanne, 1987.

Galignani. *New Paris Guide For 1873.* Paris, n.d. [1873].

Gautier, Hippolyte, and Adrian Desprez. *Les Curiosités de l'exposition de 1878. Guide du visiteur.* Paris, 1878.

Gérondeau, Christian. *Les Transports urbains.* 2nd ed. Paris, 1977.

Girard, Louis. *La Deuxième République et le Second Empire.* Nouvelle Histoire de Paris. Paris, 1981.

Gossez, Rémi. *Les Ouvriers de Paris: L'Organisation, 1848–1851.* Paris, 1967.

Gouriet, Jean-Baptiste, ed. *Panorama des nouveautés parisiennes.* 7 vols. Paris, 1824–26.

Greenhalgh, Paul. *Ephemeral Vistas: The Expositions Universelles, Great Expositions and World's Fairs, 1851–1939.* Manchester, Eng., 1988.

*Guide dans l'exposition: Paris et ses environs.* Paris, 1889. In BHVP, 29 185.

*Guide de l'étranger dans Paris.* 2 vols. Paris, 1878.

*Guide de l'étranger dans Paris et à l'exposition universelle, 1889.* Paris, n.d. [1889].

Hanagan, Michael P. *The Logic of Solidarity: Artisans and Industrial Workers in Three French Towns, 1871–1914.* Urbana, 1980.

Harsin, Jill. *Policing Prostitution in Nineteenth-Century Paris.* Princeton, 1985.

Haussmann, Georges. *Mémoires du Baron Haussmann*. 3 vols. Paris, 1890–93.

Howlett, Edwin. *Driving Lessons in Paris*. Paris, 1906.

Hubault, Edgard. *Services de transport en commun à Paris et dans le département de la Seine et service de voitures de place et de remise: Recueil annoté de documents législatifs et administratifs publié suivant la décision du Conseil Municipal de Paris*. 2 vols. Paris, 1889–92.

Husson, Armand. *Les Consommateurs de Paris*. Paris, 1875.

*Indicateur des Dames-Blanches et des omnibus; Précédé de l'historique des anciennes voitures à cinq sous, et de quelques mots sur les Trisicles [sic] . . . , les Favorites et les Citadines*. Paris, 1828. In BN, LK⁷6181.

*Indicateur général des voitures publiques de Paris et de ses environs*. Paris, 1858.

*L'Indicateur parisien. Nouveau guide du voyageur à Paris*. Paris, 1850.

Irvine, William D. *The Boulanger Affair Reconsidered: Royalism, Boulangism, and the Origins of the Radical Right in France*. New York, 1989.

*Itinéraire et indicateur générale du service de toutes les voitures publiques de Paris*. . . . Paris, 1829.

*Itinéraires des omnibus, tramways, bâteaux-omnibus, voitures de place*. . . . Paris, n.d. In BHVP, 908008.

Jardin, André, and André-Jean Tudesq. *Restoration and Reaction 1815–1848*, Translated by Elborg Forster. Cambridge, Eng., 1983.

Jennings, Jeremy. *Syndicalism in France: A Study of Ideas*. New York, 1990.

Jitoux, Georges. *Les Transports dans Paris*. Paris, 1901.

Jodot, Marc. *Carte générale de Paris pour l'usage des voitures publiques avec des notes et statistiques*. Paris, 1829.

Johnson, Christopher H. *Utopian Communism in France: Cabet and the Icarians, 1839–1851*. Ithaca, 1979.

Jones, Joseph. *The Politics of Transport in Twentieth-Century France*. Montreal, 1984.

Jouy, Victor-Joseph-Étienne. *L'Hermite de la Chaussée-d'Antin, ou observations sur les moeurs et les usages français au commencement du XIXe siècle*. 5 vols. Paris, 1815–18.

Jouy, Victor-Joseph-Étienne, and A. Jay. *Les Hermites en liberté, pour faire suite aux hermites en prison, et aux observations sur les moeurs et les usages français au commencement de XIXe siècle*. 4 vols. 6th ed. Paris, 1824.

Judt, Tony. *Socialism in Provence, 1871–1914*. Cambridge, Eng., 1979.

Julliard, Jacques. *Fernand Pelloutier et les origines du syndicalisme d'action directe*. Paris, 1971.

Kaplan, Steven Laurence, and Cynthia J. Koepp, eds. *Work in France: Representations, Meaning, Organization, and Practice*. Ithaca, 1986.

Katznelson, Ira, and Aristide R. Zolberg, eds. *Working-Class Formation: Nineteenth-Century Patterns in Western Europe and the United States.* Princeton, 1986.

La Bédollière, Émile de. *Les Industriels, métiers et professions en France.* Paris, 1842.

Labourieu, Théodore. *Le Cocher Collignon.* Paris, n.d.

Lagarrigue, Louis. *Cent ans de transports en commun dans la région parisienne.* 2 vols. Paris, 1956.

Landouzy, Louis, Henri Labbé, and Marcel Labbé. *Enquête sur l'alimentation d'une centaine d'ouvriers et d'employés parisiens.* Paris, 1905.

Laneyrie, Philippe. *Le Taxi dans la ville: L'Envers du mythe.* Paris, 1979.

Lapommerage, Berdalle de. *Publicité universelle: Le Bon Conducteur dans Paris.* Paris, 1852.

Laux, James M. *In First Gear: The French Automobile Industry to 1914.* Montreal, 1976.

Lavedan, Pierre. *Histoire de l'urbanisme à Paris.* Nouvelle histoire de Paris. Paris, 1975.

Lavolée, C. *Les Omnibus à Paris et à Londres.* Paris, 1868.

Lazare, Louis. *De la circulation des voitures dans Paris.* Paris, n.d.

Legendre. *Indicateur-Guide contenant les renseignements utiles aux cochers de voitures de place et de remise.* 2 vols. Paris, 1888.

Lequien, Émile. *Les Merveilles de l'exposition en 1889: Guide du visiteur à l'exposition universelle dans Paris et ses environs.* Paris, 1889.

Lequin, Yves. *Les Ouvriers de la région lyonnaise (1848–1914).* 2 vols. Lyon, 1977.

Le Roy Ladurie, Emmanuel, ed. *La Ville classique: De la Renaissance aux Révolutions.* Paris, 1981. Vol. III of *Histoire de la France urbaine,* edited by Georges Duby.

Lespinasse, René de. *Les Métiers et corporations de la ville de Paris.* 3 vols. Paris, 1886–97.

Levine, Louis. *Syndicalism in France.* New York, 1914.

Loth, Johann Thomas. *Loth's Guide to Paris and Its Environs.* London, n.d. [1878].

Louet, Eugène. *Nouveau Manuel des cochers.* Paris, 1878.

Marchand, Jean-Henri. *Requête des fiacres de Paris contre les cabriolets.* [N.p., n.d.].

Marchant, F.-M. *Le Nouveau Conducteur de l'étranger à Paris.* Paris, 1817.

Mareschal, Georges. *Les Voitures de place: Étude de la règlementation parisienne de la circulation.* Dijon, 1912.

Martin, Alfred. *Étude historique et statistique sur les moyens de transport dans Paris, avec plans, diagrammes et cartogrammes.* Paris, 1894.

Martin-Fugier, Anne. *La Place des bonnes: La Domesticité féminine à Paris en 1900*. Paris, 1979.

Mayeur, Jean-Marie, and Madeleine Rebérioux. *The Third Republic from Its Origins to the Great War, 1871–1914*. Translated by J. R. Foster. Cambridge, Eng., 1984.

McBride, Theresa M. *The Domestic Revolution: The Modernization of Household Service in England and France, 1820–1920*. New York, 1976.

McKay, John P. *Tramways and Trolleys: The Rise of Urban Mass Transport in Europe*. Princeton, 1976.

Mercier, Louis-Sébastien. *Tableau de Paris*. New ed. 12 vols. Amsterdam, 1783–89.

Mercier, Pol, and Léon Morand. *Les Cochers de Paris*. Paris, 1864.

Merlin, Pierre. *Les Transports parisiens: Études de géographie économique et sociale*. Paris, 1967.

Merriman, John M., ed. *Consciousness and Class Experience in Nineteenth-Century Europe*. New York, 1979.

———, ed. *French Cities in the Nineteenth Century*. New York, 1981.

———. *The Red City: Limoges and the French Nineteenth Century*. New York, 1985.

Montigny, le Comte de. *Manuel des piqueurs, cochers, grooms et palefreniers*. Paris, 1905.

Montigny, Louis-Gabriel. *Fragmens d'un miroir brisé*. Paris, 1823.

———. *Le Provincial à Paris, esquisses des moeurs parisiennes*. 3 vols. Paris, 1825.

Montorgueil, Georges. *La Vie des boulevards*. Paris, 1896.

Moonen, Charles. *Cook's Guide to Paris and Its Exposition, 1878. With a Plan of Paris*. London, n.d. [1878].

Moss, Bernard H. *The Origins of the French Labor Movement, 1830–1914: The Socialism of Skilled Workers*. Berkeley, 1976.

Nord, Philip G. *Paris Shopkeepers and the Politics of Resentment*. Princeton, 1986.

Nougaret, Pierre. *Bibliographie critique de l'histoire postale française: Poste aux lettres, poste aux chevaux, messageries et diligences, télégraphe*. Montpellier, 1972.

Ory, Pascal. *Les Expositions universelles de Paris*. Paris, 1982.

Palmade, Guy P. *French Capitalism in the Nineteenth Century*. Translated by Graeme M. Holmes. New York, 1972.

Papayanis, Nicholas. *Alphonse Merrheim: The Emergence of Reformism in Revolutionary Syndicalism, 1871–1925*. Boston, 1985.

Parent-Duchatelet, A. J.-B. *De la prostitution dans la ville de Paris*. 3rd ed. 2 vols. Paris, 1857.

*Le Parfait Cocher, ou l'art d'entretenir et conduire un équipage en ville et en compagne.* Liège, 1777. In BN, 8°Z Le Senne 5841.

*Paris, fin au XIXe siècle.* Paris, 1894.

*Paris: Guide par les principaux écrivains et artistes de la France.* 2 vols. Paris, 1867.

*Paris, ou le livre des cent-et-un.* 15 vols. Brussels, 1831–34.

Paris Universal Exposition, 1889. *Guide to the Exposition.* London, 1889.

Pelletier, Émile. *Code pratique des usages de Paris.* Paris, 1890.

Perdiguier, Agricol. *Statistiques du salaire des ouvriers: En réponse à M. Thiers et autres économistes de la même école.* Paris, 1849.

Pereire, Gustave. *L'Exposition et les transports parisiens.* Paris, 1895.

———. *Les Transports dans Paris.* Paris, 1895.

Périssé, L. *Les Fiacres automobiles à Paris.* Paris, 1908.

Perrot, Michelle. *Les Ouvriers en grève, France, 1871–1890.* 2 vols. Paris, 1974.

———. *Workers on Strike: France, 1871–1890.* Translated by Chris Turner, with Erica Carter and Claire Laudet. New Haven, 1987.

Perrot, Michelle, and Annie Kriegel. *Le Socialisme français et le pouvoir.* Paris, 1966.

*Pétition des cochers de voitures de place à M. le Préfet de Police et à MM. les conseillers municipaux.* N.p., n.d. In APP, D/B 505.

Petrot, Albert. *Les Conseillers municipaux de Paris et les conseillers généraux de la Seine.* Paris, 1876.

Pinkney, David H. *Napoleon III and the Rebuilding of Paris.* Princeton, 1958.

*Plan topographique et raisonné de Paris.* Paris, 1758.

Plessis, Alain. *The Rise and Fall of the Second Empire, 1852–1871.* Translated by Jonathan Mandelbaum. Cambridge, Eng., 1985.

Préfecture de Police. *Étude sur la circulation.* Paris, 1951.

Price, Roger. *An Economic History of Modern France, 1730–1914.* Rev. ed. London, 1981.

———, ed. *Revolution and Reaction: 1848 and the Second French Republic.* London, 1975.

Publicité universelle. *Le Bon conducteur dans Paris.* Paris, 1852.

Raison-Jourde, Françoise. *La Colonie auvergnate de Paris au XIXe siècle.* Paris, 1976.

Ramée, D. *La Locomotion: Histoire des chars, carrosses, omnibus et voitures de tous genres.* Paris, 1856.

Reddy, William M. *Money and Liberty in Modern Europe: A Critique of Historical Understanding.* Cambridge, Eng., 1987.

———. *The Rise of Market Culture: The Textile Trade and French Society, 1750–1900.* Cambridge, Eng., 1984.

Reid, Donald. *Paris Sewers and Sewermen: Realities and Representations*. Cambridge, Mass., 1991.

Reinhard, Marcel. *Paris pendant la Révolution*. Paris, 1962.

Reynaud, Françoise. *Les Voitures d'Atget au Musée Carnavalet*. Pairs, 1991.

Ridley, F. F. *Revolutionary Syndicalism in France: The Direct Action Movement of Its Time*. Cambridge, Eng., 1970.

Robert, Jean. *Histoire des transports dans les villes de France*. Neuilly-sur-Seine, 1974.

Rougemont, Michel Nicolas Balisson de. *La fille du cocher: Comédie-Vaudeville en deux actes*. Paris, 1834.

Rousseau, Pierre. *Histoire des transports*. Paris, 1961.

Sauval, Henri. *Histoire et recherches des antiquités de Paris*. Vol. I of 3 vols. Paris, 1724.

Say, Horace. *Études sur l'administration de Paris et du département de la Seine*. Paris, 1846.

Scott, Joan W. *Gender and the Politics of History*. New York, 1988.

————. *The Glassworkers of Carmaux: French Craftsmen and Political Action*. Cambridge, Mass., 1974.

Seilhac, Léon de. *Les Ouvriers des transports en France (chemins de fer et tramways et voitures de place de Paris)*. N.p., n.d. In Musée Social, 12.233/868.

Sewell, William H., Jr. *Structure and Mobility: The Men and Women of Marseille, 1820–1870*. Cambridge, Eng., 1985.

————. *Work and Revolution in France: The Language of Labor from the Old Regime to 1848*. Cambridge, Eng., 1980.

Shorter, Edward, and Charles Tilly. *Strikes in France, 1830–1968*. Cambridge, Eng., 1974.

Singer-Kerel, J. *Le Coût de la vie à Paris de 1840 à 1954*. Paris, 1961.

Société de Statistique de Paris. *Paris 1960*. Paris, 1961.

Société Protectrice des Animaux. *Exposé de l'oeuvre*. Alençon, 1891.

————. *Lettre aux cochers de Paris par G. de M., membre de la Société Protectrice des Animaux*. Paris, 1890. In BN, 8°S Pièce 4975.

————. *Nouvelle Lettre aux cochers de Paris, par l'administrateur de la Société Protectrice des Animaux*. Paris, 1898. In BN, 8°S Pièce 7692.

*Stationnement, itinéraire et tarifs des fiacres, cabriolets, omnibus, Dames Blanches, Coucous, à volonté ou à destination fixe, pour Paris ou la banlieue . . . [et] obligations imposées aux cochers*. Paris, 1828. In BN, Lk⁷ 6179.

Stearns, Peter N. *Lives of Labor: Work in a Maturing Industrial Society*. New York, 1975.

————. *Revolutionary Syndicalism and French Labor: A Cause Without Rebels*. New Brunswick, 1971.

Stendhal [Marie Henri Beyle]. *The Red and The Black*. Translated by Lloyd C. Parks. New York, 1970.

Sutcliffe, Anthony. *The Autumn of Central Paris: The Defeat of Town Planning, 1850–1970.* Montreal, 1971.

Thiery, Henri, and Adolphe Dupeuty. *Un Joli Cocher: Vaudeville en un acte.* Paris, 1863.

Thompson, E. P. *The Making of the English Working Class.* New York, 1966.

Tilly, Charles. *The Contentious French.* Cambridge, Mass., 1986.

Tilly, Louise A., and Joan W. Scott. *Women, Work, and Family.* New York, 1987.

Tomel, Guy. *Petits Métiers parisiens.* Paris, 1898.

Toutain, J.-C. *Les Transports en France de 1830 à 1965.* Paris, 1967.

Tricot, Lucien. *Les Droits des cochers.* Paris, 1896.

Tulard, Jean. *Le Consulat et l'Empire, 1800–1915.* Nouvelle Histoire de Paris. Paris, 1970.

Union des Loueurs de Voitures sous Remise de Paris. *Mémoires présentés à sa majesté l'Empereur.* Evreux, 1863. In BN, 8°V.54.

———. *Statuts.* Paris, n.d. [1882].

Vanier, C. *Le Cicerone, guide des étrangers dans Paris.* Paris, 1852.

Varin, P. *Considérations sur la Compagnie Impériale des Voitures.* Paris, 1860.

Viator, Narratius. *Vingt jours de route et généalogie historique de la famille des coches, messageries, diligences, voitures publiques, malles-postes . . . , avec des notes.* Paris, 1830.

Vigier, Philippe. *Paris pendant la Monarchie de Juillet (1830–1848).* Nouvelle Histoire de Paris. Paris, 1991.

Ville de Paris, Direction des affaires municipales. *Coins d'autrefois.* Paris, 1900.

*Des Voitures publiques à Paris.* Paris, 1866. In BN, VP 22838.

Weber, Eugene. *France: Fin de Siècle.* Cambridge, Mass., 1986.

———. *Peasants into Frenchmen: The Modernization of Rural France, 1870–1914.* Stanford, 1976.

Willard, Claude. *Le Mouvement socialiste en France (1893–1905): Les Guesdistes.* Paris, 1965.

## Theses

Bouchet, Ghislaine. "L'Utilisation civile du cheval à Paris, 1850–1914." Thèse, l'Ecole des Chartes, Paris, 1983.

Boudou, Anne. "Les Taxis parisiens de la fondation des Usines Renault aux 'Taxis de la Marne' 1898–1914." Mémoire de maîtrise, Université de Paris X, Nanterre, 1981.

Offerlé, Michel. "Les Socialistes et Paris, 1881–1900: Des Communards aux conseillers municipaux." 2 vols. Doctorat d'État, Université de Paris I, 1979.

## Articles

"A propos de fiacre." *L'Intermédiaire des chercheurs et curieux*, March 10, 1866, pp. 135–36.

Arbellot, Guy. "Arthur Young et la circulation en France." *Revue d'histoire moderne et contemporaine* (April–June, 1981), 323–34.

d'Avenel, Georges. "Le Mécanisme de la vie moderne." *Revue des deux mondes*, I (1903), 580–610.

Bachmann, Henri. "Les Cochers parisiens et l'exposition." *La Vie illustrée*, June 1, 1900, pp. 130–31.

Baudry de Saunier, Louis. "Les Fiacres à pneumatique." La Nature: Revue des Sciences, I (1896), 193–94.

Bernac, Jean. "Physiologie du cocher de fiacre." *Le Figaro*, June 6, 1893.

Bersaucourt, A. de. "Cochers de fiacre." *L'Opinion*, July 25, 1925, pp. 15–17.

Bouchet, Ghislaine. "La Traction hippomobile dans les transports publics parisiens (1855–1914)." *Revue historique* (January–March, 1984), 125–34.

"Cochers en Sorbonne." *Le Matin*, July 10, 1911.

Collomb, Gérard. "Nouveaux citadins ou ruraux émigrés? Les Amicales de Savoyards à Levallois-Perret." *Ethnologie française* (April–June, 1980), 185–90.

Desprez, Adrien. "Paris à vol d'oiseau." *Le Brésil*, August 25, 1887.

Du Camp, Maxime. "Les Voitures publiques dans la ville de Paris: Les fiacres et les omnibus." *Revue des deux mondes*, May 15, 1867, pp. 318–52.

Dumaine, Gustave. "La Société protectrice des animaux, ses origines, son histoire." *La Nouvelle Revue*, CXL (December 1, 1935), 193–201.

d'Elbourg, Jean. "L'École des cochers." *La Vie populaire*. Clippings file of BHVP, Actualité, Série 125, carton no. 23.

Farman, H. "Les Nouveaux Fiacres éléctriques." *Magasin pittoresque* (1899), 132–33.

"Les Fiacres à Paris." *Revue scientifique*, May 2, 1908, p. 566.

Foville, Alfred de. "Statistiques des salaires en France, de 1853 à 1871." *Journal de la Société de Statistique de Paris* (February, 1875), 36–46.

———. "Les Transports: Le Prix des voyages." *L'Economiste français*, September 30, 1876, pp. 435–37.

————. "Les Transports: Les Voitures publiques." *L'Economiste français*, August 26, 1876, pp. 273–75.

Grison, Georges. "Les Moyens de transport." *L'Exposition de Paris de 1889*, May 18, 1889, p. 95.

Hauser, Fernand. "Les Femmes-Cochers." *Le Journal*, November 15, 1906.

"Haussmann à la Préfecture de la Seine." *La Vie urbaine* (July–December, 1953), 161–317.

Lagarde, L. Denis de. "Nécrologie [Maurice Bixio]." *Bulletin mensuel de l'association amicale des élèves de l'Ecole Nationale Supérieure des Mines* (February, 1906), v–viii.

Larique, M. "Les Derniers 'Sapins.'" *Le Journal*, August 19, 1923.

Loua, Toussaint. "Les Voitures publiques à Paris." *Journal de la Société de Statistique de Paris* (July, 1875), 191–95.

Mareschal, Georges. "Alimentation du cheval à la Compagnie Générale des Voitures à Paris." *La Nature*, I (1901), 88–90.

Mauclère, G. "Note sur les voitures tramways à chevaux et les voitures automotrices." *Revue générale des chemins de fer* (November, 1899), 295–317.

McBride, Theresa M. "A Woman's World: Department Stores and the Evolution of Women's Employment, 1870–1920." *French Historical Studies* (Fall, 1978), 664–83.

"La Mort du fiacre." *Mercure de France*, February 15, 1922, pp. 282–84.

Nomis, Ernst. "L'Éducation d'un cocher de fiacre." *Le Monde et les sports* (April, 1901), 556–59.

"Notes et impressions [on the coachmen's strike of 1879]." *La Revue politique et littéraire*, August 17, 1878, pp. 165–66.

Papayanis, Nicholas. "The Coachmen of Paris: A Statistical Profile." *Journal of Contemporary History*, XX (1985), 305–21.

————. "The Development of the Paris Cab Trade, 1855–1914." *Journal of Transport History* (March, 1987), 52–65.

————. "La Prolétarisation des cochers de fiacres à Paris (1878–1889)." *Le Mouvement social* (July–September, 1985), 59–82.

————. "Un Secteur des transports parisiens: Le Fiacre, de la libre entreprise au monopole (1790–1855)." *Histoire, économie et société* (1986), 559–72.

"Le Premier Fiacre automobile à Paris." *La Nature: Revue des sciences*, December 5, 1896, pp. 1–2.

Quicherat, J. "Notice sur Alexandre Bixio." *Memoires de la Société d'Émulation au Doubs* (1866), 372–84.

Ratcliffe, Barrie M. "Classes laborieuses et classes dangereuses à Paris pendant la première moitié du XIXe siècle?: The Chevalier Thesis Reexamined." *French Historical Studies*, XII, no. 2 (Fall, 1991), 542–74.

————. "Urban Space and the Siting of Railway Stations, 1830–1847." In *Proceedings of the Annual Meeting of the Western Society for French History*, XVI (1988), 224–34.

Rougerie, Jacques. "Remarques sur l'histoire des salaires à Paris au XIXe siècle." *Le Mouvement social* (April–June, 1968), 71–108.

Saunier, Jean. "La Circulation parisienne." *Le Voltaire*, August 19, 1890.

"Statistiques des salaires en France, d'après des documents officiels." *Journal de la Société de Statistique de Paris* (February, 1875), 36–43.

Tulard, Hélène. "Le Crime du cocher Collignon." *Revue trimestrielle de la fondation Louis-Lépine* (1959), 6–9.

"Les Voitures et les rues de Paris." *Le Magasin pittoresque* (1851), 118–19.

# INDEX